PLEADINGS WITHOUT TEARS

A GUIDE TO LEGAL DRAFTING UNDER THE CIVIL PROCEDURE RULES

PLEADINGS WITHOUT TEARS

A GUIDE TO LEGAL DRAFTING UNDER THE CIVIL PROCEDURE RULES

Seventh Edition

William Rose

OXFORD

UNIVERSITY PRESS

OXFORD
UNIVERSITY PRESS

Great Clarendon Street, Oxford OX2 6DP

Oxford University Press is a department of the University of Oxford.
It furthers the University's objective of excellence in research, scholarship,
and education by publishing worldwide in

Oxford New York

Auckland Cape Town Dar es Salaam Hong Kong Karachi
Kuala Lumpur Madrid Melbourne Mexico City Nairobi
New Delhi Shanghai Taipei Toronto

With offices in

Argentina Austria Brazil Chile Czech Republic France Greece
Guatemala Hungary Italy Japan Poland Portugal Singapore
South Korea Switzerland Thailand Turkey Ukraine Vietnam

Oxford is a registered trade mark of Oxford University Press
in the UK and certain other countries

Published in the United States
by Oxford University Press Inc., New York

© W. M. Rose, 2007

The moral rights of the author have been asserted
Database right Oxford University Press (maker)

Crown copyright material is reproduced under Class Licence
Number C01P0000148 with the permission of OPSI
and the Queen's Printer for Scotland

First edition published by Blackstone Press 1990
Seventh edition, 2007

British Library Cataloguing in Publication Data

Data available

Library of Congress Cataloging in Publication Data

Rose, William M., 1949-
Pleadings without tears: a guide to legal drafting under the civil procedure rules / William M. Rose.--
7th ed.
p. cm.
ISBN-13: 978-0-19-928077-3 (alk. paper)
1. Pleading--Great Britain. 2. Legal composition. I. Title.
KD7453.R67 2007
347.42'072--dc22

2006034957

Typeset by Cepha Imaging Pvt. Ltd., Bangalore, India
Printed in Great Britain
on acid-free paper by
Ashford Colour Press, Gosport, Hampshire

978-0-19-928077-3

3 5 7 9 10 8 6 4 2

Contents

Acknowledgments

With grateful thanks to Alistair, Heather, and all the staff at Blackstone Press and Oxford University Press. To Robin Ray for the cartoons. To Wayne Beglan, Nicholas Grundy, and Martin Russell, who have graciously allowed me to use their excellent skeleton arguments as the basis for some of the examples in this work — their originals far exceed the examples for quality. To all those who have so kindly written to me about the book and for their (mostly unprintable) comments. Finally to Sue, without whose encouragement this work would not have seen the light of day.

To Sue, who almost convinced me
that I know what I am talking about!

Preface

I confess that when I completed the first edition of *Pleadings Without Tears* in October 1990, I thought there would be very little need for any form of revision to the work for a long time to come. Pleadings tend to be relatively immutable in the everchanging swirl of legal fashion and development. Additionally, of course, there was the not insignificant possibility that critical reception of the work would render any thoughts of subsequent editions completely hypothetical in any event. I therefore heaved a sigh of relief, had a long drink, and looked forward to the royalties.

Well, fortunately the reviews were not too bad! One kindly went so far as to describe the work as a 'joyous exposition of how to do it'! I suggested to my publishers that they might wish to emblazon this across the front of the book, and display it in some of the more lurid bookshops in our city centres. For some reason they declined the opportunity!

However, since the first edition was published (although not because of it, I am sure), there has been a continual evolution of civil procedure, the culmination of which has been the Civil Procedure Rules (CPR), which came into force on 26 April 1999, although there have been several modifications and amendments since. Even before that, we saw changes to the jurisdiction of the civil courts, together with giant strides towards the laudable end of providing for 'clear English' prescribed forms, all of which meant that there had to be some revision and updating to some of the examples in this work. I also took the opportunity of making various minor alterations consequent upon the helpful advice of colleagues and friends — one or two of whom had even read the book!

Now of course, we have experienced massive and fundamental changes to our system of civil justice — changes which are not merely procedural, but which require us to approach the process of civil litigation in a different spirit. The nature and extent of these reforms are outside the modest scope of this work, which will continue to concentrate on the art of good drafting, rather than its formal context. Even the word 'pleadings' has now been abolished, to be replaced by the more practical (if inelegant) 'statements of case', although I will still use the old generic title from time to time.

Pleadings under the old rules were much criticised for being over-stylised and complex, using anachronistic language and obscure terminology. However, I am firmly of the view that such criticisms, however justified, were not due to inherent defects in the system itself, but to the way in which it was employed in practice — which led to this humble work being written in the first place! In fact, although the formal mechanism by which a party now states its case may be different from hitherto, the general principles of legal drafting appear to remain substantially unaltered, although there is now considerably greater scope for setting out details of facts and law supporting a claim than existed previously.

Thus, I consider that the CPR require not so much a fundamental re-adjustment of approach to legal drafting, but a **refocusing** on the original aims and purposes of the drafting process — these being the concise and clear identification of subject matter of the action, the issues in the case, and the parties' respective positions in respect to those issues. Experience in the years since the Rules, has, I think, proved this to be right. A firm grasp of the essential elements of good drafting will continue to be an invaluable asset to practitioners, and the ability to set out relevant matters with clarity and precision will rank high amongst the qualities which distinguish the good lawyer from the mundane. This new edition has generally brought the work up to date as at November 2006, and incorporates several revisions consequent upon experience under the CPR. Additionally, the increased use and importance of skeleton arguments in everyday litigation has led me to write a chapter on that subject, which I hope will be of assistance to those seeking to encapsulate their cases in a condensed yet powerful manner. The form may well be different, but much of the substance remains as before. Enjoy!

Introduction

Alice laughed. 'There's no use trying',
she said: 'one can't believe impossible
things.'
'I daresay you haven't had much practice', said the Queen. 'When I was your
age, I always did it for half-an-hour
a day. Why, sometimes I've believed as
many as six impossible things before
breakfast.'

Many (many) years ago, whilst I was studying for my Bar finals, I was 'taught' drafting by a visiting lecturer, whom I will call Mr Prout. It was not his real name.

Mr Prout was a barrister of the old school. Doubtless of not inconsiderable forensic ability, he nevertheless presented as an 'old codger' in his mid-60s, shortish, with wispy grey hair, and a complexion that bore testament to his affection for G and T, and doubtless (in the finest traditions of the Bar) for some of the more famous liquid assets exported from Portugal. His black jacket and striped trousers were of a cut which was probably all the rage in pre-war days, and he wore a bowler hat, which rested on the desk beside him as he gave his lectures.

He read his notes in a voice ponderous and gravelly. He spoke of 'striking out your opponent's pleadings' and used words like 'contumacious'. He dealt both 'in extenso' and 'ad nauseam' with something called a 'setorf', which apparently was connected with a counterclaim, although I never did discover how.

I had no idea what he was talking about!

Being an enthusiastic sort of chap, I sought to rectify my ignorance, and consulted some of the major respected tomes on the relevant shelf in the Middle Temple Library. They were heavy, fat, and impressive, and were clearly written by Very Clever People.

Mr Prout

The trouble was, I found, one had to be a very clever person oneself in order to understand the learned authors. I began to get 'the doubts'.

In some confusion I then tried to purchase one of those little paper-backs, so beloved of students, which are generically known as 'idiot's guides'. They are published by a number of houses under different names, and have an embarrassingly large circulation. Nevertheless, I could not find one on the subject.

The gentle reader may at this stage be wondering how in all the circumstances, it came about that I passed the examination. The answer is simple. First, the exams were somewhat easier in those days than they are now. Secondly, I learned my notes more or less parrot fashion, and used the word 'contumacious' liberally in my essays. The actual plead-ings were cobbled up, and I hoped that the results would be sufficiently legally 'streetwise' to get me through. They apparently were! But I knew, as they say in Russia, from nothing!

Such knowledge of drafting as I now possess has been gained first through the advantage of a good pupillage, but increasingly through experience. Although there is, of course, no substitute for the latter, I try hard not to think too much about the hapless clients who were subjected to the full blast of my forensic abilities (such as they were), during the early years. Fortunately, the level and quality of work at that time was not usually such as to demand the drafting skills necessary in more complex litigation, but I am now convinced there are certain fundamental rules which are common to all drafting (and to advocacy for that matter), and the earlier such rules are understood and applied, the better the service that will be provided.

In recent years, an age of enlightenment has dawned upon legal education, and considerable research has gone into the best way of training both potential barristers and solicitors. It is now clearly appreciated that a need for a sound basic understanding of the principles of drafting and advocacy is vital for both branches of the profession, in the light of the reforms in civil procedure that have now taken place.

This book is not intended to contain precedents which can be used as a basis for your future drafting. So, if you have bought this volume for such a reason, I'm afraid that you have wasted your money. No refunds will be given! However, now you are stuck with it, you might as well read it; and who knows, the need for precedents may diminish.

There are several books of precedents commonly available. Many of them are specialist works, although the most famous ones cover almost all subjects you are likely to come across in the average practice. Some of these precedents are very good indeed. Others are still firmly rooted in the nineteenth century. All are for the guidance of wise men and women, and for the obedience of fools! For my part, I consider that each case has an identity and a 'personality' of its own, and that it is rare for a precedent precisely to cover the situation. It has to be adapted, and if you have to do that, why not do your own from the beginning?

I have deliberately tried to keep the style of this book both informal and readable. Save in the case of discursive examples, there are no footnotes[1] and any form of references will be kept to a minimum. I have, however, provided an 'annotated' Opinion in Chapter 13, in order to illustrate various techniques of the art.

Again, in the finest traditions of the legal profession, the responsibility for all errors, omissions, ignorance of the law and general blunders

---

[1] Actually there are two, including this one.

lies with my publishers, instructing solicitors, the au pair, the dog and/or anybody but myself. I will, of course, still be delighted to hear from anyone who has found glaring errors or omissions, or who has any helpful suggestions to make. This means that my publishers will be able to bring out yet another edition, and we will all make a lot (?) more money. Now read on …

Chapter One

Pillars of Understanding (General Principles)

'I don't think they play at all fairly',
Alice began, in rather a complaining
tone, 'and they all quarrel so dreadfully
one can't hear oneself speak — and they
don't seem to have any rules in particu-
lar: at least, if there are, nobody attends
to them.'

The trouble with Mr Prout was that although he was extremely good
at expounding rules and regulations, and even had a go at explaining
why it was necessary for pleadings to exist, he was never very convincing as to the latter, nor was he able to communicate what I might
pompously describe as the philosophical underlay to the process of legal
drafting. After all, it seems fundamental to the founding of competence
in any subject, for one to have a good conceptual grasp of its underlying
principles. To put it another way, before writing his ninth symphony,
Beethoven had a pretty good idea not merely of the theory of music, but
as to the effect he was trying to create. This understanding went much
further than the mere expression of joy or sadness, fast or slow — the
complex subtleties that give the work its unique character did not arise
merely by fortunate accident! He didn't actually tell me such, but

a comparison with lesser works of the age, and the consistency of his own art surely make the above premise beyond argument.

No one is expecting you to produce statements of case of symphonic excellence (it is to be hoped they will be somewhat shorter!), but the point still holds good. If you do not understand what it is you are trying to achieve, the chances of ultimate success are slim.

It is conventionally stated that the system of statements of case exists to inform the other side and the Court of what your case is all about.

Beethoven's Defence and Counterclaim in E♭ Minor

It is a fundamental rule of justice that, if a party is going to be called upon to spend time and money on answering claims made against him (let alone possibly meeting the claim at the end of the day), he should be given a clear indication as to what is being demanded of him, and the reasons therefor. Even though we have thankfully grown away from the ancient practice of pleadings having to be so exact that a mere word out of place would invalidate the action, precision in the formulation of the claim is still rightly of paramount importance. The same, of course, is equally true of any defence, counterclaim or other statement of case in the action. However, there are other more subtle points which can also be expressed in the course of a statement of case, which can have almost as important an ultimate effect on the case as mere compliance with the rules. Let's look at a few of them.

The first of these is the manner in which the case is drafted. Although there is of course no one 'right' way to draft a matter (notwithstanding the way that the subject is sometimes taught!), a tight, logical and well-expressed case cannot but have a good psychological effect upon the Judge who reads it. He or she is, after all, only human, despite the odd indication to the contrary. We will examine the way to do this in a later chapter. It is largely a matter of practice once the basic ground rules are applied.

Next, it is quite possible not merely to give a statement of your case or defence, but to do so in such a manner as to maximise its strength. This is often more easy to do in a Defence than in a Particulars of Claim, because you can play on the weak points in your opponent's case in such a way as to enhance the strengths of your own. In all too many cases, I have seen Defences which correctly deny liability, and which technically meet all the rules as to 'traversing' the claim, but which fail to set out matters concerning the defence case, which are not merely proper to set out, but which could and should be drafted and to devastating effect! Let us take an hypothetical example:

> The Claimant claims £20,000. He alleges that the Defendant ordered 5 tons of shot-fired, nut-cased widgets from him, to be paid for 7 days after delivery. He says they were delivered, and the Defendant thereafter refused to pay.
>
> The Defendant, for whom you have the privilege and pleasure to act, says that he rejected the consignment because they were cracked and pitted with rust, and that he did this on the strength of a written report from the Independent Association of Widgetfirers, which said they were defective.

The relevant part of the Particulars of Claim reads as follows:

> 1. At all relevant times the Claimant carried on business as a manufacturer and supplier of widgets and other artefacts.
> 2. By an oral agreement made on 5th January 2004, the Defendant ordered, and the Claimant agreed to supply, 5 tons of shot-fired, nut-cased widgets, in consideration of the sum of £20,000, to be paid within 7 days of the delivery thereof.
> 3. The Claimant duly supplied and delivered the said widgets on or about 19th January 2004, but, in breach of the said agreement, the Defendant has refused to pay the agreed price, or any part thereof.

All good, simple, plain boring stuff! Your riposte therefore states:

> 1.   Paragraphs 1 and 2 of the Particulars of Claim are
> admitted.
> 2.   It was an express, alternatively an implied term of the
> said agreement, that the said widgets should be of satisfac-
> tory quality, and/or in entire condition, without cracks or
> blemishes such as might weaken them.
> 3.   Save that it is admitted that the Claimant purported to
> deliver the said widgets on 19th January 2004 and that the
> Defendant thereafter refused to pay for the same, paragraph 3
> is denied.
> 4.   In breach of the said agreement, the said widgets were
> defective and/or of unsatisfactory quality, in that the vast
> bulk of the same were cracked and were pitted with rust. As
> a result, the Defendant, as he was entitled to do, rejected the
> said consignment.
> 5.   In the circumstances, it is denied that the Claimant is
> entitled to the sum claimed or any part thereof, for the rea-
> sons alleged or at all.

That's actually not a bad effort.The case for each side is perfectly clear, the
rules of drafting have not been broken sufficiently to cause any problems,
and the matter would thereafter ordinarily proceed on its weary way.

However, let us look at the situation from the point of a Judge reading
the papers. The issues are there to be decided, but on the case as drafted
he has no way of gaining any preliminary opinion as to whether the
Claimant is a purveyor of faulty goods, or whether the Defendant is
simply impecunious and looking for an excuse to delay payment. Now
it is arguable that this is good and proper — the Judge **has** to be impar-
tial. It would be wrong if he was to form any preliminary view of the
case, having merely read the papers.

That's his problem! Yours is to do the best for your client, whilst not
breaking (or even bending) the rules. Consider the following alternative
to the previous draft:

> 4.   In breach of the said agreement, the said widgets were
> defective and/or of unsatisfactory quality in that the vast bulk
> of the same were cracked and pitted with rust. The Defendant
> will rely, as part of his case, on a report from an inspector
> from the Independent Association of Widget-firers dated

19th January 2004, as to the condition of the said widgets.
The said report is annexed to this Defence. As a result, the
Defendant, as he was entitled to do, rejected the said con-
signment.

What you have done, of course, is to alert your opponent to a report of
which disclosure would have had to have been given within a short
time in any event, and as you have nothing to fear from it, the earlier it
is disclosed, the better.

Now, from a tactical point of view, however, the instant psychological
effect is to give the Claimant an uphill task. Any Judge looking at the
papers will, consciously or not, be looking to the Claimant to justify
supplying widgets in a poor condition. The question of the Defendant's
bona fides is now out of the window — even if he **may** be impecunious.

More importantly, if the strength of your case looks devastating on
paper, the other side (assuming they are properly advised) may be far
more keen to negotiate an out of court settlement than might otherwise
be the case. Remember there are few exceptions to the general rule in
any case: your task is to get your client out of the problem as quickly,
and cheaply, as possible. Sometimes that will mean taking a 'bullish'
line and fighting a case through to the bitter end. However, in the present
example, why run a case all the way through trial, if a spot of judicious
drafting might present the other side in such a bad light that they will be
far more keen to settle than to fight?

Let me put it another way. It is always a little unwise to assume that
your client is being full and frank. If you were the solicitor for the
Claimant, you may not have been told of the independent report, and
may not have found out until discovery, perhaps many months later.
The Claimant himself may be in financial trouble, or simply a shyster.
The sooner his legal advisers are apprised of the strength of your case, the
better it may be for you — after all, you can hardly rely on the Claimant
himself to do your job for you!

Lastly, there is **no** substitute whatsoever for a good command of the
English language. We are blessed with a means of communication which
is capable of great subtlety and conciseness of approach. It is perfectly
possible to express one's ideas in exactly the mood and to the exact
degree desired. Not only is a good and flexible vocabulary an asset here,
but so is a proper command of grammar. However pedantic it may
sound, the authority of an otherwise good piece of work is considerably
lessened by the unnecessary use of split infinitives and sentences ending
with prepositions.

There is presently a laudable trend away from the pomposity and 'stuffiness' of earlier legal language. Campaigns have been waged against 'legalese' and 'gobbledegook', which have my full support. However, being clear and modern does not mean being sloppy, or even slovenly, in approach. Modern language carries with it the virtues of clarity and easy comprehension. It is equally capable of style, elegance, precision, wit — in short all the 'old-fashioned' virtues which have prevailed throughout hundreds of years of literature.

You may ask, 'Well, what is the **point** of elegant drafting? After all, so long as I have made myself clear, why should style be of any relevance?' The answer can be summed up in one word — **authority**.

Assuming a basic legal competence, the most important additional attribute that will distinguish good drafting (or advocacy for that matter) from the mundane, is authority. To be able to stamp your mark on the case, pick it up by the scruff of its neck, dictate the action, and essentially show yourself to the Court to be in command and the master of your subject, gives you an incalculable advantage over your opponent. For a start, and have no doubt about this whatsoever, it shows! Your opponent will know, the Judge will know, and if you are at the Bar your solicitor will know. In terms of prestige and sheer psychological 'clout', you are ahead. Don't be mistaken, these things matter.

Although I would not wish to overplay the above strengths, I know, from personal experience, the effect that a well-drafted statement of case can have on an opponent. In the course of many years in the profession, I confess invariably to a tightening of the stomach when I was confronted with a piece of work drafted by someone who clearly knew what he or she was doing. I knew that I was not going to be able to get away with anything, that the weaknesses in my case would almost certainly be ruthlessly exploited, and that if I had any reservations about the wisdom of proceeding with the action, now was the time to see if a 'deal' could be done. Don't be confused with the rude or 'bull in a china shop' approach beloved of some, whose lack of ability is sometimes concealed beneath a pompous and arrogant exterior. These people are best answered in kind, with the legal equivalent of a swift kick in the fundament! But someone who knows their job inside out — that's a different matter. If you are of the same ability, good business (or battle) can be done, and the best interests of all parties are properly served.

Now, I confess that along with many of my brethren, I had a tendency to use the rather old-fashioned 'roll-up' words such as 'hereinbefore' and 'thereafter', which form no part of our everyday language, spoken or written. Personally, I see nothing wrong in this provided that the words are used properly, economically, and in order to clarify rather than to confuse. Most of these archaic words have the virtue of enabling a conventional idea to be expressed simply and conveniently, in an almost 'codified' manner. I do, however, object to unnecessary antique verbiage, such as 'now this Deed witnesseth' and 'these presents', all of which are well past their 'sell by' date and should have been heaved out in a verbal house clearance decades ago. They are frequently the products of minds rooted in the past or rooted to the precedent book (1st edition). If the intention (by conscious desire or by default) is to surround the law with an aura of mystique, forget it. If the aim is to clarify and render comprehensible that which would otherwise be cumbersome, so be it. The 'modern language' approach that should be adopted in drafting under the CPR will mean that even these words will be used less frequently than hitherto (sorry, before). Just make sure, however, that your language smacks of precision, and does not sound casual or sloppy. Here endeth the lesson!

I suppose that has wound me up to the most important point of all. It's almost brutal in its simplicity: how on earth can you expect to draft in a competent manner, if you have little or no conception of what it is you are trying to do?

I appreciate that, at this early stage, I may well lose the remaining few readers who have stuck with me this far. You may say, 'Of course I know what I am doing, I know what comprises a breach of contract/act of nuisance/negligence etc. How dare you suggest that I don't?' But apart from the obvious matters such as knowing that the action involves contract, tort, or an alleged breach of trust, can you always put your hand on your heart and state that you are fully aware not only of all the causes of action available to you, but of their relative merits *vis-à-vis* your case, and that you are certain not merely of the remedies available, but of the circumstances in which each one may arise, and of their preferential order? Have you fully thought through the best logical way to draft the various causes of action that you wish to set out, so that the alternatives will flow one from the other without unnecessary repetition or confusion? Have you planned out the best possible way of making your case look formidable, having regard to the nature of the Defence or reply that may be raised? Indeed, have you thought tactically as well as legally? You have? Always? Well, you can always give this book to someone as a Christmas present, or use it as a doorstop!

May I take the liberty of supposing, even hypothetically, that some of us are not always as '*au fait*' with the case as we should be. Occasionally we all tend to get a bit 'litigation happy', and the exigencies of time and other work lead to a temptation to take the easy way out — getting it generally right on the basis that we can always amend later. This may have been possible under the old system of pleadings, but will be far harder to achieve now. Thus it is essential not only to have a grasp of the facts and cause of action right from the start, but also to ensure that the overall **style** of the document is right as well. No amount of amendments can cure defects in the style of a statement of case, and only a complete redraft can cure any inherent defects in the document. Even allowing for the fact that we all have different styles, you should still be aware of the way in which a document can be subtly shaped in order to impart a more authoritative approach, or to give different emphasis to varying parts of the action. Such a 'slant' or personality can greatly enhance a statement of case, yet so many are drafted without consideration to these subtle, yet important effects.

It may sound trite, but inevitably, there is no substitute for a full understanding of the case itself, and the relevant law. In the absence of either of the above, the drafting is bound to be second-rate. On the other hand, let's face it, the advice given to the client (or instructing solicitor) will also suffer in such circumstances. So a general concentration of the mind may be beneficial in many different ways — after all, a happy client is a regular client, and that can include instructing solicitors as well.

What I will attempt to demonstrate in the following chapters is the means whereby you can produce statements of case tailor-made to your requirements, employing the desirable concepts outlined above, and without recourse to the precedent books! A word of warning (and self-protection). Inevitably, we all have our personal styles. Statements of case are not statutes, and within the parameters of what is acceptable, we all have our individual tastes both in language and layout. It is not my wish to persuade anyone that my personal style is superior to others, that my grammar is beyond reproach, or that my analysis of either facts or law is unimpeachable. I wish merely to demonstrate various ways in which statements of case can be constructed, and the merits or demerits of each. From an understanding and appreciation of the **concepts** employed, you can formulate your own style, it is hoped to devastating effect. Good luck!

Chapter Two

Getting the Show on the Road (The Claim)

Of course the first thing to do was to make a grand survey of the country she was going to travel through. 'It's some-thing very like learning geography', thought Alice, as she stood on tiptoe in hopes of being able to see a little further.

Fortunately for all (except the lawyers), a high proportion of matters in respect of which solicitors are instructed never require the institution of proceedings. In all but the most urgent cases, it is expedient (and less expensive) to make one or more requests to the other side to 'cough up' or comply with their alleged obligations, etc. before hitting them with the big stick. Indeed, if you do not do so, it is highly unlikely that you will recover your costs of commencing proceedings if the other side immediately does what is required of them, especially if the cause of action is governed by a pre-action protocol, under the CPR.

The way in which such preliminary correspondence is written, and the manner in which pre-action negotiations should be conducted, are out-side the scope of this work. A good measure of common sense combined with a shrewd appraisal of the matters in issue, will normally suffice to get the message across. After all, 'Dear Sir, Unless ...' (in one of its various disguises) should be clear enough to most people, whereafter negotiations can take place if there is any possibility of settlement. Such letters do, however, normally set out the basic cause of complaint, and it is thus necessary, even at that stage, to be able to formulate the nature of the claim fairly precisely, in order to avoid later contradictions in the drafted statements of case.

However, let us assume that your letters have met with no response, or that it appears a negotiated resolution of the dispute is unlikely. It is thus considered necessary to issue proceedings. This may not be because all other methods have failed — possibly it may be felt that service of proceedings may act to assure the other side of your serious intentions. Sometimes, of course, the limitation period is looming, and proceedings have to be issued in order to protect your client's position (to say nothing of avoiding a claim for negligence!).

So, there you are, be you solicitor or Counsel, sitting at your desk, with a blank sheet of paper in front of you. What you are about to institute may be a 5-minute wonder, or the beginnings of megalitigation which will ultimately end up in the House of Lords, and reported in august legal journals and the national press. What are the principles that should be applied?

As this is a book on drafting, I shall seek, wherever possible, to avoid delving too deeply into matters of law or civil procedure. Nevertheless, in order to give a title to the case, you will have to decide who are to be the parties, and before which Court or tribunal the matter should be commenced. The former is important for obvious reasons — if only for the fact that it is both expensive and humiliating to have to climb down and withdraw an action which has been commenced against the wrong Defendant, particularly if he is someone who may bear the moral, but not the legal, responsibility for the present dispute. Your competence is impugned, and your client/instructing solicitor thinks that you are a wuzzock!

Thus it is important to advise your client in advance (as I had once to do) that it was inappropriate to sue 'The Directors of Bloggs Ltd', when the action was in respect of monies owed under a contract with the company, and there was no suggestion of misfeasance by the directors. The fact that the company was insolvent, and that the directors were smugly playing their rounds of golf safe in the knowledge that their personal bank accounts could not be touched, was unfortunate, but no ground for founding an action which would be doomed to failure.

The rules relating to the jurisdiction of the County Court and High Court are to be found in the CPR and their accompanying Practice

Directions, and should be studied carefully. Note, for example, the restrictions on the jurisdiction of the County Court to grant freezing injunctions, as it's very embarrassing (and expensive) to turn up at Court, armed to the teeth, only to be told that you are in the wrong place!

Let us look at the way in which we might approach Particulars of Claim in a straightforward 'running down' action, of the type which is altogether too familiar today. I shall assume that all relevant pre-action protocols and procedures have been followed, and will concentrate only on the drafting aspects of the case.

EXAMPLE

Jack Penn, a 30-year-old labourer, is driving his Y registration Ford Focus down Putney Hill in London, at about 4.00 pm on Monday, 17th October 2005. His girlfriend, Jill Carrot, aged 26 and presently unemployed, is sitting in the front passenger seat. Both are wearing seat belts.

As they approach the traffic lights with the Upper Richmond Road, they notice that they are green and that the road is clear ahead, into Putney High Street. They cross the lights at about 25 mph, but as they do so, they are struck by a Bedford light van driven by Dennis Haystack. He is an emergency plumber on a job for Stoppadrip Ltd, but has over-indulged his fondness for drink at lunchtime, and had been driving far too fast along the High Street, weaving in and out of traffic. He struck a Fiat Uno parked on his left-hand side, went out of control, and skidded sideways across the road into the path of the oncoming Focus.

Jack Penn was temporarily knocked out, but came to shortly afterwards. He was taken to hospital and found to have a broken arm, which was set under general anaesthetic. He was released 2 days later, and spent 8 weeks off work, during which time he received sickness benefit. Fortunately he will suffer no long-term disability. His car will cost £6,000 to repair.

Jill Carrot suffered a severe cut to her arm from flying glass, but was otherwise uninjured. She had 8 stitches in her arm, which will leave an unsightly scar which will gradually improve, but which will always be visible. Some of her clothing was damaged in the accident.

Dennis Haystack suffered minor bruising. He was breathalysed and found to be slightly over twice the legal limit. On 14th December 2005 he pleaded guilty at Wimbledon Magistrates' Court to driving with excess alcohol in his blood, was fined £500, and disqualified from driving for 2 years. The front offside tyre of his van was found to be underinflated, due to a faulty valve, but no further action was taken in respect of this.

Both the company and Dennis Haystack have refused to acknowledge any correspondence from solicitors. There is no alternative to commencing proceedings.

STEP 1

Let us identify the parties to the proposed action. These, in this simple example, are going to be Jack Penn and Jill Carrot. There is also no reason why they cannot both be Claimants in the same action, i.e. it is not necessary to bring separate proceedings for each of them. Note however, as an example of the type of decision that has to be made, that their causes of action are separate from each other, and thus they are not **joint** but **first** and **second** Claimants. Although PD16 tells us to number multiple parties as if they were jointly suing (or being sued), I would respectfully suggest that the old system of distinguishing between joint and separate parties be maintained, to assist clarity. I do not think that anyone will be struck out or penalised for doing so!!

Now let us look at the Defendants. Applying the usual principles of law, we have, it appears, a claim against Dennis Haystack in negligence. Additionally, we have a claim against his employers, as they are vicariously liable for the torts of their employees committed whilst in the course of their employment. As it appears in the present case that Mr Haystack was on his way to a job, an action can properly be commenced against them as well. Once again, the actions are separate, and thus the Defendants should, I suggest, be first and second, rather than joint.

STEP 2

It is virtually certain that this case will be tried in the County Court, probably on the fast track, and therefore there would seem to be no advantage in starting it elsewhere. We shall assume that a hearing of the action will have to take place, and will therefore found the action in the Defendants' home Court.

STEP 3

Now we should make a brief note of the **causes of action**, and the **nature of the remedies sought**. Taking first the case of Jack Penn, we will be looking for:

1. General damages for personal injury.
2. Loss of earnings.
3. Special damages — being the cost of repairing the car, together with any other necessary expenditure incurred in hospital visits etc., and any other recoverable loss.

In Jill's case, we will require:

1. General damages for personal injury, this time including some sum to compensate her for her residual scarring and the consequent personal embarrassment.
2. Special damages — being the cost of clothing together with other recoverable loss and damage as above.

STEP 4

Finally, at this stage, we should take stock of any **procedural requirements** which will have to be satisfied. In personal injury actions, it is necessary to serve a medical report with the Particulars of Claim, and we will bear this in mind, particularly when dealing with the Particulars of Injury to both parties.

So, we entitle the case:

IN THE VERULAM COUNTY COURT   Case No. VL0000

BETWEEN:

Mr JACK PENN

1st Claimant

and

Miss JILL CARROT

2nd Claimant

— and —

Mr DENNIS HAYSTACK

1st Defendant

and

STOPPADRIP LIMITED
<u>2nd Defendant</u>

PARTICULARS OF CLAIM

So far so good!

Paragraph 1
In most cases, and certainly in the present instance, the first (and usually
the second and possibly third) paragraph should be 'definitive', i.e. it
should contain (hopefully) non-contentious matters to set the scene for
the ensuing claim (the pun was not intentional!). However, it is important
to remember that even the identity or status of the parties can be open to
dispute, and these matters should thus be set out in such a manner so as
to allow a proper response to be drafted.

Although it is usual for the first paragraph to contain an identification
of the relevant parties, it is not essential to do this when their status is
not of great importance. Thus, it is not necessary to commence:

> The First Claimant is and was at all relevant times, a
> labourer … etc.

whereas something to that effect would be necessary if you were asserting the identity and status of the Claimant in order to set out his legal
basis for bringing the claim, i.e.:

> The Claimant is and was at all relevant times, a Limited
> Company carrying on business, among other matters, as
> manufacturers and suppliers of earth-moving equipment.

In the present case, other than as required in all cases by the CPR, there
appears to be no reason for setting out the identity of the Claimants, save
in the course of stating their reasons for bringing the proceedings.
However, in the case of the Defendants, the position is different, in that
the relationship between Dennis Haystack and the Second Defendant
Company is clearly of legal importance. Although I consider that there
are better ways of setting out the matter, it is quite possible to set out

this relationship in the first paragraph, and to deal with the facts in the next, thus:

> 1.   At all relevant times, the First Defendant was the employee or agent of the Second Defendant Company acting in the course of his employment.
> 2.   At about 4 pm on Monday, 17th October 2005 ... etc.

Note that the use of the phrase 'At all relevant times' is used to avoid tedious phrasing to explain why it is alleged that the Second Defendant company is liable for the First Defendant's tortious acts and omissions. The allegation that he was acting as the Second Defendant's employee or agent at all material times is clearly meant to cover the subsequent accident, and the company is thus placed firmly 'in the frame'. It is, of course, still at liberty to dispute the allegation.

Also observe that I have described the company in the singular. I confess to some ambiguity on this point. Technically of course, the company is a separate, singular legal personality. It is thus possible simply to describe it as 'The Second Defendant'. On the other hand, in the natural course and flow of language, it is conventional to refer to a company in the plural — thus 'The Second Defendants are a company ... in the course of their said business ...' etc.

Strictly speaking, the proper course is to refer to 'The Second Defendant Company', thus complying with the demands both of legal propriety, and clarity of explanation. However, this course can be both cumbersome and pompous in a draft which requires constant reference to the company.

In my view, it does not matter whether you elect ultimately to describe corporate parties in the singular or the plural, provided that you maintain a consistent approach. Don't refer to the 'Second Defendants' in one paragraph, and the 'Second Defendant' in another.

The phrasing used in the above example has the advantage that there can be no doubt as to the basis upon which the Second Defendant is being brought in to the action. It also provides it with an easy method of admitting or denying the allegation in its Defence. However, I consider it to be inelegant for a number of reasons. First, it does not appear to be the most logical approach to commence a claim by a description of the Defendants, without reference to the Claimants. Secondly, the involvement of the Second Defendant is passive, i.e. its liability does not arise out of its **physical** involvement in the accident, which has not yet been alleged, and it is thus being introduced before its due time. Thirdly, there

is an alternative method of setting out its involvement, which is altogether more logical and comprehensive. How about:

> 1.   On Monday, 17th October 2005, at about 4 pm, the First
> Claimant was driving his Ford Focus motor car, registration
> number Y123 ABC down Putney Hill, London SW15 at the
> junction with Upper Richmond Road, when a collision
> occurred between his said vehicle and a Bedford van regis-
> tration number CFL 204Z driven by the First Defendant, who
> was at all relevant times the employee or agent of the Second
> Defendant Company, acting in the course of his employment.
> 2.   At the time of the said accident, the Second Claimant was
> the front seat passenger in the First Claimant's said vehicle.

In this example, the involvement of the company has been interwoven
with the narrative in a logical and natural manner, yet in such a way as
to enable it easily to admit or deny the allegation. There are a number of
other matters in these paragraphs which are also worth examining.

The date
It used to be a rule of practice that, in order to avoid any technical
defences based on minor inaccuracies, a date would not be pleaded
specifically, but would be qualified with the words 'on or about'. Thus,
if the accident, for example, took place just after midnight, the words 'on
or about 17th October 2005' would suffice to defeat any argument that
the matter had not been properly alleged.

This rule of practice still holds good, but where there is no possible
dispute that the date is accurate, it seems somewhat ponderous and inflexible invariably to include the words 'on or about'. In the present case, the
police were called (as a breath test was administered to Mr Haystack),
the date will therefore be certain, and there thus seems little point in
putting in the additional verbiage.

The time
Note that I have included the **time** that the accident took place. It is almost
certain that this will not be in dispute, but although it may not strictly be
relevant, in that there is no allegation that the First Defendant should have
been using lights and was not doing so, it does not hurt to put it in.
Technically of course, the time of the accident is a matter of evidence, and
falls outside the bare bones that have to be drafted in order that the case can
be fully understood. The CPR do not fundamentally alter the distinction
between what was formerly known as 'material particulars' and 'evidence',

and there is no general encouragement, let alone a requirement, to set out evidence in a statement of case. However, in the present case, there seems no reason to omit the time, and we shall therefore put it in.

The place
The place of the accident has to be set out sufficiently clearly to enable the case to be understood and a Defence filed. Once again, however, we should be careful not to forget the difference between relevant matters and evidence, although sufficient details of how it is alleged the accident occurred should be set out in the Particulars of Negligence, which will follow in due course. In the present instance, it should be sufficient for the general area to be set out in the first paragraph — the actual positions of the relevant vehicles on the road can appear later.

The description of the parties
As a matter of law, it will be necessary to state the driver's interest in the car, should he wish to recover in respect of the damage to his car. If the car does not belong to him, he may not be able to claim that **he** has suffered damage as a result of the negligence of the Defendants — something which is an indispensable prerequisite to the successful foundation of a claim under this cause of action. It is of course possible to plead ownership by the inclusion of a specific line to this effect thus:

> 1.   The First Claimant is and was at all material times the owner of a Ford Focus motor car registration number Y123 ABC.
> 2.   At about 4 pm on Monday, 17th October 2005, the First Claimant was driving his said motor car down Putney Hill ...

but this does seem a prolix and unnecessarily cumbersome way of going about things. By setting things out as I have done, the word 'his' makes it quite clear that ownership is being asserted, and that should be sufficient.

On the other hand, ownership of his vehicle is not a precondition of liability of the First or Second Defendants, and thus the draft uses the word 'driver' (which is).

Paragraph 2
The Second Claimant has earned a whole paragraph to herself. This is because she was not an active party to the events which have given rise to the present claim. Her cause of action arises out of an alleged breach of a duty of care towards her by the Defendants, and thus falls outside the immediate narrative of the first paragraph. The second paragraph thus succinctly introduces her into the action, and states her position in the car.

Paragraph 3
Taking stock of the situation, we have now introduced the parties, and alleged that an accident took place at a certain place at a certain time, and on a certain date. It is highly unlikely that any of the above matters will be in dispute. No responsibility has yet been alleged for the events that happened. It is now time to do so. So:

> 3.   The said collision was caused by the negligence of the First Defendant as set out below:

Note that I have used the word 'collision' rather than 'accident', as that was the word used in paragraph 1. I suppose that, were one to be really impossibly pedantic, this could be justified on the basis that the collision may have been deliberate — and not an accident. However far-fetched that may be, 'collision' is the proper word to use in the first paragraph as it properly expresses the events that happened without giving rise to unnecessary complications. There therefore seems no reason to substitute any different word in paragraph 3.

You will (I hope) have also observed that I have said nothing about the Second Defendant Company in this paragraph. It is in this action as a result of being vicariously liable for the tort of one of its employees committed in the course of his employment. Thus we are concerned only, at this stage, in establishing that a tort has been committed, upon which such vicarious liability will hang.

As a matter of style, it is not necessary that the words 'as set out below' be added to the paragraph. (Under the old rules, I may have used the words 'as hereinafter set out', but the spirit of modern drafting requires the more mundane, but recognisable, words that I have actually used.) However, I consider them to be an elegant introduction to the Particulars which, you may have guessed, are now to follow.

PARTICULARS OF NEGLIGENCE

(It is perfectly permissible to use the simple heading <u>PARTICULARS</u> should you so wish.)

Within the bounds of reason, it has long been a legal tradition that one can throw in just about anything under this paragraph that one thinks will stick. This has led to some traditional phrases being almost invariably included. Sometimes these phrases are justified, sometimes not. Presumably the rationale behind the above is to ensure that, so far as possible, the Particulars are sufficiently intimidating to 'put the willies up' the other side, and induce a speedy and favourable offer of settlement in your favour. At the risk of being accused of spoiling the fun, I would suggest that the inclusion of Particulars that are short, sharp and to the point, will be more effective than a long *mélange* of general accusations, only some of which will have any relevance to the Claimants' case. Remember that you should be able to justify each Particular as being a breach of a duty of care.

Therefore, before cataloguing the various alleged acts of wickedness committed by Mr Haystack, let us first take stock of what we consider to be the relevant lapses of duty, and then review the chronological order in which they took place:

1. Driving too fast along the High Street.
2. Weaving in and out of traffic.
3. Drunken driving.
4. Hitting the parked car.
5. Going out of control.
6. Skidding into the path of the Focus.
7. Driving with an underinflated tyre.

'… Particulars sufficiently intimidating to put the willies up the other side'

These are not necessarily all concerned with the **direct** cause of the accident, but may be relevant to various departures from the duty of care owed to the Claimants. It will now be necessary to translate these into relevant Particulars of Negligence. In order to do so, it may be helpful to divide up the above into various types of allegation. Let us examine:

1.   Matters relating to the active manner of his general driving.
2.   His physical and mental capacities at the time.
3.   Any defects in his vehicle which may be relevant.
4.   The causation of the accident itself.
5.   Consequent specific allegations of departure from the duty of care owed to the Claimants.

1.   It seems clear that Mr Haystack was driving too fast, and was weaving in and out of traffic. The reasons for this may well be that he was drunk, but we will deal with this under the next heading. However, analysing his driving *vis-à-vis* the Claimants, we have to decide whether or not his driving down the High Street can be translated into any allegation of negligence towards them. Clearly, both the speed and the initial weaving in and out of traffic may have been unlawful, but they were not directly causative of the accident. However, the **nature** of the driving can be described in such a way as to constitute a breach of duty towards other drivers on the road (and in the particular circumstances towards the Claimants), and that is by use of the word **aggressive**. The fact that the First Defendant was driving aggressively along the road towards the Claimants, indicates that he had departed from his proper duty to drive with care for the safety of other traffic, and is thus a relevant allegation. In the present case, the actual acts of aggression may, I suggest, be omitted from the Particulars as being more in the way of evidence than relevant particulars.

2.   It is obvious that some of these categories will overlap. Thus, aggression may describe not merely the manner of driving, but the driver's mental state as well. Additionally, however, Mr Haystack was found to have been driving with over twice the legal limit of alcohol in his blood. That can be looked at in two ways. First, he was committing a criminal offence directly relating to his driving. This will have a paragraph to itself in due course. Secondly, however, it is going to be very hard, if not impossible, for him to resist an allegation that he was driving 'whilst under the influence' of alcohol — which has a direct bearing on the manner of driving which we wish to allege was the cause of the collision.

3. The only defect in the vehicle of which we are aware, is that the front offside tyre was underinflated, due to a faulty valve. It is true that there is presently no evidence that this was directly causative of the collision, but it is nevertheless an act of negligence, which may well have played some part in the driver's failure to control his van once it had struck the Fiat Uno. Thus, it seems appropriate that this item should appear in the Particulars.

4. The cause of the collision has to be described in terms sufficiently comprehensive (and comprehensible) for the First Defendant and the Court to understand precisely what is being alleged, together with the relevant positions of the vehicles before and at the time of the collision. Thus, it is necessary to set out the fact that the van struck a vehicle on its nearside, that it glanced off that vehicle and went out of control, and that it skidded into the path of the Focus which was an oncoming vehicle and then collided with it.

5. Finally, let us look at the departures from the duty and standard of care which we allege are exhibited by the above acts and omissions. Looking at the events in chronological order, the fact that Mr Haystack struck a parked vehicle may have been due to the fact that he did not see it. Even if he did see it, he should have been able to take avoiding action to prevent colliding with it. Once the collision had taken place, he should have been able to control his van rather than skidding across the road and colliding with the Focus. Finally, the whole sorry affair demonstrates, we allege, a completely selfish manner of driving, without any concern for other road users.

Let us now put all this into the Particulars of Negligence. It will first be necessary to decide on the most appropriate format.

It is, of course possible to start each paragraph of the Particulars with a declaration of the First Defendant's misdeeds, for example:

> 1. The First Defendant negligently drove in an aggressive manner and/or at an excessive speed.
> 2. The First Defendant drove with a defective front offside tyre.

but this is an awfully clumsy way of going about things. In this particular example, as in so many cases, stop and consider whether what you are intending to do can be expressed more neatly. Thus, as we are going to be describing a number of different acts of alleged negligence, let's use a general heading to set out the allegation, and then detail the individual acts below:

The First Defendant was negligent in that he: 1 ... 2 ... etc.

In fact, we can be very clever indeed, and do this in relation to some of the general allegations of negligent driving as well, resulting in a taut and authoritative statement:

The First Defendant was negligent in that he:

(1)   Drove his said vehicle along the said road:—
    (a)   in an aggressive manner and/or at an excessive speed;
    (b)   whilst the front offside tyre thereof was underinflated and/or defective;
    (c)   whilst his blood alcohol was more than twice the legal limit, and/or whilst under the influence of alcohol.
(2)   Failed, in time or at all, to observe or heed a Fiat Uno parked at the side of the said road, to his nearside.
(3)   Failed to take any or any sufficient steps to brake, steer or otherwise manoeuvre his said vehicle, so as to avoid colliding with the said Fiat Uno.
(4)   Collided with the said Fiat Uno, and thereafter glanced off the same, lost control of his said vehicle, and skidded sideways across the said road into the oncoming path of the First Claimant's said vehicle, and collided with the same.
(5)   In the circumstances, drove his said vehicle without reasonable concern for the safety of other road users, and in particular the First and Second Claimants.

It's worthwhile analysing these particulars in the light of the principles discussed above.

The first paragraph deals with the first 3 categories of allegation: the active manner of his general driving, his physical and mental capacity at the time, and the defects in the vehicle. In the particular circumstances of the case, these can conveniently be set out under particulars of the way in which the vehicle was being driven along the road. None of them is descriptive of the way in which the accident actually occurred, but each is possibly an important contributory factor. The grouping of these matters in three sub-paragraphs under one heading is, I suggest, not merely convenient but comprehensibly conveys the matters we wish to express in the minimum possible space.

I repeat my earlier warning, and accept that you may not agree with this. If, having considered the principles that I have discussed, you feel that you can do a better job, then good luck to you. At least you will have come to your conclusion having consciously considered the other options.

In particular, I accept that there may be those of you who dislike the use of 'and/or'. I have, of course, used them in each sub-paragraph, and purists may argue that there are a possible 6 allegations set out, and that each should be alleged separately. I respectfully disagree. It is highly unlikely that either of the alternatives will be contentious without the other, and each alternative protects the Claimants against technical defences.

In (a), the speed itself is put as being part of the aggression alleged, or as a separate allegation of negligence. The manner of aggressive driving will be a matter of evidence, but, in the absence of speed, we will also be alleging the weaving in and out of vehicles. The relevance of the speed is as being indicative of the general manner of driving, rather than a direct cause of the accident (although even this has not been entirely discounted in the way in which the particulars have been drafted).

In (b), the underinflation of the tyre is alleged either as an act of negligence on its own, or as being an allegation of driving with a defective tyre. Again, both are interconnected, and prevent any silly defence that no basis for negligence existed merely because the tyre was underinflated.

In (c), the allegations are again linked. It is technically possible for the First Defendant to allege that the fact that his blood alcohol was over the limit did not necessarily cause or contribute to the accident, or that it did not affect his driving. Although there is authority on the subject, this nonsense can simply be prevented by drafting in the way that I have suggested.

The subsequent Particulars deal chronologically with the events which happened, and (I hope) convey sufficient to describe the relevant circumstances in which the collision occurred with enough clarity and precision to permit the Defendants (and the Judge) immediately to comprehend the scene. It is quite possible, of course, to group the various allegations under headed sub-paragraphs as before, i.e. 'Failed...', 'Caused...', etc., but here I do not think that this will assist matters. First, the overall effect will be more clumsy than if set out as I have done. Secondly, we are now dealing with chronological matters, and thirdly the hammer blows of separate sequential allegations have a psychologically greater impact (in my wholly unqualified opinion!). The final 'In the circumstances' is supposed to provide a logical and devastating indictment of the driver's activities.

Note that I have employed some of the conventional phraseology to cover possibilities which might otherwise lead to the case not being fully stated — for example, 'in time or at all', 'any or any sufficient steps' — and a short word on these devices is in order.

One of the difficulties about drafting a case, is that one must take account of all possible eventualities. If we are to make allegations that a Defendant has acted, say, in breach of a duty of care, his precise lapses from grace must be set out. For example, if one was to state:

> Failed to observe a Fiat Uno parked at the side of the said road ...

it is always possible for the Defendant to say 'No, that isn't true, I did see it (although far too late to do anything about it),' or (albeit in desperation) 'No, I saw it all along — I just didn't take any notice of it'.

Now, being adult and sensible about such things, the chances of anyone seriously getting away with such a defence are pretty remote, and any advocate trying to run it would be best advised to stand up in Court wearing a tin hat!

On the other hand, there is no denying the fact that such a draft only alleges that the Defendant failed to observe the car — a fact which may be completely inaccurate. It does not set out the most important aspect of the allegation, which is that he may not have seen it until too late, or alternatively, having seen it, he did nothing about it. Drafting it in the way I have done in paragraph 2 leaves him no way out. However cumbersome it may be, the statement of case has the virtue of precision, and the whole purpose of this work is to encourage accurate and precise thinking, which will have its ultimate expression on paper. Likewise, the expression 'any or any sufficient steps' connotes that even if the Defendant did something, it wasn't sufficient.

Another point to observe is that there must be at least one paragraph which covers the physical events which have led to the present claim being made. Thus in paragraph 4 of the Particulars, the actual collision is described in terms which, it is hoped, are clear and unambiguous. All too often I have seen statements of case which omit to allege that the Defendant actually collided with the Claimant, even though they contain allegations of negligence starting from the way in which he ate his cornflakes in the morning! Once again, such an omission may not be fatal to the claim — but, for the reasons discussed earlier, we are not in the business of fudging our way through the case.

*'... the chances of anyone seriously getting away
with such a defence are pretty remote'*

Paragraph 4

Although in paragraph 1(c) of the Particulars of Negligence, we have
dealt with the First Defendant's driving whilst over the limit, we have
not yet pleaded his conviction which, under the provisions of the Civil
Evidence Act 1968, is admissible as proof of the offence committed.
We should be able simply to deal with the matter as follows:

> 4.   The Claimants will also seek to rely on the fact that on
> 14th December 2005 at Wimbledon Magistrates' Court, the
> First Defendant pleaded guilty to an offence of driving with
> excess alcohol in his blood at the time of the said collision,
> as evidence of his said negligence.

Paragraph 5

Having digested the above, let us consider the next logical step.

We have now identified the parties, alleged that there was a collision, and that it was caused by the negligence of the First Defendant. Further, we have set out the Particulars of Negligence. In order to establish a successful claim, it is of course necessary to show that the Claimant(s) suffered loss or damage as a **result** of the negligence. If they have not done so then there is no claim, whatever the Defendant's breaches of duty of care. So, simply:

> 5.   By reason of the First Defendant's said negligence, the First and Second Claimants suffered personal injury, loss and damage.

This simple paragraph can be expressed in a number of alternative ways, but I do not think that any of them has any advantages over the above. It expresses:

(a)   that the First and the Second Claimants have suffered loss (etc.); and

(b)   that such loss, etc. was occasioned by the negligence, particulars of which have been fully set out in the previous paragraph.

Put another way, there is a logical flow to the draft, which echoes the necessary ingredients of the tort of negligence:

1.   A collision occurred.
2.   It was due to the First Defendant's negligence.
3.   As a result of the negligence, the Claimants suffered injury, loss and damage.

What we now have to do, of course, is describe the nature of the loss (etc.) caused. This is logically divided into general and special damages, and particulars of each should be set out. Normally we will set out the particulars of injury here, but the special damages will usually be set out in a special Schedule, unless they are extremely straightforward.

PARTICULARS OF INJURY

It is now necessary to file a medical report with the claim in virtually all cases. The object of the Particulars is thus clearly not merely to repeat the report verbatim. The paragraph should give a broad idea of the heads of injury for which you are claiming, together with an indication of the seriousness thereof. There are a number of schools of thought on the matter. Some folks believe in a full exposition of the:

> The Claimant was carried on a stretcher to the ambulance, screaming with pain, with his ears hanging off…

variety, whilst others content themselves simply with:

> Lacerations to the face and scalp.
> Fractured left tibia.
> Detained in hospital 3 weeks … etc.

As you may have guessed, I think that the true approach lies somewhere between the two.

I cannot see that there is any tactical advantage to be gained from a long, whingeing Particulars of Injury. The medical report should speak for itself, and whereas there is always some argument that a good, firm Particulars of Claim may convince the Defendants that you are not to be trifled with, I do not feel the same to be true of Particulars of Injury. Negotiations will always take place on the basis of medical reports, and thus the object of a well-drafted Particulars is to ensure that all relevant heads are pleaded. This can involve not merely physical injury, but pain, inconvenience, psychological effects and loss of amenity.

In the present case, therefore, we should deal with each Claimant separately. Remember that it is essential to include any information required under the rules. This includes the Claimant's age and/or date of birth. Thus:

PARTICULARS OF INJURY OF THE FIRST CLAIMANT

> The First Claimant was born on 3rd August 1975, and was 30 years of age at the time of the said accident. As a result of the said collision, he lost consciousness for several minutes and was conveyed by ambulance to the Accident and Emergency Department of Queen Mary's Hospital. The First Claimant was discovered to have suffered a fracture to the radius of his right arm, which was set under general anaesthetic. He was detained for 2 days in hospital, and remained in plaster for 8 weeks, during which time he was unable to work. The First Claimant will also rely, as part of his case, on the report of Dr S. Padrille dated 6th February 2006, a copy of which is annexed hereto.

Although there are some purists who would argue (not entirely without justification) that it is unnecessary to include the removal by ambulance in the Particulars, I have done so because it indicates that the severity of the injury was such that Jack Penn was unable to make his own way to hospital. Apart from that, I would suggest that the matter has been set out in a straightforward manner, and all the essential elements and consequences of the injury have been particularised. We have:

(a) the age of the victim;
(b) unconsciousness;
(c) removal to hospital by ambulance;
(d) the broken arm;
(e) the operation under general anaesthetic;
(f) detention in hospital;
(g) 8 weeks in plaster;
(h) 8 weeks off work;
(i) the medical report.

It is, of course, not necessary to state that Mr Penn thereafter made a good recovery without complications. That will be shown in the medical reports (or admitted), and does not comprise particulars of injury.

At this stage, if you are feeling particularly resourceful and energetic, I would invite you to have a go at drafting the Particulars of Injury of the Second Claimant. My version is set out below in any event, so if you want to cheat, please yourself. I regret that there are no prizes! However, award yourself a double of your favourite tipple if you noticed the possible need for further particulars of any psychological effects that the scarring might have had on Jill Carrot. As I have made up the original case, I shall do the same in this regard as well.

PARTICULARS OF INJURY OF THE SECOND CLAIMANT

The Second Claimant was born on 2nd February 1979, and was 26 years of age at the date of the said accident. As a result of the said collision she suffered a deep gash to the upper part of her right arm, and was conveyed to the said hospital in the ambulance with the First Claimant. The said gash required 8 stitches, whereafter she was allowed to return home. The said injury has healed leaving an unsightly scar which may gradually improve further, but which will always be visible. As a result of the said scarring, the Second Claimant is caused considerable distress and embarrassment and thus wears clothing that covers her arms at all times, thereby diminishing her enjoyment of social occasions and holidays. The Second Claimant will also rely, as part of her case, on the report of Mr R. Chimides FRCS dated 29th March 2006, a copy of which is annexed hereto.

In the above example, I have not felt it necessary to describe how her arm came to be cut — that is a matter of evidence. It is sufficient merely to state that the cut was 'as a result of the accident'.

I also think that the above provides a good illustration of the difficulties that can be encountered in attempting to deal with a number of matters within a succinct compass. Let us take a further look at the last paragraph. Here we wish to show:

(a)   that the scarring causes distress and embarrassment;

(b)   that Jill always feels obliged to wear clothing that covers her arms;

(c)   that this diminishes her enjoyment of social events and holidays.

Now the trouble is, of course, that as I have already (it is hoped) solved the grammatical and logistic problems raised by attempting to combine the above into a comprehensible paragraph, the next bit may lose some of its impact. However, I initially found considerable difficulty in expressing the above matters without repetition or inelegance. The only way that I could find to approach such a problem, was to analyse precisely what it is I was trying to say, in as logical a manner as I could.

The first part is not too difficult — her age has to be set out. The actual injury caused at the time is next, followed by a brief statement that she had to be taken to hospital. Immediate treatment is next, followed by a statement as to the subsequent history (including, if relevant, any particular pain and suffering experienced in the interim). As no full recovery has been made, the permanent disabilities or disfigurements should then follow. Then I dealt with any psychological or physical effects suffered by the victim as a result of the permanent effects of the injury. Here the effect is cumulative. First, the scarring causes general distress and embarrassment at all times. This leads to her feeling obliged to wear long-sleeved clothing at all times. In turn, there are obviously times when this is itself embarrassing or distressing, e.g. when she would otherwise have been enjoying the sunshine on holiday but now feels self-conscious.

Once it is reasoned out in that manner, it is to be hoped that the subsequent drafting becomes merely a matter of good grammatical expression.

So what remains? We have stated the identity of the parties, the accident, the allegations of negligence, and of personal injury suffered as a result of the negligence. We have still, of course, to set out particulars of special damage. In very straightforward cases, it will be sufficient to set these out in the body of the Particulars of Claim. However, in most events, you will have to annex a Schedule of Damages, the preparation of which lies outside the scope of this work. In the present case, it is almost certain that a separate Schedule will be required, annexed to the Particulars of Claim, so that, for example, interest calculations can be properly set out. If the Particulars of Special Damage are to be inserted in the body of the text, simply set out the heading:

PARTICULARS OF SPECIAL DAMAGE

or, if required:

PARTICULARS OF SPECIAL DAMAGE SUFFERED BY THE FIRST CLAIMANT

and tabulate the claim accordingly.

For the sake of clarity, all that will happen in the present case is that we will insert:

PARTICULARS OF SPECIAL DAMAGE

Particulars of the special damage suffered by the First and Second Claimants are set out in the Schedule of Special Damage attached to this Particulars of Claim.

and that should be sufficient for our purposes.

Next, it is necessary to claim interest on the damages awarded. The rules require that if the Claimant is seeking interest, he must state whether he is doing so under the terms of a contract, or under an enactment (which must be specified), or on some other specified basis. Additionally, if the claim is for a specified amount of money, the Claim for Interest must include the percentage rate claimed, the date to which it is calculated (not later than the date of issue of the Claim Form), the total interest to date, and the daily rate at which it accrues thereafter. For example, in a case, say, for breach of contract:

> The Claimant further claims to be entitled to interest at the rate of 8%, on the said sum of £60,000 from 1st May 2004 until 5th June 2006 (being the date of the issue of the Claim Form in this case) being £[whatever], and thereafter at the daily rate of £[whatever] until judgment or sooner payment, pursuant to Section 35A Supreme Court Act 1981.

In this case, we are not claiming a specific sum of money (save for the special damages) and thus a general claim only will be made. In so far as interest on the special damages is concerned, this should be set out in the separate Schedule of Special Damage. For the sake of clarity (and through sheer idleness), I am not going to set out the precise calculations here, but if you insist, you can do these yourself! So:

> The Claimants further claim to be entitled to interest on such general damages as may be awarded, at such rate and for such period as the Court shall deem just, and on the special damages claimed herein at the rate and in the amount set out in the Schedule of Special Damage attached hereto, pursuant to Section 69 of the County Courts Act 1984.

Now we should pause for a moment to consider the **statement of value** of the action which must, under the rules, be inserted in the Claim Form, and which it is wise also to include in the Particulars of Claim. This is done in order to assist case management, and in particular the allocation of a case to the appropriate trial track. It is important, therefore, to ensure that you comply strictly with the rules. In this case, the value of the claim for personal injury, in the case of each Claimant, exceeds £1,000, and this must be stated if the value of the overall action does not exceed £5,000 (as otherwise the claim would assigned to the small claims track). In this case, however, the overall value of the action in respect of each Claimant will almost certainly exceed £5,000, but will not exceed £15,000 (an important figure, beyond which the case will, in the absence of consent, almost certainly be assigned to the multi-track). Therefore it will be necessary for us to insert:

> In the case of each Claimant:
> The value of this action exceeds £5,000 but does not exceed £15,000.

And so we shall!

Now for a word on the Second Defendant Company. We haven't heard much of it in the course of the draft. Although you will not be castigated for including a paragraph claiming against it specifically through its vicarious liability for the torts of its employee, I do not consider this to be necessary. We have claimed that the First Defendant committed the torts complained of whilst in the course of his employment with the Second Defendant Company. We have set out our claims for damages under the various heads. The case against the Second Defendant Company is thus, in my opinion, properly and fully drafted, and more is unnecessary. So we can continue to the next stage.

Prior to the CPR, all pleadings contained what was called a 'prayer', in which the Claimant would conclude his claim with a statement of the relief claimed, thus:

> AND the Plaintiff claims:
> 1.   Damages
> 2.   Interest as aforesaid
> 3.   (Anything else that he could possibly think of)
> 4.   Costs

Under the CPR, there is no express requirement for a claim to contain a 'prayer' (and it would almost certainly not be referred to as such under the new terminology). The Claim Form itself, which contains a space for the inclusion of a short Particulars of Claim, does not specifically require a summary of the claim, but I would nevertheless advise that the old 'prayer' format (whatever we call it today) should be retained, so that there is a clear summary at the end of the case of the relief being sought by the Claimant. Of course, this work assumes that your Particulars of Claim will be contained on a separate sheet and will be served with, or within the prescribed period after, the Claim Form. So we will proceed as follows:

> AND the First and/or Second Claimants claim:
> 1.   Damages;
> 2.   Interest as aforesaid.

Strictly speaking, it is not necessary to claim costs, as these will be dealt with by the Court at the conclusion of the trial. Nevertheless, I confess to being one of those who usually slip in a claim for costs at the end, just for the sake of completeness (and to remind the other side that this could be a very expensive exercise for them if they don't cough up now). (On the other hand, if we lose it could be a very expensive exercise for us as well, but there's no harm in being reminded of that either!) Note that once again, coward that I am, I have included the words 'the First and/or Second Claimants', in order to avoid any possible argument that they stand or fall together. Possibly silly, but sometimes a desperate Defendant will try anything!

Remember, before concluding the draft, the rules require the Particulars of Claim to be verified by a statement of truth. Although this work is confined to drafting technique and does not extend to civil procedure, remember that the responsibility for signing the statement of truth is that of the **client** and that it is not sufficient or proper for you to sign in the general belief that your client must be telling the truth. The general rule should be that once you have finished and signed your draft, the client should then sign the statement of truth. If you choose to sign it (if you are a solicitor), you should have obtained express instructions from your client that the facts stated therein are true, and will be taken to have warned him or her of the consequences of such a statement being proved subsequently to be false! If you are Counsel, it is best not to sign the statement of truth in any circumstances. Most importantly of all, ensure that it is included in the draft.

> Statement of Truth
> I believe* (the Claimant believes) that the facts stated in these particulars of claim are true.
> *I am duly authorised by the Claimant to sign this statement.

(In future, I will abbreviate the above.)

So for the sake of completeness, here is our *grande oeuvre* in full:

IN THE VERULAM COUNTY COURT   Case No. VL0000

BETWEEN:

Mr JACK PENN

1st Claimant

and

Miss JILL CARROT

2nd Claimant

— and —

Mr DENNIS HAYSTACK

1st Defendant

and

STOPPADRIP LIMITED

<u>2nd Defendant</u>

PARTICULARS OF CLAIM

1. On Monday, 17th October 2005, at about 4 pm, the First Claimant was driving his Ford Focus motor car, registration number Y123 ABC down Putney Hill, London SW15 at the junction with Upper Richmond Road, when a collision occurred between his said vehicle and a Bedford van registration number CFL 204Z driven by the First Defendant, who was at all relevant times the employee or agent of the Second Defendant Company, acting in the course of his employment.

2. At the time of the said accident, the Second Claimant was the front seat passenger in the First Claimant's said vehicle.

3. The said collision was caused by the negligence of the First Defendant as set out below:

PARTICULARS OF NEGLIGENCE

The First Defendant was negligent in that he:
 (1)   Drove his said vehicle along the said road:
  (a)   in an aggressive manner and/or at an excessive speed;
  (b)   whilst the front offside tyre thereof was underinflated and/or defective;
  (c)   whilst his blood alcohol was more than twice the legal limit, and/or whilst under the influence of alcohol.
 (2)   Failed, in time or at all, to observe or heed a Fiat Uno parked at the side of the said road, to his nearside.
 (3)   Failed to take any or any sufficient steps to brake, steer or otherwise manoeuvre his said vehicle, so as to avoid colliding with the said Fiat Uno.
 (4)   Collided with the said Fiat Uno, and thereafter glanced off the same, lost control of his said vehicle, and skidded sideways across the said road into the oncoming path of the First Claimant's said vehicle, and collided with the same.

(5)   In the circumstances, drove his said vehicle without reasonable concern for the safety of other road users, and in particular the First and Second Claimants.

4.   The Claimants will also seek to rely on the fact that on 14th December 2005 at Wimbledon Magistrates' Court, the First Defendant pleaded guilty to an offence of driving with excess alcohol in his blood at the time of the said collision, as evidence of his said negligence.

5.   By reason of the First Defendant's said negligence, the First and Second Claimants suffered personal injury, loss and damage.

PARTICULARS OF INJURY OF THE FIRST CLAIMANT

The First Claimant was born on 3rd August 1975, and was 30 years of age at the time of the said accident. As a result of the said collision, he lost consciousness for several minutes and was conveyed by ambulance to the Accident and Emergency Department of Queen Mary's Hospital. The First Claimant was discovered to have suffered a fracture to the radius of his right arm, which was set under general anaesthetic. He was detained for 2 days in hospital, and remained in plaster for 8 weeks, during which time he was unable to work. The First Claimant will also rely, as part of his case, on the report of Dr S. Padrille dated 6th February 2006, a copy of which is annexed hereto.

PARTICULARS OF INJURY OF THE SECOND CLAIMANT

The Second Claimant was born on 2nd February 1979, and was 26 years of age at the date of the said accident. As a result of the said collision she suffered a deep gash to the upper part of her right arm, and was conveyed to the said hospital in the ambulance with the First Claimant. The said gash required 8 stitches, whereafter she was allowed to return home. The said injury has healed leaving an unsightly scar which may gradually improve further, but which will always be visible. As a result of the said scarring, the Second Claimant is caused considerable distress and embarrassment and thus wears clothing that covers her arms at all times, thereby diminishing her enjoyment of social occasions and holidays. The Second Claimant will also rely, as part of her case, on the report of Mr R. Chimides FRCS dated 29th March 2006, a copy of which is annexed hereto.

PARTICULARS OF SPECIAL DAMAGE

Particulars of the special damage suffered by the First and Second Claimants are set out in the Schedule of Special Damage attached to this Particulars of Claim.

6.   The Claimants further claim to be entitled to interest on such general damages as may be awarded, at such rate and for such period as the Court shall deem just, and on the special damages claimed herein at the rate and in the amounts set out in the Schedule of Special Damage attached hereto, pursuant to Section 69 of the County Courts Act 1984.

7.   In the case of each Claimant:
     The value of this action exceeds £5,000 but does not exceed £15,000.

AND the first and/or Second Claimants claim:
1.   Damages;
2.   Interest as aforesaid.

POLLY VINYL-CHLORIDE

<u>Statement of Truth</u>
I believe* (the Claimant believes) that the facts stated in these particulars of claim are true.
*I am duly authorised by the Claimant to sign this statement.

I hope that the above exercise will have demonstrated that there are certain factors which are common to all drafting, of whatever nature. The whole point of this tome is to divert attention away from the precedent books, and to illustrate that one can make a good 'stab' at a set of papers founded on a few basic principles, an understanding of the case (and of the law), and some sound common sense.
    Let me suggest that you should adopt a philosophy of drafting which I shall call 'The 4 Cs':

1.   The draft should be as **concise** as possible.
2.   The draft should be as **comprehensive** as possible.
3.   The draft should be as **comprehensible** as possible.
4.   The draft should be as **accurate** as possible.

The more astute amongst you may have noticed that the fourth listed matter does not begin with the letter C. I hope it will enable you to remember it all the better!

1.   When I say 'concise', I mean that you should not be any longer than is necessary. This can be achieved not merely by rigid exclusion of all that is irrelevant, but also by good use of language and the adoption of taut phraseology whenever it can be of service.

2.   'Comprehensive' is not at odds with the first idea. The draft should contain all that is necessary, albeit within the shortest possible compass.

3.   'Comprehensible' means that the finished product should be easy to assimilate. It should not be confusing or confused. It should 'look good', or to put it in modern terminology, it should be 'user friendly'. This can be achieved by consistent use of good layout, including the use of sub-paragraphs where it would lead to greater clarity, such as I have done in the Particulars of Negligence of the First Defendant, in the above example.

4.   'Accurate' should be self-explanatory. It requires, as I have stated, a thorough knowledge of your case and the applicable law (including any specialised rules of drafting relevant to the particular instance).

'… one can make a good stab'

The above principles should be applicable to **all** statements of case or documents of whatever nature. Indeed, they can be applied to advocacy and to the writing of opinions as well. By way of further illustration, let's take another set of facts, and analyse the appropriate statement of case.

EXAMPLE

Julian Spratt purchased a flat in a mansion block in Bassett Road, Bitterne, Southampton. He intended to have it 'done up', with a view to letting it. He enlisted the services of Albert Grumble, who was the sole proprietor of Grumble Builders. In the course of various conversations (mainly in the local pub, the 'Admiral Rowe' in Bitterne) during June 2004, the parties agreed that Mr Grumble would undertake the refurbishment of the flat. A schedule of works was drawn up and agreed between them. Mr Grumble said that he would do the job for £12,500, inclusive of VAT. (Those are your instructions — we'll leave any suspicions to HM Revenue & Customs!)

Mr Spratt is adamant he told Mr Grumble that he wanted to let the flat, and that it was agreed that the works would start during the last week of July 2004, and would take between 2 and 3 weeks. It was also agreed that he would pay £10,500 'up front', and the balance of £2,000 would be paid on completion.

In a letter dated 29th June 2004, Grumble Builders wrote: 'I confirm our agreement that I should do the works to your flat for £12,500, and that I will start during the last week in July.'

Mr Spratt paid the sum of £10,500 on 24th July, and works duly commenced almost immediately, but they continued at a slow pace. By the end of the first week in September, it was clear that they were far from finished. Mr Spratt complained bitterly at the delay, but on 6th September, Mr Grumble left the site.

On 8th September, Mr Spratt received a letter from Mr Grumble apologising for the delay, stating that he was 'on the sick, with my nerves', but would hope to return within 2 to 3 weeks.

Nothing having happened in the interim, on 4th October 2004, Mr Spratt sent Mr Grumble a letter making time the essence of the agreement, and requiring him within 3 days to confirm that he would resume work at the premises within 7 days thereafter, and to ensure that all matters were finished within a further week, otherwise the contract would be treated as having been repudiated by him.

No reply having been received, Mr Spratt then engaged another firm of builders to finish the works. They were able to start on 30th October, and finished by 6th November. A tenant was found for the premises,who moved in on 24th November.

The new builders charged £6,750 to complete the works. Mr Spratt wishes to recover for the additional cost, and for his loss of rental in the meantime.

Applying the same procedure as in the previous example, we will commence by identifying the parties. This should not be difficult, but we must make sure that the Defendant is sued in his proper capacity. The Claimant is Julian Spratt; the Defendant is not a corporate entity, so he must be sued as:

Mr Albert Grumble (trading as Grumble Builders).

As to the Court of trial, we are going to sue for £6,750 (being the additional cost of completing the works) **less** the retainer of £2,000 presently held by Mr Spratt. Additionally, we understand that there is to be a claim for loss of rent. At the moment we do not know the exact amount. However, the works were to take about 2 to 3 weeks, and were to commence in late July. It would be reasonable to assume that the flat would have been available for letting as from the 1st September. Presumably Mr Spratt could have been advertising for tenants in the interim period, although this is a matter which will have to be canvassed with the client, and argued at trial if necessary.

The works were actually completed by 6th November, and the new tenant moved in on the 24th. Although the Defendant may well wish to know why a tenant could not have been sought in the meantime, and moved in on the 7th, or may argue that in the circumstances Mr Spratt might have been unable to procure a tenant until some time after 1st September had the contract been fulfilled, we obviously do not have to worry about this at the present moment. The appropriate dates of loss to set out will be between 1st September and 24th November 2004.

Even without knowing the precise rental (which is subsequently confirmed at £200 per week), it is clear that this case must be commenced in the County Court. The obvious venues are either the local Court of the Defendant, or that of the area in which the property in question is situated. Coincidentally, in this example, they are one and the same!

The causes of action and the remedies to be sought should be the next matter to concern us. We should here also take note of any points which may complicate the statement of case, or which may require special care. Here we will be seeking:

Damages for breach of contract being:

1. Additional cost of completing the building works.
2. Loss of rental caused by the delay.
3. Interest.

We must take care about setting out the terms of the contract, and in particular the fact that time limits were to be observed. Additionally, we must consider the legal effect of the letter of 4th October. What effect (if any) did this have on the existing terms of the contract?

We should also bear in mind the relevant law relating to remoteness of damage. As a result it may be necessary to show (and therefore to allege) that the builders were at all times aware of the fact that the property was to be 'done up' for letting, such that they would have known that any delay in completing the contract would have caused loss of rental income.

Finally, we will have to deal with the way in which we are going to set out the termination of the contract, such as entitled Mr Spratt to put in another firm of builders to complete the job.

Bearing all these in mind, we will start with the easy bit:

IN THE SOUTHAMPTON COUNTY COURT   Case No.

BETWEEN:

Mr JULIAN SPRATT

Claimant

— and —

Mr ALBERT GRUMBLE
(Trading as GRUMBLE BUILDERS)

Defendant

PARTICULARS OF CLAIM

Now it's your turn ...

I hope that, applying the principles set out in the earlier example, you will have decided that the first paragraph should contain some form of identification. There seems no reason to set out the identity of the Claimant at this point, but that of the Defendant **is** relevant here, as he is being sued on a contract which he entered in the course of his business. I would have put:

> 1. The Defendant is and was at all relevant times a builder and decorator carrying on business under the name of Grumble Builders.

Again, the use of the phrase 'is and was at all relevant times' makes it plain that the Claimant is going to allege that the subject matter of the present claim is going to concern the Defendant in his stated capacity. Although this obviously does not preclude the Defendant from claiming that he may at some time have been dealing with the Claimant in another capacity (perhaps because he did not trade under the name of Grumble Builders at some relevant moment), the Claimant's case is clear and unambiguous.

There is no need to set out the Claimant's identity. After all, what would you say? The Claimant is a bloke? Admittedly, you could say should you wish:

> The Claimant is and was at all relevant times the owner of a flat situated at and known as 2 Tumbledown Mansions, 115 Bassett Road, Bitterne, Southampton,

and then set out the contract without repeating the above, but I do not think it would add anything to the narrative clarity of your case. If you did wish to pursue that course, your draft would run:

> 1. The Defendant is and was at all relevant times a builder and decorator carrying on business under the name of Grumble Builders. The Claimant is and was at all relevant times the owner of a flat situated at and known as 2 Tumbledown Mansions, 115 Bassett Road, Bitterne, Southampton.

Or more succinctly:

> 1. At all relevant times the Claimant was the owner of a flat situated at and known as 2 Tumbledown Mansions, 115 Bassett Road, Bitterne, Southampton, and the

Defendant was a builder and decorator carrying on business under the name of Grumble Builders.

2.   By an oral agreement made in about June 2004, the Defendant, in the course of his said business, agreed with the Claimant that he would carry out various building and redecoration works to the Claimant's said flat for a total price of £12,500 inclusive of VAT. The said agreement was evidenced, amongst other matters, by a letter from the Defendant dated 29th June 2004, and an undated schedule of works agreed between the parties.

The other way would be to put:

1.   The Defendant is and was at all relevant times a builder and decorator carrying on business under the name of Grumble Builders.

2.   By an oral agreement made in about June 2004, the Defendant, in the course of his said business, agreed with the Claimant that he would perform various building and redecoration works to the Claimant's flat at 2 Tumbledown Mansions, 115 Bassett Road, Bitterne, Southampton, for a total price of £12,500 inclusive of VAT. The said agreement was evidenced, amongst other matters, by a letter from the Defendant dated 29th June 2004, and by an undated schedule of works agreed between the parties.

As I have indicated, I prefer the second version, as I consider it to be more fluent, and compatible with the narrative. That is not, of course, to say that the first is in any way incorrect or unacceptable.

Note, however, the way in which the existence of the contract has been stated in both instances. The agreement is 'oral', it was made in 'about' June 2004 (as the precise date is unknown and probably not contentious), and the subjectmatter of the contract has been alleged as 'various' building works. The reason for this last is that it is probable that the dispute will not concern the 'identity' of the works to be performed, and in any event they are later identified by reference to the schedule agreed between the parties. Therefore, rather than complicate the issue with some form of explanation of the works that were to be done, it is perfectly permissible to describe them generically, and then by reference to the schedule, as has been done.

You may be interested to enquire why it is that I have set out 'evidence' of the contract, and why such evidence has been stated to be 'amongst other matters'. This is merely in order to identify the existence of the agreement — it was oral, but in case there was any ambiguity, the Defendant acknowledged its existence in a letter. Further, the schedule of works was orally expressly agreed to be incorporated into the agreement. The Defendant is thus left in no doubt as to precisely what is being alleged. The 'amongst other matters' is there for two reasons. First there will, of course, be oral evidence of the agreement given by the Claimant. Secondly, it implies that the Claimant is not committing himself merely to the matters alleged in the statement of case. Thus if, for example, other relevant documentation comes to hand, or unforeseen circumstances occur to bolster the case, no embarrassment will be caused. It's a safety net to a certain extent, and although in an ideal world one should not be necessary, this is far from being an ideal world!

Now we have identified the parties and alleged the existence of the contract, we must set out the particular terms which we allege were contained therein, and which we say were broken by the Defendant. It is, of course, unnecessary to state all the terms of the agreement, particularly as it was oral, and even more particularly because only certain of them are relevant to this cause of action. It is not (for once) alleged that such works as were done were done badly, so, for example, there is no need to allege an implied condition that the work was to be done in a competent and professional manner.

The centre of attention here will be time. Both the commencement date of the works and the length of time which they were to take were, we say, express terms of the contract, such that failure to adhere to the same justifies the present claim for damages. As time is not invariably of such importance that delay is inevitably actionable, we must make it quite clear that it was so in the present case.

However, before we put pen to paper, let us think the whole thing through logically, i.e., map out the basis of our case:

Grumble agreed to start at or about the end of July.
He agreed to do the works within 2–3 weeks.
He knew that time was important, as Spratt wished to let the premises.
He didn't finish within the agreed period.
He later left the site.
He never returned.

Now all that certainly expresses our case as we have been instructed. However, I can see one further way in which our case could be advanced, and additionally there is one small legal hurdle to overcome.

The additional advancement of our case comes in so far as the necessary time for completing the works is concerned. The agreement is oral, and there is no indication in the Defendant's letter of 29th June that he would complete them within 2 to 3 weeks. Although it is wrong to 'jump the stile' and anticipate potential defences, there is no reason why one cannot take advantage of alternative forms of setting out the case where the opportunity properly exists.

As you are of course aware, even where time is **not** of the essence in a contract, there is an implied term that work will be completed within a 'reasonable' time. In order thereafter to succeed in an action for breach and/or repudiation of contract, it is necessary for a Claimant to indicate to the Defendant that in his view, a reasonable time has now elapsed, and that unless the Defendant withdraws his digit pretty quick (within a stated time), he will have been held to have broken and/or repudiated the agreement.

As it happens, this is what, in any event, has happened in the present case. On 4th October, Mr Spratt gave the Defendant 3 days to reply, confirming that he would complete the outstanding works within a further 7 days. This was in fact the small legal hurdle which I mentioned above, as it is legally incompatible with time having been of the essence in the first place. However, laymen are by definition not lawyers, and the mere fact that Mr Spratt may have been disposed to have given some additional time in the circumstances may not deprive him of his original legal rights.

Nevertheless, even without the express term as to time that we allege, there is therefore another ground upon which we are able to allege breach of contract, and we should take advantage of it. Of course, we would rather not, as the measure of damages for loss of rental would only run, in that case, from the date of expiry of the ultimatum, i.e., 14th October, and we would prefer to claim from 1st September. Still, if needs must, beggars cannot be choosers, and we should set out the alternative just in case. Our second line of attack is therefore:

Grumble agreed to commence the works during the last week in July.
The works were to be completed within a reasonable time.
They weren't.
Spratt gave notice making time the essence.
This was ignored.
The contract was therefore broken, and Spratt is entitled to damages.

All that remains is for us to combine the two, as merely to allege one after the other would be cumbersome. Once again, therefore, before wasting the ink, let's map out the way in which we will put the matter:

It was an express term that the work would commence in the last week of July 2004.

It was an express term that the works would be completed within 2–3 weeks thereafter.

Even if it wasn't, there was an implied term that the works were to be completed within a reasonable time.

We say that a reasonable time would have been 3 weeks.

We paid him the agreed down payment, and he started work on time.

He didn't finish within the agreed period.

He left the site after the agreed period had ended, without having finished the works.

He sent a letter stating that he wasn't going to come back for 2 or 3 weeks.

Even then he didn't come back.

We made time of the essence.

He ignored our letter.

We were forced to bring in other builders.

As a result, we suffered loss and damage.

Having performed the above exercise, the rest should be straightforward. We must set out:

1. The relevant terms.
2. Any relevant narrative.
3. The breaches of contract.
4. The letter making time the essence.

5. The failure to reply, and legal consequences.
6. The alleged loss and damage.

Remember that where a claim is based on a written agreement, the
CPR require that a copy of the contractual document(s) constituting
the agreement should be attached to or served with the Particulars of
Claim; and where the claim is based on an oral agreement, the
Particulars of Claim should set out the contractual words used, stating by
whom, to whom, and when and where they were spoken. Our draft must
therefore contain the required information — at least in so far as it is
available.

At this stage, it's time to have a go yourself. Your finished product
will, of course, look like this:

IN THE SOUTHAMPTON COUNTY COURT   Case No.

BETWEEN:

Mr JULIAN SPRATT

Claimant

— and —

Mr ALBERT GRUMBLE
(Trading as GRUMBLE BUILDERS)

Defendant

PARTICULARS OF CLAIM

---

1. The Defendant is and was at all relevant times a builder and decorator carrying on business under the name of Grumble Builders.

2. By an oral agreement made in about June 2004, in the course of
and as a result of several conversations between the Claimant and
the Defendant in the 'Admiral Rowe' public house in Bitterne,
Southampton, the Defendant, in the course of his said business, agreed
with the Claimant that he would perform various building and redecoration works to the Claimant's flat at 2 Tumbledown Mansions, 115 Bassett
Road, Bitterne, Southampton, for a total price of £12,500 inclusive of VAT.

The said agreement was evidenced, apart from other matters, by a letter from the Defendant dated 29th June 2004, and by an undated schedule of works agreed between the parties, copies of which are appended to this Particulars of Claim.

3.   At all relevant times the Defendant knew that the said works were required by the Claimant in order that he could let the said premises immediately after the conclusion thereof.

4.   There were, amongst others, the following express terms of the said agreement:
 (1)   That the Defendant would commence the said works during the last week of July 2004.
 (2)   That the same would be completed within 2–3 weeks of the commencement thereof.
 (3)   That the Claimant would pay the said price by means of one payment of £10,500 immediately prior to the commencement of the said works, and the balance of £2,000 upon the completion thereof.

5.   Alternatively, it was an implied term of the said agreement that the said works would be completed within a reasonable time of their said commencement. The Claimant will contend that 3 weeks was and would have been such a reasonable time.

6.   The Claimant duly paid the Defendant the sum of £10,500 on 24th July 2004, and the Defendant duly commenced the said works immediately thereafter.

7.   In breach of the said agreement, the Defendant:
 (a)   failed to complete the said works within the agreed time or at all;
 (b)   left the said site on 6th September 2004 whilst the said works had not been completed;
 (c)   by a letter dated 7th September 2004 informed the Claimant that he was 'on the sick with my nerves' but would hope to return to complete the said works within 2–3 weeks;
 (d)   Thereafter failed and/or refused to return to the said premises and complete the same.

8.   By reason of the said breaches (and without prejudice to the matters set out in paragraphs 3 and 4 hereof), by a letter dated 4th October 2004,

the Claimant required the Defendant to confirm, within 3 days of the receipt thereof, that he was prepared to return to the said site and complete the said works within 7 days thereafter, failing which the Claimant would treat the Defendant as having repudiated the said agreement.

9. Notwithstanding the aforesaid, the Defendant thereafter failed, within the said time or at all, to answer the said letter, give the said undertaking, and/or to complete the said works, as a result whereof the Defendant repudiated the said agreement and/or was treated by the Claimant as having done so.

10. By reason of the Defendant's said breaches of contract and/or repudiation of the same, the Claimant has suffered loss and damage:

PARTICULARS

(1) The Claimant was obliged to instruct PDQ Builders to complete the said works. The said firm were unable to commence the same until 30th October 2004, and finished on 6th November 2004 at a cost of £6,750.

(2) The Claimant was unable to let the said premises until 24th November 2004, and thereby lost rental at the rate of £200 per week from 1st September 2004, being a total of £2,400.

The Claimant will give credit for the sum of £2,000 presently retained by him under the said agreement.

11. The Claimant also claims interest at the rate of [x%] on

(1) the sum of £4,750 from [date] to [date of issue of Claim Form] being [£], and thereafter at the daily rate of [£] until judgment or sooner payment, and

(2) on the sum of £2,000 from [date] until [date of issue of Claim Form] being [£], and thereafter at the daily rate of [£] until judgment or sooner payment,

pursuant to Section 69 of the County Courts Act 1984.

12. The value of this action exceeds £5,000 but does not exceed £15,000.

AND the Claimant claims:

1. Damages;

2. Interest as aforesaid.

Statement of Truth
I believe* (the Claimant believes) that the facts stated in these particulars of claim are true.
*I am duly authorised by the Claimant to sign this statement.

LAURA NORDA

Let us look at some points that arise from the above.

Paragraph 3
It is, of course, essential to set the case out in these terms in order to be able to make a claim for the loss of rental. Once again, the phrase 'at all relevant times' is used to ensure that we have made clear that at no relevant time was the Defendant **unaware** of this fact.

Paragraph 4
Here, sub-paragraphs have been used to plead the various express terms which we claim are relevant to our case. Stylistic variations on this could include:

> There were, amongst others, express terms of the said agreement that ...

although I prefer the way that has been used above. The words 'amongst others' are used for accuracy, to impart that there were (or may have been) other terms of the agreement, but we are not interested in them for present purposes.

Although it is a matter of taste, I have preferred economical use of language in paragraph 4(2) by use of the words 'same' and 'thereof'. I could have put:

> That the said works would be completed within 2–3 weeks of their having been started

and I suppose there's nothing wrong with that. I simply prefer the drafted version as being more taut and authoritative. It may be that you will disagree, and consider that the alternative version is less 'legal' and has greater clarity.

That just goes to prove my point that there is no statutory way of drafting, and of course the whole point of this *magnum opus* is, if possible, to assist you to develop your own style of drafting, in the way that you find most comfortable.

In paragraph 4(3) I have again preferred economical language. I am as guilty as the next person of overuse of the word 'said', although I use it in order to avoid any possibility of ambiguity. Thus 'the said price' avoids any likelihood of confusion with any other possible payment, and 'the said works' makes it abundantly clear that no other works fall into consideration. Having 'said' this, I freely concede that the present instructions do not suggest that there were any other works or any other price. My suggestion is still that you should err on the side of caution and use 'said', unless to do so will make the finished product grammatically indigestible.

Paragraph 5
I have already mentioned the necessity for setting out the implied term as to time. The contention as to 3 weeks makes it clear that no concessions are being made on the point, so that even if there had been no specific agreement on the point, the time suggested was more than sufficient. The words 'was and would have been' are included to show that our case is that both with foresight and hindsight, 3 weeks was reasonable. It may be 'belt and braces', but it's better than being caught with your trousers down!

Paragraph 6
The word 'duly' is used to denote that the acts were done in pursuance of an **obligation**, by virtue of the contract.

Paragraph 7
Again, note the use of sub-paragraphs to give clarity to the expression of the various breaches of contract complained of.

Paragraph 8
The Claimant's letter is expressed to have been 'by reason of the said breaches' — i.e. the statement of case carries through the narrative in logical form. In case it should be thought this shows any weakening in the original contention that there was a specifically agreed time for performance, this second argument is expressed to be 'without prejudice' to the first.

Paragraph 9
The words 'failed, within the said time or at all,' make it clear that the work was not completed, even at a later date. This is another example of the need to ensure that the case is expressed with the greatest possible precision. It is probably adequate to put that the Defendant failed to

answer the letter, give the undertaking, and/or to complete the works. However, it is a more exact statement of the case to state that the various acts did not take place **either** within the time given, **or** indeed at any time. Psychologically I think it enhances the Claimant's claim — the Defendant did not merely ignore the time limit, he abandoned all of his obligations under the agreement.

The remainder of the Particulars of Claim is, I hope, straightforward, and continues the narrative with an exposition of the degree and extent of loss and damage allegedly suffered by the Claimant.

My final illustration in this chapter concerns the way in which we should approach commencing proceedings when we have reason to believe that part of our case may be defective in law.

Obviously, we all have a duty not to commence proceedings which we believe to be wrong in law. This duty is owed not only to the client (who is, after all, directly or indirectly paying the bill), but also to the Court itself. Thus, in the event of a client insisting that a claim be started in cases when you are positive that there can be no cause of action, you must regretfully invite said client to take his business elsewhere.

However, there may, from time to time, be circumstances in which you have a very strong conviction that the case will not be successful, but the ultimate result may depend on an assessment of the evidence rather than of the law. Sometimes a set of facts exists, the interpretation of which will, in your expert view, almost inevitably be against your client. In such circumstances, one gives the appropriate advice. Although, as a solicitor, you are not obliged to take on a case, once you have done so you may often feel professionally bound to continue even if your advice is ignored, unless you are positive that the action must fail. If you are Counsel, you must of course continue to act unless to do so would result in your being professionally embarrassed.

I give below an example of a case in which one of the contentions is decidedly 'iffy', and we will take a quick look at the way in which I suggest it should be set out.

EXAMPLE

On 8th August 1983, Miss Maureen Flight was granted a 'holiday let' of 2 Aerodrome Cottages, Elstree, Herts by the then owners Grottylet Ltd, at a monthly rental of £90. The original letting was in writing and for a period of 3 months, but it was then continued by agreement for a further 3.

At the end of that period, Miss Flight simply remained in possession, and the landlords accepted rent.

Our clients, The Perfect Property Company Ltd, purchased the property early in 2002. They continued to accept rent from Miss Flight, but in April 2004 she began to fall into arrears, gradually at first, so that by 1st November 2004 the amount owing was only £90. However, from that day on, no rent whatsoever was paid.

In August 2005, the landlords instructed their previous solicitors to issue a Notice to Quit, as is required under the relevant legislation covering the period when the property was originally let. They originally made a mess of it, and stated the landlord to be Grottylet Ltd. They then served a Notice in proper form on 10th November 2005, but which purported to determine the tenancy on 22nd September 2005. Fortunately, the Notice contained the printed 'catch-all' provision, that alternatively it expired after 4 weeks from the beginning of the rent period next following service.

For some unexplained reason, the landlords then became dissatisfied with their then solicitors! New solicitors have been instructed, and the pleasant task of drafting proceedings has fallen to you.

Nowadays of course, possession proceedings are usually drafted on a standard form and now must be in accordance with CPR Part 55. But this is a somewhat unusual case, and in any event, this is a book on drafting techniques, not form-filling. So bear with me.

Applying the principles with which I trust we are now most familiar, we should have no difficulty in identifying the appropriate parties to the action. The Court of trial will be the County Court.

The **cause of action** is obviously for possession, together with arrears of rent and/or mesne profits. However, here we hit the first snag.

Although the case will have to be determined on the facts, it's quite obvious that the 'holiday let' either was, or became a sham. Fortunately (as this is an exercise in drafting, and not in the law of landlord and tenant), a Notice to Quit was served, which should nevertheless give the landlord grounds to claim possession under Case 1 of Schedule 15 to the Rent Act 1977, which covered the period in question, provided that the Court was satisfied there were arrears of rent and that it was reasonable to make an Order. However, here we hit the second snag, in that the Notice was not exactly straightforward.

As I have said, we will claim that the Notice was not invalid, as it gave an alternative date of expiry that was correct. That should leave us in the clear. So, bearing all the above in mind, we will have to set out:

1.   The Landlord's interest in the property.
2.   The contract with the Defendant (or the reason for which she is in occupation of the property).
3.   The determination of the tenancy.
4.   The reason(s) for which we claim possession.
5.   The remedies that we seek.
6.   All other matters that we are specifically required to insert in the Particulars of Claim, by virtue of CPR Parts 16 and 55 and the associated Practice Directions.

IN THE WATFORD COUNTY COURT   Case No.

BETWEEN:

THE PERFECT PROPERTY COMPANY LIMITED
                                                         Claimant
— and —

Miss MAUREEN FLIGHT
                                                         Defendant

PARTICULARS OF CLAIM

That was the easy bit! The next bit's not too bad either. We must state the landlord's title, and his alleged right to possession of the property.

Paragraph 1

1. The Claimant Company is the freehold owner and entitled
to possession of residential premises situate at and known as
2, Aerodrome Cottages, Elstree, Hertfordshire.

Here I have 'killed two birds with one stone', by introducing the Claimant and also alleging that the Claimant is entitled to possession of the premises. The Rules require that we state that the claim relates to residential premises.

Paragraph 2
Here we have to use a little mental dexterity. We wish to set out the fact that the Defendant was granted a holiday letting by the former landlords, and that the Claimant purchased the premises with a sitting tenant. We must also here give consideration as to what approach we are going to take with regard to the tricky problem of the 'holiday let' itself.

Dealing with the latter point first, we have to face the fact that it must be set out, as we have to give an accurate account of the circumstances in which the Defendant took up residence at the property. However, as I have said, we are fortunate in that we can dispense with any reliance on the nature of the original letting, as we can, on our instructions, make out a perfectly good case for possession of a protected and then a statutory tenancy. We could deal with the paragraph thus:

> 2.   By a written agreement dated 8th August 1983, made between the Claimant Company's predecessors in title, Grottylet Ltd, and the Defendant, the Defendant was granted a holiday letting of the said premises for a period of 3 months at a monthly rental of £90.
> 3.   The said letting was subsequently extended for a further 3 months, whereafter the Defendant continued to occupy the said premises at the said rental.
> 4.   The Claimant Company acquired the said premises by purchase in about early 2002, at which time the Defendant was still occupying the same.

The above paragraphs have the advantages of logic, accuracy and detail. They are also long-winded, cumbersome and totally unnecessary, so:

> 2.   The Claimant Company purchased its said interest in the premises in about early 2002, at which time the Defendant was the occupier and/or a tenant thereof, having been granted a holiday letting of the same by the Claimant's predecessors in title, Grottylet Ltd, on 8th August 1983. In 2002 and at all relevant times thereafter, the rental for the letting was £90 per month.

All done in one paragraph! We have followed on from the first paragraph, and thus can refer to the Claimant's 'said interest'; the Defendant was resident in the premises at the time, and the circumstances of her residence are set out in detail as is necessary. Note the stylistic variation of 'a tenant thereof', and then, 'a holiday letting of the same', rather than using 'thereof' twice.

Paragraph 3
The above does not, of course, get us around the problem of the holiday let. So let's come clean:

> 3. Further or alternatively, at the time of the said purchase by the Claimant Company, the Defendant was a contractual periodic tenant of the said property, at a monthly rental of £90.

OK, I admit it, this is a bit of a fudge. The 'further or alternatively' hardly hides the fact that we obviously don't think much of the argument that the Defendant was still resident in the property under a holiday let (if she ever was) at the time that the Claimant Company took over the property. In any event, we continued to take the rent, so we might as well get around any suggestion that the holiday letting was not bona fide from the beginning, and nail our colours to the mast.

Paragraph 4
Having 'explained' the position as it stood when we took over, there seems no reason to set out that the Defendant was treated as a tenant by the new landlords. She cannot possibly have any right to stay there for nothing, and we are taking the approach most favourable to her — i.e. that she is a tenant. Let's therefore get on with setting out why we claim to be entitled to possession. This can be done in 6 words:

> 4. The said rent is in arrears.

However, it is always considered polite in such circumstances to condescend to a few particulars, and in any event we are required to do so under the CPR, so our task is to simplify the matter as much as is consistent with properly stating our case. We will have to provide a schedule of all payments which have been missed (which can be attached to the Particulars of Claim), but the remainder of the matters can be set out succinctly as follows:

PARTICULARS

Since April 2004 the said rent has always been in arrears. No payments whatsoever have been received since the

beginning of November 2004, at which time the arrears of
rent amounted to £90. A schedule of payments between April
and November 2004 is attached to this Particulars of Claim.
The arrears of rent at the start of these proceedings amount to
£[whatever]. The Claimant is unaware of any previous history
of late or under-payment, and does not believe that any previous steps have been taken to recover these, or any, arrears of
rent. The Claimant is unaware of the Defendant's circumstances, save that her rent is not paid directly to it under the
Social Security Contributions and Benefits Act 1992.

It seems to me that the above is quite sufficient. We have set out the
arrears, attached the schedule and given the information required by the
Rules in cases of non-payment of rent. (Additional information required
by the CPR will be set out shortly.) It is, of course, perfectly permissible
to set out the required particulars under the heading:

<u>PARTICULARS REQUIRED UNDER CPR PARTS
16 AND 55</u>

and then tabulate them, and you can, of course, do this should you so
wish. It is a matter of preferred style. My preference is as I have set out
above.

Paragraph 5
Due to the arrears a Notice to Quit was served. (I didn't say we served
it!) Our case is, of course, that despite the Notice, the Defendant didn't
go, and the rent has still not been paid. Never mind about the first
abortive attempt, as it is irrelevant. All we need to do is aver that a **valid**
notice has been served at some point. It is also not necessary to plead
that the Notice was served because of the arrears, as a Landlord was,
under the relevant Rent Act legislation, perfectly entitled to serve a
Notice at any time and for any reason. That merely converted the
Protected contractual Tenancy into a Statutory Tenancy, and did not give
a right to possession.

5.   By a Notice to Quit dated and served on 10th November
2005, the Claimant Company determined the said tenancy
on 22nd September 2005, or at the end of the period of the
same which ended next after the expiration of 4 weeks from
the service of the said Notice. Notwithstanding this, the

Defendant has failed and/or refused to vacate the said premises, and the said rent remains in arrears.

There are, of course, other variations on this, but you should by now have got the general drift. Now we have to put in any further information required by the Rules:

6.   The rateable value of the said property did not at any relevant time exceed £1,500.

7.   The Claimant claims to be entitled to possession under Case 1 of Schedule 15 to the Rent Act 1977.

(Take both the above from me!).

All that now remains is for us to deal with the 'prayer' – our claim for relief, and then the statement of truth.

AND the Claimant Company claims:

1.   Possession of the said premises.

2.   £[whatever] arrears of rent.

3.   Cost of use and occupation of the premises at the rate of £90 per month (or proportionately) from 3rd January 2006 until possession be delivered up.

4.   Interest on arrears of rent at such rate and for such period as the Court shall deem fit, pursuant to Section 69, County Courts Act 1984.

MILES A'DRIFT

Statement of Truth

I believe* (the Claimant believes) that the facts stated in these particulars of claim are true.

*I am duly authorised by the Claimant to sign this statement.

Note that the claim for use and occupation (formerly known as 'mesne profits') has to commence from the date of the expiry of the Notice to Quit. The tenancy runs from the 6th day of the month. The Notice of 10th November expires 4 weeks after the end of the following rental period, which begins on 6th December. Thus, 3rd January is the date on which possession should be given.

In accordance with hallowed tradition, the full draft is reproduced below:

IN THE WATFORD COUNTY COURT   Case No.

BETWEEN:

THE PERFECT PROPERTY COMPANY LIMITED
Claimant

— and —

Miss MAUREEN FLIGHT
Defendant

PARTICULARS OF CLAIM

---

1. The Claimant Company is the freehold owner and entitled to possession of residential premises situate at and known as 2, Aerodrome Cottages, Elstree, Hertfordshire.

2. The Claimant Company purchased its said interest in the premises in about early 2002, at which time the Defendant was the occupier and/or a tenant thereof, having been granted a holiday letting of the same by the Claimant's predecessors in title, Grottylet Ltd, on 8th August 1983. In 2002 and at all relevant times thereafter, the rental for the letting was £90 per month.

3. Further or alternatively, at the time of the said purchase by the Claimant Company, the Defendant was a contractual periodic tenant of the said property, at a monthly rental of £90.

4. The said rent is in arrears.

PARTICULARS

Since April 2004 the said rent has always been in arrears. No payments whatsoever have been received since the beginning of November 2004, at which time the arrears of rent amounted to £90. A schedule of payments between April and November 2004 is attached to this Particulars of Claim. The arrears of rent at the start of these proceedings amount to £[whatever]. The Claimant is unaware of any previous history of late or under-payment, and does not believe that any previous steps have been taken to recover these, or any, arrears of rent. The Claimant is unaware of the Defendant's circumstances, save that her rent is not paid directly to it under the Social Security Contributions and Benefits Act 1992.

5.   By a Notice to Quit dated and served on 10th November 2005, the Claimant Company determined the said tenancy on 22nd September 2005, or at the end of the period of the same which ended next after the expiration of 4 weeks from the service of the said Notice. Notwithstanding the aforesaid the Defendant has failed and/or refused to vacate the said premises, and the said rent remains in arrears.

6.   The rateable value of the said property did not at any relevant time exceed £1,500.

7.   The Claimant claims to be entitled to possession under Case 1 of Schedule 15 to the Rent Act 1977.

AND the Claimant Company claims:

1.   Possession of the said premises.

2.   £[whatever] arrears of rent.

3.   Cost of use and occupation of the premises at the rate of £90 per month (or proportionately) from 3rd January 2006 until possession be delivered up.

4.   Interest on arrears of rent at such rate and for such period as the Court shall deem fit, pursuant to Section 69, County Courts Act 1984.

MILES A'DRIFT

Statement of Truth
I believe* (the Claimant believes) that the facts stated in these Particulars of Claim are true.
*I am duly authorised by the Claimant to sign this statement.

Now it is, of course, perfectly possible to continue this chapter with a series of further examples, each one demonstrating another series of difficulties which can arise from time to time in drafting a Particulars of Claim. However, it may come as some relief to you if I tell you that I do not propose to do so! It is quite impossible to anticipate each and every potential complication that can obstruct the easy flow of drafting. Some of these complications can arise from the particular areas of law which the case may concern, and cannot be dealt with here.

Finally, there comes a time when the law of diminishing returns sets in. As I have said before, and it is important enough to repeat, the aim of this work is not to provide you with a series of precedents, but to give you sufficient insight into the technique of drafting to be able to work out potential difficulties unaided. By applying the thought processes that are relevant to the particular type of document that you wish to draft, and by using appropriately clear and unambiguous language, it is hoped that most matters can safely be tackled in a more than competent fashion. Additionally, the finished article will not merely be correct, but will, in presentation and content, be as dynamic and effective a presentation of your case as is possible in the circumstances.

The remaining chapters in this book will draw on these thought processes, and will attempt to adapt them to the needs of the individual types of drafting which I propose to examine. I make no apology for any repetition of basic approaches from time to time, as these should serve as additional exercises in general drafting, and will consolidate what we have so far explored in this chapter. Let us therefore proceed boldly onward, turn the tables, and consider how we should deal with a claim that has been served upon **us**.

Chapter Three

Making a Fight of It
(The Defence and Counterclaim)

'You will observe the Rules of Battle, of course?' the White Knight remarked, putting on his helmet too.
'I always do', said the Red Knight, and they began banging away at each other with such fury that Alice got behind a tree to be out of the way of the blows.

THE DEFENCE

Although we have spent a good deal of time examining the way in which we should draft proceedings, our time is, of course, equally spent in responding to claims which have been served on our clients. As often as a client (or solicitor) comes through the door crying 'I want to sue the !?@*£', another traipses in brandishing a claim form and wants to know how to defend the matter.

I am not a cynical person, but experience and common sense have made it quite unrealistic for me to pretend that all Defences are drafted in the sincere belief that the claim is untenable or misconceived, or that the Claimant is going to be laughed out of Court (with costs) as soon as he has opened his case. However, most, if not all, books on procedure and drafting seem to me to be based on this premise, and thus to a certain extent ignore certain practicalities which often fall to be considered when sitting down to draft the Defence.

Now it may be that the above paragraph will raise a few eyebrows, but I do not think that one should flinch from examining the reasons for which some Defences are drafted, if only to reiterate certain immutable rules of ethics, practice and procedure which should **never** be broken.

The first and most important rule of all is that you should never ever 'make up' a Defence for your client. This may seem obvious to all, but there are occasions when it is quite easy unconsciously to let one's enthusiasm for the job stray over the border into that land of fabrication which is (and should be) the graveyard of all professional careers. Don't get carried away — remind yourself from time to time that you are acting on instructions, not that you are acting on instructions from time to time!

Secondly, it is never proper unquestioningly to accept instructions. Although you are not judge and jury of the facts, a great deal of time and money can be saved if the client is diplomatically informed at an early stage that there is more chance of the Devil taking Holy Orders than of his case being believed by the Court. If the client nevertheless insists that his version is correct, you have no option than to proceed according to your instructions, unless to do so would result in professional embarrassment. (The above is, of course, equally applicable to instructions on certain facts, rather than the whole of the case.)

Thirdly, even if you have advised the client that he has a case, you should never put the possibility of settlement out of your mind. It is this which may require the most examination when it comes to the question of 'tactical' defences, which, although perhaps diminished in importance after the CPR, may not nevertheless be completely extinct.

Thus, we should by now have accepted the fact that a Defence should never be drafted unless it is on the face of it capable of defeating the claim, and is based on genuine instructions received from the client, which appear to have some realistic foundation in law and/or in fact. Having said that, however, it should also be apparent that there are many occasions on which Defences are drafted which it is hoped will never have to be tested in Court, even if they do comply with the above criteria. Think of it this way — the vast majority of cases settle before they reach trial — and many of these have had Defences filed.

The route to a successful negotiated settlement is often by demonstrating that you are capable of putting up a good fight, even if there is no certainty that you are going to win in the end. Even in this age of the CPR, when it is likely that most negotiation will have taken place prior to starting the case, a good Defence may still persuade the Claimant that the risks are just not worth it, and that it would be wiser to settle.

It may not be too cynical an approach to divide Defences into two broad categories: those which are genuinely intended to continue all the way to trial (unless a practical compromise is reached); and those which are calculated to mitigate the effect of the claim by inducing a compromise, notwithstanding that it may, from the inception, be considered too expensive and/or risky to pursue the matter to the bitter end. The second may now be a dying breed, but experience has proved that the death throes are protracted!

'... capable of putting up a good fight'

Even today, our legal system is imbued with administrative and financial impediments which provide a powerful disincentive to protracted litigation. I strongly suspect that one of the reasons why this state of affairs was allowed to continue for so long before the present reforms, was that parties were provided with an equally powerful incentive to compromise their differences wherever possible so as to avoid the inevitable delays and expense of having a case come to trial. Now it may well be that once again I am invoking on myself a thunderbolt from my elders and betters, but I remain quite convinced (as I believe do many practitioners in the profession) that the above was true, so let's be open about it. After all, negotiation is a far less expensive solution than legal fisticuffs, and even if it did mean that both parties went away grumbling about the expense and inconvenience of the law having caused them to abandon their 'cast iron' case against each other, I remain firmly convinced that in most cases justice usually triumphed, and thus the law had the last laugh — even if the clients did not appreciate the fun! The intention of the CPR was to reduce the number of cases settling for such reasons, although it is hoped (piously or otherwise!) that the expected climate of cooperation in fulfilling the overriding objective will mean that parties settle on the merits, rather than because of the deficiencies of the system. Time will tell, time will tell, although present experience shows little or no diminution in the enthusiasm to settle cases at the last minute.

Another way of looking at matters is by appreciating that, as in all matters touching upon human relations, the merits of a case can vary from the completely justified, to the utterly indefensible — with a vast range of other possibilities in between. In keeping with our professional duty to do the best for our client, we must take the benefit of every fair and legitimate possibility for achieving as advantageous a result as possible. I always told a client that I considered it my duty, in every case, to get him or her out of his or her predicament as quickly and as cheaply as possible. If that meant fighting through to the bitter end, so be it. If it meant an undignified withdrawal, thus likewise. Therefore, in a position where proceedings have been served, one must take advantage of all legitimate ways of effecting as beneficial a solution as possible as the problem allows.

At the top end of the scale, this may require the prompt and 'high profile' filing of as abrasive and full a Defence (and Counterclaim if required) as is possible to demonstrate the weaknesses and inadequacy of the Particulars of Claim, thereafter accompanied by a searching Request for Further Information, designed to highlight every weak point of the claim and strong point of the Defence. Down in the lower reaches of the barrel, there is the 'nuisance' Defence, where the merits are slim, possibly just sufficient to avoid a successful application for summary judgment (or the Court disposing of the case of its own volition), but which is basically designed to induce the Claimant to settle for less than that to which he may be entitled, or even to go away altogether, on the basis that the time and expense that will be involved in pursuing the claim will be out of all proportion to the potential gain at the end of the day. Of course, pursuance of the overriding objective may well lead a legal adviser to consider whether such a course of action would be professionally proper — but having brought this to your attention, I shall say no more.

Even in the latter example, there is no excuse for not doing as full and proper a job as is possible if you are professionally able to do so — it is just that the raw material may be inadequate to allow you to draft the masterpiece that you would have wished.

So, whatever the reasons for which we may wish to draft the Defence, let us start from the premise that there is adequate material to justify our doing so with propriety, and without being in breach in any way of our professional standards. We also propose to do the best possible job of ensuring that the Claimant will be sufficiently 'put-off' as a result, so as either to 'go away', or to negotiate a settlement.

You will doubtless be delighted to hear that I do not propose to repeat the general principles of drafting which have been propounded in the previous chapters. After all, it increases production costs substantially, and it seems unfair to charge more simply for duplicating matters (something which is not entirely irrelevant to drafting as well)! Thus, the fundamental principles of knowing your case etc. apply equally to the drafting of a Defence as to the initiation of proceedings.

Before taking that entirely as read, may I suggest that you start by examining the Particulars of Claim and asking yourself if you are quite certain that you understand **precisely** what is being alleged and claimed against your client. Sometimes you may have to draw a distinction between understanding the case only once you have read all the relevant documentation (including that from your own client) and having taken instructions, and understanding the case solely from the Particulars of Claim. In the former instance, you may then wish to consider whether the statement of case is itself in some way defective, which may enable you to attack the case procedurally or by the clever use of a Request for Further Information.

If you cannot fully understand the case, do not immediately upbraid yourself for your stupidity, plunge into the deepest gloom, and consider a life of seclusion and meditation, away from the pressures of litigation. It may well be that the party drafting the proceedings has not purchased this handy work, and does not know what he is doing. Maybe his case is inherently weak, or founded on a misconception as to the law. Possibly his instructions have been vague, and he has not sought to obtain clarification from his client before launching the action. This serves to highlight a facet of drafting a Defence which does not occur in originating proceedings, and that is that you are **responding to someone else's work**. Thus you have to deal with your own case, but according to a format dictated by the other side. There are ways round this, at which we will look in a moment, but generally speaking one does not have quite the same freedom of manoeuvre that attends the drafting of a Particulars of Claim.

Thus, before even formulating your own response, it is wise to start by questioning all aspects of the document to which you have to plead. Does it disclose a cause of action? Has it been founded within the limitation period? Has it sued in the proper name, or sued the correct Defendant? Is it issued in the appropriate Court? Does the statement of case itself (even if disclosing a cause of action) make it clear what is being alleged, so as to enable you to reply to it? Is the relief claimed available as a matter of law, or within the jurisdiction of the Court in which the action is founded? All these are matters which should be considered before deciding on the way in which you intend to respond to the claim.

As a result of the above, you may, in addition to any Defence that you may wish to plead, consider it appropriate to deal with points of procedure or law which ought properly to be taken at this time. At this stage, you should list the various matters which you intend should be contained in the Defence. (For the sake of simplicity, I shall leave the question of counterclaim for the moment.) It is at this point that you should remind yourself that the whole purpose of a Defence is not merely to answer the points raised in the Particulars of Claim, but also to deal with matters in your instructions which provide a Defence to the claim. So many times I have seen Defences which deal, point by point, with the allegations set out in the claim, but which wholly neglect to aver to matters which are not raised but which are highly relevant to the Defence. Thus, the job is only half done. In fact it is less than half done, as the other side will remain unaware of the strength of your case, you will be in breach of the Rules, and you will find that the failure fully to set out matters in the Defence will be prejudicial to credibility when you seek to put them forward at a later stage, assuming that your case hasn't been struck out first.

Having mapped out the nature of your response, you may find yourself unable to put your points in precisely the order that you would have liked, due to the manner in which the claim itself has been set out. However, never feel yourself completely hidebound by the format of the claim. For a start, it is completely unnecessary to deal blow by blow with the matters in the claim, before asserting the rest of your defence. Provided that the overall result is logically referable to the claim, there is no reason why relevant parts of your case cannot be interposed at suitable moments in the overall layout.

Let us take a very simple example. The claim against us alleges a breach of contract:

IN THE HARTLEPOOL COUNTY COURT   Case No. HL99000

BETWEEN:

Mr PANTAGRUEL KNEECAP

Claimant

— and —

Mr C. FOODSAUCE

Defendant

PARTICULARS OF CLAIM

---

1. By an oral agreement made on 8th January 2005 at the Claimant's house at 2 Bouverie Road, Hartlepool, the Defendant agreed to sell his Honda motor cycle 00 51 CPR to the Claimant, for £8,250.

2. It was a term of the said agreement between the parties, and stated in the conversation, that the Defendant would deliver the said motor cycle to the Claimant's house by no later than 3pm on Tuesday, 10th January 2005.

3. The Claimant paid the Defendant the sum of £8,250 in cash on 8th January 2005, despite which, in breach of the said agreement, the Defendant thereafter failed and/or refused to deliver up the said motor cycle at the time and place agreed, or at all.

4. By a letter to the Defendant dated 17th January 2005, the Claimant demanded the delivery up of the said motor cycle or (without prejudice to his claim for damages herein), the return of the said £8,250. Despite this, the Defendant thereafter unlawfully failed and/or refused to deliver up the said motor cycle or refund the said money.

5.   By reason of the Defendant's said breach of contract, the Claimant suffered additional loss and damage, in that he was forced to purchase a similar motor cycle elsewhere, on 29th January 2005 at a price of £8,750.

6.   The Claimant further claims to be entitled to interest on (etc.) ... pursuant to section 69 of the County Courts Act 1984.

7.   The value of this action exceeds £5,000 but does not exceed £15,000.

AND the Claimant claims:

1.   Refund of the said purchase price of £8,250, further or alternatively.

2.   Damages for breach of contract.

3.   Interest as aforesaid.

JOSIAH FISHPOOL

Statement of Truth
I believe (the Claimant believes) that the facts stated in the Particulars of Claim are true.

Your instructions are very simple — the agreement was never made, the Defendant ignored the letter as it made no sense to him, and he was in Texas between 15th December 2004 and 15th January 2005, and could thus not possibly have entered into the alleged bargain.

The **wrong** way to do it is as follows:

1.   Paragraph 1 of the Particulars of Claim is denied.

2.   Paragraph 2 of the Particulars of Claim is denied.

3.   Paragraph 3 of the Particulars of Claim is denied.

4.   Save that the Defendant admits having received the said letter, and that he did not thereafter deliver up the said

motor cycle, or refund the monies demanded, it is denied that his failure to do so was unlawful as alleged in Paragraph 4 of the Particulars of Claim, or at all.

5.   Paragraph 5 of the Particulars of Claim is denied.

6.   Paragraph 6 of the Particulars of Claim is denied.

7.   In the circumstances it is denied that the Claimant is entitled to the relief claimed or any relief for the reasons alleged or at all.

CHRIS MASCARROL

Statement of Truth
I believe (the Defendant believes) that the facts stated in the Defence are true.

Now the reason why you couldn't get away with it, using the above, is that although Mr Mascarrol has actually done quite a good job on bits of it, what he has not done is put the defence! He merely seeks, in a rather cumbersome way, to counter the points raised in the Particulars of Claim.

A couple of stylistic points to start with. First, I do not consider it necessary for the words 'Particulars of Claim' to be repeated time after time, as long as it clear to which document you are referring. Some Counsel I know, will merely put:

1.   Paragraph 1 is admitted.

2.   Paragraph 2 is denied ... etc.

although I prefer to mention the document the first time, and then use the more simple form, thus:

1.   Paragraph 1 of the Particulars of Claim is admitted.

2.   Paragraph 2 is denied ...

and so on. The most important thing is to avoid the whole thing becoming unnecessarily top-heavy. If it is clear to what you are referring, there seems no need to weight your draft down with unnecessary repetition.

Next! The style of Mr Mascarrol's petition is beloved of many law students. Many of my pupils proudly presented me with their first efforts at drafting, slavishly following the format of the above example. They seldom did it twice. If they did, the lesson was reinforced with a good bang on the head with a suitably heavy volume — 1982 Current Law Statutes is particularly useful in this regard! It was one of the most rewarding thrills of being a pupil-master, to observe the wonder of enlightenment in the eyes of a pupil, when I took the draft:

1.   Paragraph 1 of the Particulars of Claim is admitted.

2.   Paragraph 2 is admitted.

3.   Paragraph 3 is admitted...

struck it through, and substituted:

1.   Paragraphs 1, 2 and 3 of the Particulars of Claim are admitted.

Well, one would think that it would be obvious, but I tell you it is not. See how many times you have done it yourself!

Looking at the present claim, we can see that, on our instructions, we will deny there was an agreement between the parties. Following on logically from that, paragraph 2 will be denied, as will paragraph 3. Therefore, there is no problem in commencing:

1.   Paragraphs 1, 2 and 3 of the Particulars of Claim are denied.

However, there is every good reason why we should, at this stage, state the reason **why** we deny that an agreement took place. Although some may argue that we are about to disclose evidence, as we have previously seen, the statement of any case must do this to a certain extent, and it is perfectly permissible to do so provided that it is kept within the strict boundaries of providing the other side with an exposition of your case, which will enable the issues to be clear to one and all as required by the Rules. Furthermore, in the present instance, the disclosure of our defence should be tactically advantageous, as it will give the Claimant and his legal advisers some considerable food for thought. After all, if the Defence is true, the Claimant is in a lot of trouble. Additionally, of course, the burden of proof lies on the Claimant, although for all practical purposes the Defendant's case will collapse unless he can show that he was truly abroad at the time. So, with just the tiniest hint of malice, we finish the paragraph:

> 1. Paragraphs 1, 2 and 3 of the Particulars of Claim are denied. At all relevant times, the Defendant was in Texas, USA and did not return to England until 15th January 2005.

To complete the effect, and taking advantage of our ability to do so under the CPR, let us add:

> A copy of the Defendant's air ticket confirming the above, is attached to this Defence.

Get out of that one!

Note that I have added the date of the Defendant's return, as we do admit that we were within the jurisdiction so as to receive the Claimant's letter dated 17th January. To try and explain this later may cause complications, so I have done it now. I have not set out the date of the Defendant's departure for Texas, for three reasons. First, the situation is adequately covered by the words 'at all relevant times'. Secondly, the date of departure is irrelevant to the nature of the defence. Thirdly, the information can be seen from the attached ticket.

The response to paragraph 4 has been quite nicely set out by Mr Mascarrol. Applying the same principles of drafting that we have discussed in the previous chapter, we can see that it is necessary:

(a) to admit that the letter was received;
(b) to agree that no action was taken as a result; but
(c) to assert that the Defendant was under no liability to take any action, and that his failure to do so was in no way unlawful, as there was no contract between the parties.

All (!) that remains, is to express the above, as elegantly as possible. I prefer to use no more than one sentence if possible, each part flowing logically from the last. However, there is nothing wrong in using more than one if you feel it absolutely necessary. Before you do though, check again to see if you can make it more 'rounded', and incorporate it all in one sentence.

Mr Mascarrol has adopted a very useful stylistic approach using 'save that'. It allows you to admit or deny something with the exception (or exceptions) listed. It can enable you to avoid having tediously to list all that is agreed and all that is denied, particularly if you are stating your reasons at the same time. Look at the difference between:

> 2.   It is admitted that the Claimant sent the letter dated 17th January 2005, and that the Defendant thereafter failed and/or refused to deliver up the said motor cycle or refund the monies demanded. The Defendant avers that he was not obliged to do so by reason of the matters set out above, and that he did not therefore act unlawfully as alleged in paragraph 4 of the Particulars of Claim or at all.

And

> 2.   Save that the Defendant admits having received the said letter, and that he did not thereafter deliver up the said motor cycle, or refund the monies demanded, it is denied that his failure to do so was unlawful as alleged in paragraph 4 of the Particulars of Claim, or at all.

I contend that the second version is far more fluent and 'professional' than the first. That is not to say that the first version is either incorrect, or does not make sense. It is just that it is a bit cumbersome, and contains 74 words as opposed to 51 in the second draft. Also, note how the first attempt has to go deliberately out of its way to refer to the relevant paragraph in the Particulars of Claim, whilst the second seems to flow more naturally.

You may also have noticed that Mr Mascarrol does not specifically state the reason why it is denied that the failure to comply with the terms of the letter was unlawful. Bearing in mind the shortness of the draft, and the close proximity to the only other preceding paragraph, it seems quite unnecessary to do so. I stress once again, however, that drafting is a personal art, and if you ultimately decide that you would do something different, or to combine parts of the two versions, then at least that decision will have been taken in the light of a consideration of all (or most) of the various possibilities.

Our response to paragraph 5 of the Particulars raises a number of interesting points. First, as is our habit, let us consider what we may wish to assert in our paragraph:

> (a)   We deny that the Claimant has suffered any loss or damage as a result of anything we may have done or failed to do.

(b)   We haven't the foggiest idea as to whether or not the Claimant purchased another motor cycle, or as to the price if he did, or as to whether or not that price was grossly inflated.

That brings me conveniently to a discussion of various 'keywords' which are commonly used in Defences to set out the Defendant's position. The first such word is 'deny' or 'denies'. This is simply a positive (or rather negative!) assertion that what has been alleged is not true. Thus:

> 1.   It is denied that the said motor car was defective as alleged or at all ...

amounts to a specific statement that there was nothing wrong with the car. If the Claimant says otherwise then he is either sorely mistaken, or lying through his teeth! It further carries with it the implication that you will cross-examine the Claimant's witnesses, and call your own evidence on the point.

Next, we have the words 'does not admit', or 'makes no admissions' or 'it is not admitted that'. These phrases are capable of more than one subtle meaning. Take:

> 1.   It is not admitted that the said motor car was defective as alleged or at all.

This amounts neither to an admission that the car was defective, nor to an assertion that it was not. Why should this be?

There are many times when something may be peculiarly within the knowledge of the other party. In the above little example, we may not have had a chance to inspect the car. We are therefore certainly not in a position to be able to say that there was nothing wrong with it, although we are of course not going to admit that it was faulty, merely on the Claimant's say so. Thus we make no admissions, which leads on to my second point.

In (almost) every case, the burden of proof lies on the Claimant, on the balance of probabilities. It is thus open to the Defendant to say 'prove your case', provided of course that sufficient defence is raised to take the matter outside the realms of summary judgment procedure. However, there are aspects of almost every case, often as to the quantum of damage suffered, to which the Claimant may be put to strict proof — possibly because the Defendant is unable to say whether or not the

Claimant is correct when assertions as to damage are made. It is possible (and sometimes psychologically desirable) to add the phrase:

> and the Defendant puts the Claimant to strict proof of each
> and every item of loss and damage alleged,

or even:

> and the Defendant puts the Claimant to strict proof of each
> and every item of loss and damage alleged, together with the
> cause or causes thereof.

Used judiciously the phrase 'puts the Claimant to strict proof' can carry the implication that he is clearly over-egging the pudding, and is going to look a right charlie at the end of the day when he cannot come up to proof. Do not be fooled into thinking that the term 'strict proof' imposes any form of additional burden on the other side. It does not. The term 'strict' is actually redundant — but sounds nicely 'bullish'. On the other hand, used as a matter of routine, the phrase rings distinctly thin, and can look as if that is your only defence.

Of course, often, it is! It may be that you know that you have no defence on the merits, but may have as to quantum. You can, if you are big and brave, boldly plead:

> The Defendant admits that the said vehicle was defective,
> but makes no admissions as to the said or any loss or damage
> suffered by the Claimant.

However, I must confess to having seen very few such examples in the course of a reasonably long career. The reason may well be that, in such cases, negotiations are well under way, and the Defence will be drafted so that, if possible, judgment will not be signed and all options will be left open, thus:

> No admissions are made as to the alleged or any defects in
> the said vehicle and the Defendant puts the Claimant to strict
> proof of each and every defect and/or every item of loss and
> damage alleged together with the cause or causes thereof.

Of course, it fools nobody, but it looks less damning on paper — to the uninitiated!

Next, we have the word 'admit'. This is fairly self-evident, and concedes an allegation made in the claim. Although it is often used in respect of any concurrence with something set out in the claim, it does not hurt to remember that you can also use the word 'agree' if the overall effect will be less pejorative, and the context allows. So, for instance it is usual to 'admit' that the parties came to an agreement. One can also 'admit' that, for example, a party took place on a Friday, although it is possible also to agree this. I tend only to use 'agree' if to do otherwise might give the paragraph a defensive flavour which I consider inappropriate in the particular circumstances. Be aware though, that by making an admission, the Claimant is then relieved from having to bring any evidence on the matter, if the case goes to Court.

Another useful word is 'aver'. It means to assert, or contend, and **is** a more neutral form of making a statement. Some Counsel used to use the phrase 'it is admitted and averred that ...' which I am sure is very learned and important, but which does not, in my humble opinion, add very much if anything to the overall strength of the case, and the phrase is now probably redundant.

Now, as this is a discursive text, I will continue at this little tangent for a moment more, in order to demonstrate the various ways in which the above keywords can be used in the course of a draft. There are I think, two basic ways, although the second can sometimes be used in two styles. Each has its own advantages and drawbacks. However, it is rarely advisable to mix them. Normally it is better to find the one that best suits the draft (or your preferred style), and stick to it throughout. We can have:

> The Defendant does not admit paragraph 1 of the Particulars of Claim.

Or

> Paragraph 1 of the Particulars of Claim is not admitted.

The latter style can, however sometimes be expressed:

> No admissions are made as to paragraph 1 of the Particulars of Claim;

although this can only be used in limited ways. It is highly unusual (to say the least) to state:

> Admissions are made as to paragraph 1.

Of the two main formats, the first has the advantage of directness, and psychologically brings the person of the Defendant to the forefront. 'He' does not admit this. 'He' avers that … etc. However, it is also a relatively unsophisticated way of drafting, and although this is by no means always a disadvantage, it can tempt one to get too 'chatty', particularly if the sentence has to go on to get more complicated. It may be a *reductio ad absurdum*, but it's not possibly too difficult to get into:

> The Defendant does not admit Paragraph 1 of the Particulars of Claim, but does contend that he was present at the scene of the accident and saw everything that happened. He will say that the Claimant was driving far too fast, and crossed a red traffic light before swerving to the right and hitting the shop front. The Claimant got out of his car in a horrible rage and swore at a poor old lady whom he had narrowly avoided knocking over a couple of minutes before … etc.

Now there's them as would say that the above possibly gives a more clear and graphically compelling statement of the situation than all the finely tuned phrases the lawyers like to use, and had it been endorsed on the Defence Form N9 by a Defendant in person I'm sure that his case would not have been prejudiced. That may well be so. It's fine for the small claims procedure, where lawyers are not necessarily the most welcome guests and where the issues are relatively straightforward. But rules is rules, and one does not have to think very hard to realise that responding to such a paragraph may be very hard indeed. Separating the real issues from the irrelevant is not assisted by the use of such a format.

The second style is perhaps more usual. It is a little more detached, and stylistically capable of greater flexibility than the more 'personal' version. Furthermore, even more flexibility can be achieved through the use of the alternative 'sub-style' that I have outlined, particularly if the sentence will have to be quite complex, for example if only part of a paragraph is admitted, or there are caveats to your response. This may not inevitably be the case — you just have to experiment until your goal is accomplished. Compare for example:

> It is admitted that the accident took place as set out in paragraph 3, save that it is not admitted that the Claimant was thereby injured to the extent alleged or at all.

And

It is admitted that the accident took place as set out in paragraph 3, save that no admissions are made as to the existence or extent of any injuries thereby alleged to have been suffered by the Claimant.

Now, in my view, the first of the two paragraphs is far less cumbersome than the second, which falls into grammatical difficulties unless fairly tortuous language is used. Let us see whether we can achieve anything better by inverting the sentence:

Save that no admissions are made as to any injuries alleged to have been suffered by the Claimant, paragraph 3 is admitted.

Frankly, I don't care for that much either! Let's try another form of inversion:

Save that it is not admitted that the Claimant suffered the alleged or any injury, paragraph 3 is admitted.

Here, the word 'admitted' has been used twice, and therefore fails stylistically.

Paragraph 3 is admitted, save that no admissions are made as to the alleged or any injury suffered by the Claimant.

Take your pick! With luck, your client will concede liability and save you the bother.

Let us now look afresh at our response to paragraph 5 in the light of all this knowledge. Mr Mascarrol has contented himself with a simple denial of the matters pleaded therein. You may feel that you can do better, particularly in view of our planned response, some pages ago. Have a try on your own.

We could have dealt with matters in the order that we set out earlier. However, our paragraph may flow more freely if we do it the other way round. We haven't the faintest notion as to whether the Claimant purchased a motor cycle elsewhere, or the price paid if he did. What we do know is that, even if he did, it's not down to us. This could translate as:

No admissions are made as to the loss and/or damage suffered by the Claimant alleged in paragraph 5 or at all, and the

> Claimant is put to strict proof of the same together with the
> cause thereof. If, which is denied, the Claimant has suffered
> the alleged, or any loss and/or damage, it is denied that the
> same is due in any way to the fault of the Defendant, as
> alleged or at all.

Now that is a somewhat comprehensive way of going about things. It
follows a fairly standard pattern, although I concede that it is perhaps
more suited to claims of greater weight than the present. Let us nevertheless examine its structure.

Rather than deal with the specific purchase pleaded by the Claimant,
this paragraph takes an approach from the concept of loss and damage.
The Claimant asserts that the purchase of the new motor cycle constituted
loss and damage on his part. Of course, if his claim is true, that will be the
case. He claims already to have parted with £8,250 and has had to spend
an additional £8,750 in order to obtain what he should have received for
his original money. What the above paragraph does is to say that even if
he has suffered some loss and damage (which is not admitted), it has nothing to do with us! That of course begs the question as to how it could constitute loss and damage, but that is not the concern of the Defendant. It
may be that the Claimant has simply sued the wrong person. Who knows?
All we are concerned about is that the bill should not end up with us.

Observe the use of language in the first sentence. Direct reference has
been made to paragraph 5, not merely in order to indicate the
Defendant's response to that paragraph in the Particulars of Claim, but
also because it enables the matter to be pleaded concisely. Reference is
made not merely to the loss and damage which the Claimant claims to
have suffered, but to **any** loss and damage. Thus the Claimant cannot
then say that the Defendant may have implied that some lesser amount
may be 'down to him'.

Note also that the paragraph (one hopes) closes any loopholes that
may exist in the argument. Not merely does the Defendant deny that the
damage was caused by reason of his alleged breach of contract, but he
also states that it was not due to any other breach or fault of his either,
even if it hasn't been alleged. A shorter, and (in the circumstances) possibly more appropriate, way of dealing with paragraph 5 would be:

> 3.   If, which is not admitted, the Claimant suffered the
> alleged or any loss and damage, the same was not due to any
> breach of contract by the Defendant, as alleged in paragraph
> 5 or at all.

To all intents and purposes that perfectly well covers what we wish to say in respect of paragraph 5. After all, the matter is fairly straightforward, the statements of case are short, and it seems quite unnecessary to use a steam hammer to crack a nut. The above examples are set out merely to illustrate that you have a considerable variety and weight of weaponry in your arsenal, and you should consider the appropriate ones to use in the particular circumstances.

As far as paragraph 6 is concerned, Mr Mascarrol has considered that a simple denial is appropriate, and I respectfully agree with him. One does not even, in my view, need to refer the paragraph to anything that has gone before.

There then remains the question of 'wrapping up' the whole matter. There is a wonderful 'stock phrase' which (in its ancient, complete and unexpurgated form) ran:

> Save as hereinbefore expressly admitted, the Defendant denies each and every allegation set out in the Particulars of Claim, as if the same had been set forth separately and traversed seriatim. In the premises, it is denied that the Claimant is entitled to the relief claimed, or any part thereof, for the reasons alleged or at all.

I should add that the final words 'on yer bike!' are, by long tradition, omitted from the paragraph!

As a student, I was strictly enjoined to use the above phrase (or at least its cut-down form, omitting the second sentence) in all Defences as a 'catch-all'. It was years before I could remember it properly, let alone what it meant, but some garbled version or other invariably found its way into my pleadings (and those of most of my contemporaries)! The rationale was that, just in case one omitted to deal with some important aspect of the case, one could always rely on the good old 'general traverse', as it is called, to get one out of trouble. In fairness, I must confess to one occasion on which I did have to use it to paddle myself out of a well-known malodorous creek! However, it is frowned upon today, save in the most complex of drafts, and there is room for doubt as to whether it would be of any assistance under the CPR. It is unwieldy, largely unnecessary, and pretty hard to comprehend in any event. 'Seriatim' and 'traverse' are not exactly in day-to-day use in these modern times. Best avoided at almost any cost!

What it actually means is that the Claimant must treat the Defence as having specifically denied everything in the claim, line by line, unless the contrary has been indicated. Use the phrase if you really feel it necessary to incorporate a safety net in your statement of case. Otherwise don't!

The expression 'in the circumstances' (the modern word for 'premises') is quite useful. You can also use 'by reason of the matters aforesaid', although that is to be avoided in excess.

Thus, Mr Mascarrol has used a short and all-embracing paragraph to sum up the defence:

> 5.   In the circumstances it is denied that the Claimant is entitled to the relief claimed or any relief for the reasons alleged or at all.

Here, 'in the circumstances' means 'by reason of all the matters set out in the Defence'. It is not strictly speaking a general traverse (i.e., a blanket denial of the Particulars of Claim), as it refers to what has already been set out.

The words 'the relief claimed', are worth remembering. 'Relief' can mean damages, an injunction, interest, etc., and its use obviates having to list all these matters. In other words, instead of setting out:

> In the circumstances it is denied that the Claimant is entitled to the said or any refund, and/or damages and/or interest, for the reasons alleged or at all ...

we use the word 'relief', and save ourselves (and everyone else) a good deal of trouble.

The words 'or any relief' likewise make it clear that we are not only denying the Claimant's entitlement to that which he is claiming, but that we also contend that he is not entitled to anything at all! If we had made admissions in the course of our case, we may have had to put:

> Save to the extent expressly admitted,

or

> Save to the extent admitted in paragraphs 7 and 9 herein,

or

> Save that the Defendant admits that the Claimant is entitled to the sums admitted in paragraphs 7 and 9,

(usually a bit clumsy, but you've got the idea as to the various permutations), and so on.

I hope that it has become unnecessary to reiterate that the above is only an example of what I hope is an efficient, comprehensive and concise pleading, and that it is by no means definitive. I shall not say this again during the course of this work. It is to be hoped that you have now already begun to form a style of your own, which may be very different from mine. So much the better — variety is the spice of strife!

Now, just so that we can behold the whole glory of the finished product, here is the final version:

IN THE HARTLEPOOL COUNTY COURT   Case No. HL990000

BETWEEN:

Mr PANTAGRUEL KNEECAP

Claimant

— and —

Mr C. FOODSAUCE

Defendant

DEFENCE

---

1.   Paragraphs 1, 2 and 3 of the Particulars of Claim are denied. At all relevant times, the Defendant was in Texas, USA, and did not return to England until 15th January 2005. A copy of the Defendant's air ticket confirming the above is attached to this Defence.

2.   Save that the Defendant admits having received the said letter, and that he did not thereafter deliver up the said motor cycle, or refund the monies demanded, it is denied that his failure to do so was unlawful as alleged in paragraph 4 of the Particulars of Claim, or at all.

3.   If, which is not admitted, the Claimant suffered the alleged or any loss and damage, the same was not due to any breach of contract by the Defendant, as alleged in paragraph 5 or at all.

4.   Paragraph 6 is denied.

5.   In the circumstances it is denied that the Claimant is entitled to the relief claimed or any relief for the reasons alleged or at all.

HAYDN SEEK

Statement of Truth
I believe (the Defendant believes) that the facts stated in this Defence are true.

The preceding part of this chapter has, of course, been based on claims which have been drafted in a reasonably competent manner. However, there may be occasions in which you are faced with a Particulars of Claim which is the end product of a quite horrible piece of drafting. This may be for a number of reasons. It may perhaps be the product of a person whose pretensions are greater than his competence. Sometimes the claim itself may be of little substance, which makes its exposition difficult. Very often of course the claim may be of the 'home-made' variety, and may thus not comply with even the most basic rules; and the present trend of litigation may make these far more common even than they are at the moment.

A word about homemade drafts. It is quite usual for these to be scoffed at by lawyers, who naturally think that they can do much better. Sometimes this is true. On the basis that 'the man who acts for himself has a fool for a client', many such documents are full of irrelevance, bias and obscurity. On the other hand, it is also true that, due to the expense of litigation and the selectivity of the public funding system, there are many aggrieved citizens who are tempted to 'have a go themselves', particularly if the case is fairly straightforward. This seems actively to be encouraged under the CPR and the simplified claim form N1. Many of them don't make a bad job of it at all! Look at the next one that passes across your desk. It may not be in the 'officially approved' manner. However, look again and see whether its defects are more those of form rather than of substance. Many self-crafted claims do a very good job of stating the nature and elements of the claim — often just as well as if the job had been done by a professional. Where they tend to fall down is in their unconventional format, or (more seriously) where there has been an attempt to insert 'legal language' into the document to give it some clout. This I usually find occurs when the Claimant has enlisted the services of a friend to assist. The real problem that has to be faced by a professional person drafting a Defence, is that such documents are very difficult to respond to in proper form.

When faced with such difficulties, I have the following advice. First, and very importantly, **never** make the mistake of trying to be scathing, or to belittle the document to which you are responding. Unless the litigant in person is well known to be vexatious, or the history of the action demonstrates a desire to confuse and obstruct that is inimical to the proper conduct of the cause, you will be on a hiding to nothing. The Court is likely to have a degree of sympathy with the litigant, particularly if he/she has demonstrated a clear mind and an ability to deal with the relevant facts of the case. In any event, most Courts, particularly at a lower level, will do their best to put a litigant in person at his ease, and will often lean over backwards to prevent any impression of being more at home with the professional representative in the case. In other words, if you try to be smart, you will very likely incur the usual Judicial Thunderbolt from a Very Great Height!

I recall, many years ago, appearing against a litigant in person in the Court of Appeal, in front of a tribunal, the most junior member of which was noted for his irascibility. He was, however, by far the most benign member of the Court! The senior member commenced by demanding of my unfortunate opponent (who had, it has to be said, been the vexatious author of his own misfortune) why it was that he was representing himself. He replied by stating that he had represented himself in the Magistrates' Court, had also done so on appeal to the Crown Court, and thus to the Divisional Court on a (supposed) point of law. The Learned Lord Justice thereupon growled words to the effect that that seemed to be a very good reason why he should have been professionally represented before the Court of Appeal! I needed to do very little for the remainder of the case. However, do not count on the above happening to you!

Thus, when responding to a claim drafted by a lay client, do not treat your opponent with discourtesy, and do not take clever points on form, provided that you still do justice for your client. If the claim does not disclose a cause of action then you must, of course, state that in the Defence, and/or seek to have the case struck out.

On the other hand, it may be quite impossible to approach the statement of case in the manner to which you are accustomed. So my second tip is to modify your usual format so as to answer the claim in as clear a manner as possible. Where you cannot do this in responsive form, make a statement of your position, if necessary adding in relevant matters which do not appear to be in dispute, but which will, when the documents are read together, give the Court a composite picture of the dispute. Your task is not merely to put your client's case, but to assist the Court to comprehend the issues.

Thirdly, if the claim is in such a state that a proper response to it is impossible, make a concise statement denying the allegations (if those are your instructions) and then set out your Defence, almost as if it was a Particulars of Claim itself. Let me attempt to illustrate this by an example — it is, of course, handwritten on standard Claim Form N1:

IN THE BOWDEN COUNTY COURT   Case No. BW990000

BETWEEN:

Miss MAUD EMILY NIGHTINGALE

Claimant

— and —

FLOGGIT MOTORS LIMITED

Defendant

PARTICULARS OF CLAIM

---

1.   I bought a Morris Minor from Floggits in July for £750. When I took it back in July 2005 I told Mr Sharpe that it rattled. He said it was all right so I went home. Two weeks later the car broke down. The AA man told me that the gearbox had seized up. I asked Mr Sharpe for my money back, but he refused.

2.   I consider that I have been treated very shabbily, and that I should get my money back. I only had the car for 6 weeks.

3.   The value of this case is under £5,000.

MAUD NIGHTINGALE.

(Statement of Truth signed on Form N1.)

Here we have what to the layman would seem a concise statement of a claim against the garage. It reads logically, and although there is a dearth of particularity, nobody could properly claim that they could not understand what was being alleged. However, there is virtually no chance of setting out a Defence in conventional form — at least, not using the approach so far outlined in this volume.

Our instructions are as follows:

> Floggit Motors Ltd is a dealership specialising in the sale of Lamborari motor cars — a most prestigious marque. There is only one model, and it costs £240,000 (sunroof £750 extra). Present production is sold out, and orders are being taken for 2010.
>
> In December 2004 the dealership sold a Lamborari to an old lady who had just won the pools and wanted a 'bit of a fling'. She offered her old Morris Minor in exchange, but the company clearly were not very interested, until Mr Sharpe, the managing director, thought that it would be a bit of a joke to put it in the window (which only had one demonstration model in it). He put it in at a price of £1,250 as a gimmick.
>
> In January 2005 (much earlier than contended), Miss Nightingale came into the showroom and asked for a test drive of the Morris Minor. She was treated just like a customer for a Lamborari and taken out by Mr Sharpe personally. The press were hurriedly called in as part of the campaign.
>
> Mr Sharpe noted that Miss Nightingale was an appalling driver and seemed to have no inkling either of when to change gear, or of the relationship between putting her foot on the clutch and changing up or down. Most of the changes were accompanied by an horrendous crashing from the gearbox.
>
> Before agreeing to buy the car, Miss Nightingale asked if she could have an AA examination. Mr Sharpe agreed. The report stated that the gearbox was defective, and would cost about £300 to repair. In view of the reputation of the garage, Mr Sharpe told Miss Nightingale that he did not wish to take responsibility for the vehicle and was thus withdrawing it from sale.
>
> Miss Nightingale then said that if the garage would knock £500 off the price, she would get the gearbox fixed herself, as she knew a little man around the corner from her, who would do it. Mr Sharp reluctantly agreed, but insisted that this was recorded on the sales document. It read:
>
> 'Vehicle sold with a defective gearbox, as inspected by the AA. In consideration of a reduction of £500 in the purchase

price, the purchaser has agreed to purchase the vehicle as seen, and to have the works done herself. No guarantee is therefore given with respect to the gearbox. The vendors' standard 6-month warranty applies to the remainder of the vehicle, a copy of which has been received by the purchaser.'

On 10th July 2005, Miss Nightingale came into the show-room and said that the car was rattling at the back. Mr Sharpe inspected it and discovered a loose rear exhaust mounting. He personally did it up with a screwdriver, and off she went. The car sounded OK. No charge was made, even though the warranty period had expired.

About 3 weeks later, Miss Nightingale came back to the showroom without the car, and said the gearbox had failed and she wanted her money back. Mr Sharpe asked her if she had had it fixed after the purchase, and she said she had. He said that he did not think that she was entitled to her money back, and she went off in a huff.

It is quite clear that the Defence is going to occupy rather more space than the Particulars of Claim. On the other hand, we should attempt to keep the matter in proportion — it might just be thought a little oppressive to turn in a 37-page document in Defence, particularly in a matter which will be assigned to the small claims track!

There is really a choice as to how to go about the matter. The first is to try, in so far as is possible, to proceed as if the Particulars of Claim were beautifully laid out, making such adaptations as may be necessary from time to time.

1.   It is admitted that the Claimant purchased the said vehicle from the Defendant, save that it is averred that the said sale took place in about January 2005 and not as alleged in the Particulars of Claim. It is further admitted that the Claimant returned the said vehicle on 10th July 2005 and complained that it rattled at the rear. The same was due to a loose exhaust bracket, which was immediately tightened without charge by the Defendant's managing director Mr Sharpe.

2.   No admissions are made as to the alleged or any break-down, or as to the cause thereof, or as to any comments alleged to have been made by the said or any representative of the AA.

3.   If, which is not admitted, the said vehicle broke down, and that the same was due to the fault alleged in the Particulars of Claim, the Defendant will aver:

(1)   that the Claimant knew that the said vehicle had a defective gearbox at the time of sale;

(2)   that the Defendant reduced the price of the said vehicle by £500, in consequence of the same;

(3)   that the Claimant represented that, in consideration of the said reduction, she would have the vehicle repaired by a third party known to her;

(4)   that in consequence of the same, the Claimant purchased the vehicle 'as seen', that the Defendant's 6-month warranty thereon specifically excluded the said gearbox, and that the same was specifically endorsed in writing on the sales document given to the Claimant.

4.   Further or alternatively, and without prejudice to the matters set out above:

(1)   it is denied that the alleged defect (the existence of which is not admitted) would in any event have entitled the Claimant to reject the said vehicle when she purported to do so, and/or to claim the refund of the purchase price thereof;

(2)   the alleged defect occurred after the expiry of the said warranty period.

5.   In the premises it is denied that the Claimant is entitled to the relief claimed or any relief, for the reasons alleged or at all.

T. FORTU

Statement of Truth (etc.)

As it happens, that's not a bad job at all. It achieves its purpose effectively by responding to the Particulars of Claim without making any direct reference to the individual paragraphs. It works also because the claim is very short, and thus there is little to confuse anyone trying to understand what the case is all about. This approach is therefore worth considering in cases of this nature, even if the overall effect is a little unwieldy.

Before considering the alternative method, it may be useful to examine some of the construction of the above Defence. Mr Fortu has first, and correctly, pruned the instructions, and has only dealt with matters directly pertinent to the statement of case. The reasons for the car being in the window are, of course, matters of evidence, if relevant at all.

Paragraph 1 contains a skilful blend of reply to the Particulars of Claim and averments made on behalf of the Defence. He has dealt line by line (or 'seriatim' as us pleaders used to like to say) with the various allegations, and interposed matters relevant to give what the Defendant says is the full picture.

Paragraph 2 continues the process, and is still relevant to paragraph 1 of the Particulars. It has obviously been decided to split the paragraph at a suitable juncture, to avoid the whole thing being too top-heavy.

The third paragraph employs the useful method of splitting various averments into sub-paragraphs, as discussed earlier in this work. Essentially it consists of a recitation of the sale itself, once the gearbox fault had been discovered. Note that nothing has been set out concerning the AA inspection, which resulted in the **discovery** of the defective gearbox. Once again, this seems to be a matter of evidence. The **existence** of the fault has been admitted — the reasons for the discovery are not considered pertinent at this stage.

Paragraph 4 is also of interest. First, it deals with a completely separate matter of law. It has already been alleged that the Claimant had the vehicle for far longer than she liked to make out. Then it is alleged that she was not in any event entitled to reject it, or to claim her money back. In other words, even if the Defendant was liable for the defective gearbox, the allegation is that its liability extends only to its repair, and not to rescinding the transaction. Finally, the Defendant claims that the warranty period had, in any event, expired (although that may not be felt to be its strongest point)!

The paragraph also employs a useful phrase, 'without prejudice to the matters set out above'. Previously we would have put 'without prejudice to the generality of the foregoing' — a phrase rooted in 'legalese' and thus somewhat pompous. The modern version, used wisely and rarely, encodes rather more complicated language for expressing its point: 'Without in any way going back on what has already been said, if it is wrong, then get a mouthful of this!'

The Defence is then 'wrapped up' with the general denial, with which I have dealt earlier in the chapter.

As I have said, the 'modified standard' form of drafting has worked remarkably well in dealing with a homemade Particulars of Claim. It exemplifies what can be done when there is attention to the basic rules of drafting, yet the approach is not hidebound and inflexible.

The alternative form of approach is simply to ignore the layout of the claim, make a general denial as to liability (or as instructed), and then to draft the Defence in narrative form, almost as if it was an original claim. Although this may have little advantage in the instant example, it may sometimes be the only way to ensure that the case is properly set before the Court — particularly if the claim is so garbled, imprecise and inaccurate as to be misleading. First make your position clear:

> 1. It is denied that the Claimant is entitled to the relief claimed or any relief, for the reasons alleged or at all.

Then identify parties in the normal way:

> 2. The Defendant is and was at all relevant times a limited company carrying on business, amongst other things, as accredited retailers of new and second-hand Lamborari motor cars.

Then tell the story, omitting the irrelevant parts:

> 3. By a written agreement dated 5th January 2005, alternatively by an agreement the terms of which were evidenced in writing by the Defendant's sales document of the said date, copies of both of which are attached to this Defence, the Defendant sold the Claimant a second-hand Morris Minor motor car for £750. At the time of the said sale, the Claimant was fully aware that the said vehicle had a defective gearbox, which would cost an estimated £300 to repair.
>
> 4. There were, amongst others, the following express terms of the said agreement:
>   (1) That in consideration of the Defendant having reduced the purchase price of the said motor car from £1,250 to £750, the Claimant would have the same repaired by a third party.
>   (2) That the Defendant gave the Claimant a 6-month warranty in respect of faults developing in the said vehicle, save that the same expressly excluded the gearbox.
>
> 5. In about July 2005, after the expiry of the said warranty period, the Claimant returned the said motor car and complained of a rattle from the rear. The same was diagnosed by

the Defendant as being due to a loose exhaust bracket, which was rectified without charge.

6.   At about the end of July 2005, the Claimant complained that the gearbox to the said vehicle had failed, and demanded that the Defendant refund the said purchase price. For the reasons set out above, the said demand was refused.

7.   No admissions are made as to any breakdown allegedly suffered by the said motor car, or (should the same be proved) as to the cause or causes thereof. Further, and without prejudice to the matters set out in paragraph 4 above, if, which is not admitted, the gearbox of the said vehicle failed after 5th July 2005, the same did so after the expiry of the said warranty period.

AUSTIN MINIE

Statement of Truth (etc.)

The obvious benefit of this approach is that we can take maximum tactical advantage of the defects in the layout of the claim, simply by being able to ignore the whole format, and start again. Thereafter, we can use the most sympathetic method not merely of putting our defence, but also of setting out the facts. Our selection of the pertinent facts should, it goes without saying, not be inaccurate or misleading, but **we** are now setting the scene, not the Claimant. This cannot be a disadvantage. However, I repeat, flexibility is all important, and the precise method of approaching a claim that has not been set out in an orthodox manner must depend, as ever, on the exigencies of the situation.

THE SET-OFF AND COUNTERCLAIM

As often as not, you will receive instructions not merely that your client has a defence to the wicked allegations against him, but also that he himself has a substantial cause of action against the Claimant. There are those who may pass cynical comment upon the coincidence of such disputes, and indeed there is a (highly unofficial) school of thought to the effect that the Counterclaim should always exceed the claim in the hope that the Claimant will go away and find something better to do with his time and money rather than continue the action. This is a somewhat crude and obvious tactic, but is often persisted in nevertheless.

It is quite realistic to expect that a claim will often be met by a Counterclaim as well as a Defence. After all, the breakdown of any form of relationship between parties will often lead to mutual recriminations in which each alleges that he or she has suffered at the hands of the other. Sometimes a party may not wish to initiate proceedings, but is thereafter compelled to bring all matters into the open when an action is commenced against him. Certain business relationships also may lead to cross-disputes. For example, a builder may bring proceedings in respect of breach of contract, alleging that he was excluded from the site and deprived of the opportunity of finishing the works he had contracted to perform. The property owner may allege (and usually does) that the works were performed incompetently, and that he had no alternative but to employ other contractors at additional expense. It may be more realistic to look at such cases as not being brought by one party against another, but by both parties asking the Court to resolve the situation between them.

A Counterclaim need not, of course, be founded on the same set of facts as the claim. It is nevertheless usually both economical and expedient to deal with all issues between the parties at one hearing, rather than to engage in a multiplicity of actions, although this will be dealt with by effective judicial case management under the CPR. Very often, when the form of relief claimed is common to both parties (e.g. money), the main defence to an action may not be based on the merits of the claim but on the fact that the Defendant considers that he has a right to withhold the sum claimed, on account of other monies that he says are owed to him by the Claimant. Such a defence is by way of total or partial set-off, or 'setorf' as Mr Prout was prone to say.

The appropriate way of entitling a Defence and Counterclaim is by stating just that after the title of the case, and then dividing the subsequent statement of case under the titles 'Defence' and 'Counterclaim'. The Counterclaim will follow on from the Defence and so it may well, for example, commence at, say, paragraph 9.

Note that the term 'set-off' is not used as part of the title. The set-off forms part of the defence to the claim, and is set out as such. How we do this is demonstrated below.

A Defence can thus comprise the following combinations:

1.   A substantive defence to the claim.
2.   A substantive defence to the claim accompanied by a partial or total set-off.
3.   A defence comprising solely a partial or total set-off.

Where there is both a substantive defence **and** a set-off, the main
defence will be pleaded first. Of course, if that defence is successful, the
set-off will then be dealt with solely as a Counterclaim, so that in the
event of the Defendant winning the case hands-down, he will not merely
defeat the Claimant's claim but will receive judgment in his favour on
the Counterclaim. If, however, he is unsuccessful on the merits of his
substantive defence, the claim against him may still fail if he is successful on his Counterclaim, and that the amount is equal to or exceeds that
of the claim, once there has been a set-off. The justification for this is
that the Claimant should have appreciated that he was not entitled to the
value of his claim in view of the amount to be set off in favour of the
Defendant.

There are a number of ways in which the above can be set out. It is usual
to do so after the final denial of the claim, or the 'general traverse' if used. So:

> Further or alternatively, if, which is denied, the Defendant is
> liable to the Claimant as alleged or at all, the Defendant
> seeks to set off against such liability, the amount set out in
> the Counterclaim below so as to reduce it or extinguish it
> altogether.

Now that is a bit of a mouthful I do admit, even though I have discarded
the traditional 'in extinction or diminution thereof' in favour of more
modern language. Notice that it starts with the word 'Further', thus
making it clear that the set-off is without prejudice to the substantive
defence that has been set out earlier. It is only if that defence does not
succeed that the set-off comes into play. The words 'so as to reduce it or
extinguish it altogether' are designed to deal with situations either where
the set-off completely writes off the claim, or where it will serve only to
diminish the value of the claim by such amount as is found to be due and
owing to the Defendant.

Again at the risk of risking a *frisson* of disapproval from tradition-
alists, I venture to suggest that the first 'without prejudice' part of the
formula is not invariably necessary. Were we merely to put:

> Further or alternatively, the Defendant will seek to set off against
> the Claimant's claim, the sums set out in the Counterclaim
> below, so as to reduce it or extinguish it altogether.

the same purpose will have been achieved. The set-off is 'further or
alternatively' to the substantive defence, and the express statement that
it may only be relevant were the defence to fail seems unnecessary.

In the event that the Counterclaim does not extinguish the claim, it would be appropriate to omit the words 'extinguish it altogether' from the formula. However, I would advise you to beware of doing this as a matter of course, unless you have no other substantive defence to raise. Although the claim against you may be greater than the amount of the Counterclaim, it is, of course quite possible that your substantive defence may succeed 'in part', and that the balance of the claim may then be extinguished by the Counterclaim. It is, I suggest, perhaps more a matter of semantics than vital drafting technique, but once again, being aware of the various permutations should enable you to draft your statement of case with greater flexibility and definition than hitherto.

In the event of the sole defence being one of set-off, your entire Defence may be along the lines:

1. Paragraphs 1 to 5 of the Particulars of Claim are admitted, subject to the set-off and Counterclaim set out below.

2. The Defendant claims to set off the matters set out in the Counterclaim below, in extinction of the Claimant's claim.

Or more neatly:

1. Paragraphs 1 to 5 of the Particulars of Claim are admitted, save that the Defendant claims to set-off the matters set out in the Counterclaim below, in extinction of the same.

Or *con variazione*:

1. The Defendant admits the matters set out in the Particulars of Claim, save that he claims to be able to set off the matters counterclaimed below, in extinction of the same.

Or *molto cantabile*:

1. Save that the Defendant claims to set off the matters counterclaimed below, in extinction of the same, the Particulars of Claim are admitted.

Actually, I don't much care for the last example, as it seems too defensive from a tactical point of view. The Counterclaim appears to be subordinate to the admission of the claim rather than vice versa. However, by now I trust that you have the general idea, and will doubtless produce precedents of devastating ingenuity and brilliance!

That leaves us with the embarrassing situation where there is no substantial defence, save for a **partial set-off**. In such a case it may be
advisable to do some paying-up pretty quickly, and then allege the
payment or tender of payment in the Defence. Thus:

> 1.   It is admitted that the Defendant owed the Claimant the
> sum of £2,500, which sum was paid to him by way of the
> Defendant's cheque No. 222333 drawn on Barcwest Bank
> plc, dated 21st February 2005.
>
> 2.   As to the balance of £4,900, the Defendant claims to set
> off the same … etc.

The payment or tender is pleaded not only to ensure that the precise
position is clear to the Court, but also to gain the psychological advantage that the Court is aware the Defendant is not completely impecunious, and that the defence is not merely of the nature 'The Defendant
does not want to pay'. The question of payment is also not entirely irrelevant to the question of costs!

So much for the set-off. Now a brief word as to the best way to set out
the Counterclaim.

Where the Counterclaim is based on facts completely different from
those of the claim and defence, the convenient course is (if appropriate)
to insert the necessary set-off paragraph in the Defence, and then continue under the heading 'Counterclaim' and draft as if you were starting
a Particulars of Claim from scratch. Remember of course, that the
'prayer' will commence:

> **AND** the Defendant Counterclaims:

and not:

> **AND** the Claimant claims:

I hasten to add that adopting the second version will not be fatal to your
claim. You will look a bit of a twit, however, and in my experience this
is to be avoided as much as possible. There are going to be times when
it will be inevitable, but don't positively invite trouble!

Where, as is very often the case, the facts of the Counterclaim are identical to, or largely based on, the claim and Defence, it is quite unnecessary
fully to repeat these in the Counterclaim. It is perfectly proper, and much

more intelligible, simply to 'repeat' the relevant paragraphs of the Defence, or even the whole Defence, thus:

> 14.   The Defendant repeats paragraphs 1 to 7 of the Defence above.

Or

> 14.   The Defendant repeats his Defence herein.

After that, it will often be necessary to add any relevant matters that have not appeared in the Defence and which give rise to the Counterclaim. On the other hand, there are occasions where the nature of the Defence itself, or the way in which it has been drafted, gives rise to the Counterclaim, in which case it is then necessary only to set out the 'prayer'.

Perhaps we should now look at a full example of a Defence coupled with a Counterclaim. The Particulars of Claim are from a real action, although obviously heavily disguised. I have chosen it as I do not (with the greatest of respect) consider it to be a masterpiece of drafting, but it is therefore not a wholly artificial exercise.

'There are going to be times when this will be inevitable ...'

In order to break new ground, I have chosen a rather difficult Defence, which is based more on the Claimant's failure to mitigate his loss, than on any more substantive grounds.

EXAMPLE

Mr and Mrs Barnacle trade as the East England Antique Furniture Restoration Centre, in Hubble-on-Sea. They were well known in this very specialised craft, which does not have any nationally or internationally recognised qualifications.

For some years, and in addition to their business, the Barnacles had run a 2-year course, after which successful students were awarded their Diploma in Antique Furniture Restoration. This course consisted of a first year, which was mainly theoretical, and which ended with an intermediate examination. The second year consisted of a mixture of theory and practical restoration under the tutelage of the Barnacles, at the conclusion of which there was a final exam. The course was unique to the Barnacles, and although their Diploma was not officially recognised, it was nevertheless considered in the trade to be a mark of high achievement, such that any student holding the award would have an above average prospect of obtaining employment as a restorer.

Unfortunately, due to cutbacks in local authority grants, the number of students in the course declined from its usual average of 8, such that in 2004 there were 3 second-year students and 1 first-year student, and in 2005 there were no new entrants at all. As a result, and at rather short notice, the Barnacles reluctantly decided that the school was uneconomical and had to be closed, and that they would continue to trade only as restorers.

Their sole student, Gerald Chippendale, was therefore informed of the closure of the course in September 2005. He was not pleased!

IN THE HUBBLE COUNTY COURT   Case No. HB990000

BETWEEN:

Mr GERALD CHIPPENDALE

Claimant

— and —

(1)   Mr FREDERICK BARNACLE
(2)   Mrs JEAN BARNACLE
(t/a East England Antique Furniture Restoration Centre)

Defendants

PARTICULARS OF CLAIM

1.   By an agreement reached between the Claimant on the one part and the Defendants on the other part in or about September of 2004, the Defendants agreed to provide for the Claimant a 2-year Diploma Course in Antique Furniture Restoration leading to a Diploma in Antique Furniture Restoration at the end of that period subject to satisfactory performance by the Claimant.

2.   In consequence of that agreement the Claimant paid certain fees in respect of the first year of the course, namely a sum of £2,300 on 20th September 2004 and a further sum of £2,000 on 8th January 2005. A total of £4,600 representing the first year's fees.

3.   By notice dated the 9th September 2005 the Defendants summarily terminated the Course as a result of which the Claimant has suffered loss and damage.

PARTICULARS OF LOSS AND DAMAGE

(1)   The Claimant has spent one year in carrying out the first year of a Course which is unique to the Defendants' Centre and is of no value towards any other professional qualification.

(2)   The Claimant has paid fees totalling £4,600 on account of the total course which has not been completed by reason of the Defendants' action.

(3)   The value of this claim exceeds £5,000 but does not exceed £15,000.

AND The Claimant claims:

1.   The sum of £4,600 being the return of fees paid on account of the uncompleted Course.

2.   Damages limited to £2,000 for lost time and opportunity arising out of the Defendants' breach of contract.

3.   Interest pursuant to the County Courts Act 1984 at the rate of 8% per annum on the said sum of £2,300 from the 20th September 2004 to date making a total sum of £149.60 further interest under the aforementioned Act at the aforementioned rate until judgment or sooner payment at the rate of 50p per day.

4.   Interest pursuant to the County Courts Act 1984 at the rate of 8% per annum on the said sum of £2,000 from 8th January 2005 to date making a total sum of £115.60; further interest under the aforementioned Act at the aforementioned rate until judgment or sooner payment at the rate of 70p per day.

Dated ...   POLLY PHEMUS.

Messrs Mud and Crumpet,
2 Dark Alley, Hubble-on-Sea,
Solicitors for the Claimant who will accept
service of all process in this
matter on behalf of the Claimant
at the above address.

Statement of Truth (etc.)

Before turning to the Defendants' case, I hope that you will have noted the various ways in which you could have improved on the Particulars of Claim. Not wishing to intrude too much into the present discussion, I will not go through it at length, but I hope you will have observed the following.

Paragraph 1
No mention of whether the agreement was oral or written. No identification of the Defendants. Unnecessary and antiquated use of the words 'on the one part' and 'on the other part'. No allegation as to when the course was supposed to begin.

Paragraph 2

Cumbersome use of language regarding the payment of fees. Horrible last sentence. No allegation that the Claimant duly commenced the course, although this is mentioned later, but after it is alleged that the same had been terminated.

Paragraph 3

No mention as to whether the termination was oral or written. No allegation that the Claimant was unable to start another course due to the short period of notice and the close proximity of the new term. If he was able to start a new course, there is no mention of the cost of this, as any excess might be recoverable from the Defendants.

The claim

No explanation of the damages claimed for 'lost time and opportunity'. Cumbersome pleading of interest and use of the word 'aforementioned' on no less than 4 occasions! Strictly speaking, unnecessary to set out a claim for costs.

None of the above is fatal to the case, some of the missing detail may be unimportant, but the statement of case lacks the precision and authority which should at that early stage have been stamped upon the action. Anyway, let's turn to our instructions with regard to the Defence and Counterclaim.

> Although the Barnacles informed Mr Chippendale on 9th September 2005 that the course was to close, the new term was not due to start until 10th October. Although the course was unique, this was not to say that the experience gained would not have stood the Claimant in good stead were he to seek another professional qualification in the field of antique furniture restoration.
>
> However, in view of the short notice, Mr Barnacle spoke to some contacts in London, and arranged (unusually) for the Claimant to attend for 3 days per week at the Arthur Daley Restoration Centre in Pentonville, which was world famous for the quality of its furniture and the qualifications and connections of its personnel. The practical experience gained there would have been invaluable to the Claimant, who would have also got to know (and, one hopes, impress) a number of influential people in the trade.

As a result of this, the Barnacles offered to continue to provide Mr Chippendale with the theoretical side of the course, and to allow him to take the Diploma examination at the end of the year. They did this in a letter dated 20th September 2005, in which they also invited him to a meeting to discuss a suitable financial adjustment, to take account of the additional travel and inconvenience. However, the Claimant refused to meet them, or to negotiate at all.

Further, during the first year of the course, Mr Barnacle allowed the Claimant to borrow his own textbook *Barnacle's Restoration*, worth £50, and a travelling case of specialist wood dyes, valued at £750. In early September 2005, he asked Mr Chippendale to return them, but was told to 'take a running jump' and that Mr Chippendale was going to keep them to compensate him for the loss of the course. Mr Barnacle would like them back.

Before putting pen to paper, we must first, as usual, consider the legal merits of our position. It is not, of course, essential that we be convinced that the Defence will succeed, merely that it is properly arguable in law, on the basis of our instructions. It is clearly relevant that there is no denial that the course was cancelled, and at short notice. It is also probably not arguable that there was no concluded contract for a second year. The Claimant had signed on for a course that was to last for 2 years. He had successfully completed the first, and was thus entitled to enrol for the second. The first year was of no use to him on its own, save in so far as its intrinsic value may have assisted him in his chosen career. I have therefore chosen **not** to defend the case on the basis that there was no requirement for the Barnacles to take him on for the second year. Of course, should you disagree, you are free to draft the matter accordingly.

The main thrust of the Defence must therefore be that the Claimant has not suffered any loss and damage, or that if he has, he has failed to mitigate that loss. That is a perfectly arguable defence, although I fear that the Court may well hold that it was not reasonable to expect him to commute to London 3 times per week in order to mitigate damage caused by an admitted breach of contract. However, for the present purposes we shall concentrate on the way in which the Defence should be drafted, and shall assume that the appropriate legal advice has been given. Remember also the opening pages of this chapter!

Paragraphs 1 and 2

Notwithstanding the various niggles that we may have as to the way in which these paragraphs have been drafted, they give rise to no dispute between the parties, and there is therefore no reason why they should not be admitted. Furthermore, I do not consider that there is anything relevant that needs to be added. So, depending on your preferred style, you can put:

> 1. The Defendants admit paragraphs 1 and 2 of the Particulars of Claim.

Or, as I prefer it:

> 1. Paragraphs 1 and 2 of the Particulars of Claim are admitted.

Paragraph 3

Here, we should analyse our response. We clearly have to **admit** that the Defendants determined the course. However, we may wish to dispute the 'summary' aspect of the notice in view of the fact that the new term did not start for a month. (It is to be hoped that's not our best point!) What should be our position with regard to the Claimant's allegation that he has suffered loss and damage?

We could **deny** that he has suffered loss and damage. However, I feel that this is a bit extreme. After all, we have tacitly admitted that we were in breach of contract, and are not in a position to be able to show that he had not. On the other hand, if he has suffered any loss and damage, it should be for him to prove it, and we certainly do not accept that he has suffered it to the extent claimed. Another reason which, in my view, militates against our being able to deny loss and damage, is that the Particulars of Loss and Damage cannot, in principle, be denied: the Claimant **did** spend one year on a unique course; it is **not**, unfortunately, counted towards any other course; and he **has** paid the first year's fees.

Thus, the obvious answer must be to take the coward's way out, and **make no admissions** as to the loss and damage suffered.

So, to recap: we admit the termination from the commencement of the next term, we do not admit that the Claimant has suffered loss and damage, and we put him to proof of anything which he says he has suffered.

> 2. Save that it is admitted that by a written notice dated 9th September 2005 the Defendants terminated the said Course from the commencement of the following term, no admissions

are made as to the alleged or any loss and damage suffered
by the Claimant, to which he is put to strict proof.

I shall assume that by this stage in the work, you have become familiar
with various drafting styles, and shall not analyse them in as great detail
as hitherto. Notice, however, that I have decided to adopt the 'save that'
approach, in that it is both concise and places the emphasis of the paragraph in the most effective manner for our purposes. The main thrust of
the paragraph is directed to putting the Claimant to strict proof of his allegations of loss and damage. We clearly do not wish the main emphasis to
be on our admission that we closed down the course. Likewise, the saving
of the 'strict proof' to the final words of the paragraph also subordinates
that proof (which implies the possible existence of loss and damage) to
the lack of admissions. Thus, although we cannot escape from the more
embarrassing aspects of the paragraph, we have mitigated their effect to
the greatest possible extent. We could have used words to the effect:

'OK, we admit that we broke the contract, but prove that you
have suffered any loss and damage.'

What I hope we have done is to say:

'Even though we accept that we closed down the course, we
can't believe that you have suffered anything like the
amount you have claimed, and you're going to have one hell
of a job proving it.'

To those of you who ask why, if that is the case, I did not simply draft
the paragraph in the above manner, I reply that I wished to continue my
practice for a few more years yet, without incurring any more Judicial
Thunderbolts etc. than were absolutely necessary!

By this stage we have now dealt with the entire Particulars of Claim,
save for the 'prayer'. What we have **not** done, of course, is to put our
Defence. This example thus reinforces what I have said earlier in this
chapter, about the unsatisfactory nature of a Defence pleaded slavishly
in response to the individual paragraphs of the claim. We **must** set out
our version of events, both to comply with the Rules and to enhance our
credibility. Here we have to make certain admissions of fact, and have to
put the Claimant to proof of his loss and damage. Our instructions have,
however, remained untouched.

The manner in which we draft the remainder of our Defence will
be dictated by our previous analysis of the legal issues that it discloses.

We have already decided that the effect of our instructions is that the Claimant has unreasonably failed to mitigate his loss. Our thought processes should therefore be along the following lines:

> We have already admitted that we terminated the contract. We have not admitted that the Claimant suffered any loss thereby, and invited him to prove that he has. Next, in the event of his being able to show that he **has** suffered some loss and damage, we must allege that it could have been avoided had he attempted to mitigate his loss. Although he cannot be expected to do anything unreasonable, we say that our offer was most reasonable and, had he accepted it, he would not have suffered any loss and damage. Alternatively, even if he would still have suffered loss and damage, it would have been much less than that presently claimed.

The nature and layout of our next paragraph is thus already taking shape:

> 3.   Further or alternatively, if, which is not admitted, the Claimant has suffered loss and/or damage as alleged or at all, the same was wholly or partly caused by his failure to mitigate his loss.

'*Further or alternatively*'   This makes it clear that what is to follow is in addition to the arguments already raised so far in the Defence.

'*If, which is not admitted*'   This is a 'catchphrase' used to define what is to follow as being 'inconsistent drafting'. This is perfectly permissible, and is another way of expressing that what is to follow is without prejudice to the previous argument. For the one reader who may not know the story, I relate here the no doubt apocryphal tale of a future Master of the Rolls, who, early on in his prep school days, was accused of breaking a window in his headmaster's study. His defence ran as follows:

Firstly, there is no window in the headmaster's study.
If there is a window in the headmaster's study, it is not broken.
If there is a window in the headmaster's study, and it is presently broken, I didn't do it.
Anyway, it was an accident!

The above, in my view, explains the rationale and effect of inconsistent drafting better than any essay based on burdens of proof, natural justice, logic and legal theory Anyway, that's all you're getting in this book!

'Loss and/or damage as alleged or at all'   This is inserted to safe-guard against any allegation or finding that the Claimant has suffered some loss and damage of a nature different from that originally pleaded. Our position is made quite clear — no loss and/or damage, pleaded or other-wise, has been suffered.

'The same was wholly or partly caused'   This is to take account of the possibility that the Court may find that **some** of any loss and damage proved to have been occasioned, could have been avoided. Technically (and only technically), had we not pleaded the words 'or partly', it could then have been argued by the Claimant that we had alleged that the **entirety** of the loss etc. was avoidable, and that we had not alleged that **part** of the loss could have been escaped. That particular argument did not consequently form part of our Defence, and we could therefore not escape full liability to the Claimant in such an event.

I would not like to be the person instructed to put forward such an argument, but it may well have succeeded in days past, when cases stood or fell on a strict interpretation of the pleadings. In any case, such a situ-ation would arise only in the event of sloppy drafting, which it is presently our earnest intention to avoid!

The construction of the paragraph should now be clear. Nevertheless, I am afraid that we cannot rest just yet. We have stated the **principle** of our Defence, now we must come up with some **particulars**. If we do not, our credibility will be impugned, and we will almost certainly be forced to supply them at a later stage (and at our expense) or face being struck out in default.

Although the Particulars will basically follow our instructions, it will be useful to see if they can be put in a format which will best advance the nature of the Defence being raised.

It is a good thing never to ignore the weak points in your case. Sometimes it is better to grab the bull by the horns and deal openly with various deficiencies, than to pretend that they do not exist. In the present example, the Claimant has alleged that the Barnacles' cancellation of the course caused him damage, because, amongst other matters, he has thrown away a year's fees on a course which cannot be duplicated elsewhere.

I would rather not ignore this unless there is no alternative. Admittedly there's not very much that we can do, but we do have one shot in the breech — on our instructions, the experience will put him in very good stead for the future. Although, if that is accepted, it may at best knock a little bit off the damages, it's probably worth a mention. I do not, however, think that our case would die from exposure were this particular argument to be discarded!

The above 21-gun salvo will be followed by an exposition of our case — we went out of our way to offer a viable alternative to the Claimant. It would have been very beneficial to him. We offered to make appropriate financial adjustments. However, he refused even to speak to us!

PARTICULARS

(1) Whereas it is admitted that the said Course was unique to the Defendants' Centre, the experience and education gained by the Claimant in the first year thereof was, and would be invaluable in assisting him in his proposed career in antique furniture restoration.

(2) In about September 2005, in an attempt to assist the Claimant either to complete the said course, or to mitigate his loss, the Defendants made arrangements whereby:

(a) they would continue to provide theoretical tuition to the Claimant for the second year of the course;

(b) the Claimant would complete the practical side of the course by attending for 3 days per week at a well-known restoration centre in London, which would have been especially advantageous to him, in that the said centre specialised in restoration of important and high quality furniture, and would have introduced the Claimant to a greater variety of work and personnel in the trade than would have been the case had he carried out practical work at the Defendants' premises;

(c) the Claimant would have taken the Diploma examination set by the Defendants, at the end of the said course;

(d) the Defendants would have made an appropriate financial adjustment with the Claimant to compensate him for any increased expenditure and/or inconvenience in the light of the above.

(3) In a letter to the Claimant, dated 20th September 2005, the Defendants made the above proposals, and invited the Claimant to meet with them to discuss the same, but the Claimant at all times thereafter refused to do so.

4. In the circumstances, it is denied that the Claimant is entitled to the relief claimed, or any relief, for the reasons alleged or at all.

I hope that the above is self-explanatory, although paragraph 4 raises an interesting point: why is it that we are **denying** that the Claimant is entitled to the relief claimed, when we have been assiduous in making no admissions as to the loss and damage claimed?

The answer is that we have not admitted that the Claimant has suffered any loss and damage. That is, we have put him to proof of **quantum**. Thereafter, our case is that even if he is able to prove a quantum of loss and damage, he is not **entitled** to claim it from us, due to his failure to mitigate his loss. Thus, his **claim** is denied.

That I hope makes the best of such defence as we have. Now we must proceed with our next line of argument, which is that we are, in any event, entitled to set off the Counterclaim against any amount found due to the Claimant under the claim. I hope the next paragraph will come as no surprise:

> 5.   Further or alternatively, the Defendants will seek to set off against the Claimant's claim the matters set out in the Counterclaim below, so as to reduce it or extinguish it altogether.

COUNTERCLAIM

We now have to plan the way to draft our Counterclaim. The first thing to note is that although it arises as a result of the relationship between the parties, that is the only ground that is common between claim and Counterclaim. It is thus irrelevant and unnecessary formally to repeat the entire Defence. The only part which may require formal restatement is the fact that the Claimant was a student of the Defendants, as it was in the course of this relationship that the items were lent. However, even this can safely be omitted, as the nature of the Counterclaim does not require us to establish any form of relationship between the Barnacles and Mr Chippendale. I shall do so, notwithstanding, merely in order to illustrate what I consider to be the proper approach to adopt when it **is** necessary to restate such facts.

There is no technical reason why we could not set the matter out in detail, so:

> 6.   As a result of an agreement made between the Defendants and the Claimant in about September 2004, the Claimant enrolled as a student in the Defendants' course in Antique Furniture Restoration.

However, that's all common ground, as it has been set out in paragraph 1 of the Particulars of Claim, and admitted in the first paragraph of the Defence. It would perhaps be a little peculiar to commence the Counterclaim:

> 6. The Defendants repeat paragraph 1 of the Particulars of Claim ...

if only for the fact that the Defendants have never stated paragraph 1 of the Particulars of Claim in the first place! Additionally of course, it may be thought somewhat cumbersome to 'hijack' a paragraph from a different statement of case. One can 'adopt' the paragraph, but this is still unsatisfactory.

The appropriate way out is to 'repeat' the paragraph in the Defence which admits the relationship between the parties. In the present example, we would merely state:

> 6. The Defendants repeat paragraph 1 of their Defence.

Or, more accurately:

> 6. The Defendants repeat paragraph 1 of their Defence above.

Thus, we have used our admission of the relationship as the foundation for the claim which we, in turn, are about to make against the Claimant.

Having successfully accomplished the transition between Defence and Counterclaim, we will now proceed in the normal manner, as if we were drafting a Particulars of Claim from the beginning. As a result, we must identify our cause of action, the nature of the relief that we wish to counterclaim, and any points of law peculiar to our case. As Caesar said to Brutus — I think you should have a stab first!

It seems appropriate that we should claim an order for specific delivery of the articles, which obviously have some rarity or specialist value. Alternatively to this we should claim delivery up or the value of the goods. In both instances we should claim damages for conversion. Remember that the CPR require, in every case in which a claim is brought to enforce a right to recover possession of goods, the claim to include a statement of the value of the goods.

I do not propose to go through the drafting of the remaining paragraphs in any detail, as you have hopefully followed the principles

discussed in the preceding chapter. The Counterclaim should be quite
short. Having repeated the first paragraph of the Defence, we go on:

7.   On a date unknown, but after the commencement of the
said course, the First named Defendant lent the Claimant a textbook entitled *Barnacle's Restoration*, together with a travelling
case of specialist wood dyes, both belonging to the Defendants.

8.   In about early September 2005, the First named
Defendant orally requested the Claimant to return the said
property, notwithstanding which the Claimant at all times
thereafter failed and/or refused to do so.

9.   In the circumstances, the Claimant has unlawfully detained
the said property, and converted the same to his own use.

10.   The said book is valued at £50, and the said case and
dyes are valued at £750. The value of this Counterclaim
does not exceed £5,000.

11.   The Defendants further claim interest on such amount
as they may be awarded under this Counterclaim, (etc.)
pursuant to section 69, County Courts Act 1984.

AND the Defendants Counterclaim:

1.   An Order that the Claimant do specifically deliver the
said property to the Defendants, together with damages for
its detention, and interest as aforesaid.

Further or alternatively:

2.   Delivery up of the said property, or the said value
thereof, together with damages for its detention, and interest
as aforesaid.

Further or alternatively:

3.   Damages for conversion, together with interest as
aforesaid.

IVAN EDEK

Statement of Truth (etc.)

By way of brief comment, I ask you to note the following.

Generally
I have continued to refer to the parties as Claimant and Defendant(s), as I consider that to refer to them in any other manner in the body of the statement of case would be unnecessarily cumbersome and confusing.

Paragraph 7
Due to the difficulty in ascertaining the exact time when the property was lent, I have drafted the matter by reference to the diploma course. I was enabled to do so by virtue of having referred to it already by repeating paragraph 1 of the Defence. Had I chosen not to refer to the course, I would have commenced the Counterclaim as follows:

> 6.   On a date unknown in about 2004 or 2005 the First named Defendant... etc.

Paragraph 8
This sets out the request for the return of the property. Once again, the date is inexact, so 'In about' is used. It's the best we can do. Note the particulars that the request was oral, and the use of the words 'at all times thereafter', to make it clear that the Claimant did not return the property at a later date.

Paragraph 9
This draws the alleged legal conclusions from the wrongful act of the Claimant.

Paragraph 10
Here we have set out the value of the property, for the purposes of being able to claim for the same in the event of specific delivery being refused, or not being possible, and to comply with the CPR, both in respect of the value of goods claimed and in respect of the requirement to insert a statement of value of the Counterclaim.

The '**prayer**' has been drafted along conventional lines, as can be found in any decent book of precedents (which this is not!). It claims, in the alternative where necessary, the various remedies which can be awarded when property has been converted. So, according to custom, here's a look at the entire finished product:

IN THE HUBBLE COUNTY COURT   Case No. HB990000

BETWEEN:

Mr GERALD CHIPPENDALE

<u>Claimant</u>

— and —

(1)   Mr FREDERICK BARNACLE
(2)   Mrs JEAN BARNACLE
(t/a East England Antique Furniture Restoration Centre)

<u>Defendants</u>

DEFENCE AND COUNTERCLAIM

---

1.   Paragraphs 1 and 2 of the Particulars of Claim are admitted.

2.   Save that it is admitted that by a written notice dated 9th September 2005, the Defendants terminated the said Course from the commencement of the following term, no admissions are made as to the alleged or any loss and damage suffered by the Claimant, to which he is put to strict proof.

3.   Further or alternatively, if, which is not admitted, the Claimant has suffered loss and/or damage as alleged or at all, the same was wholly or partly caused by his failure to mitigate his loss.

PARTICULARS

(1)   Whereas it is admitted that the said Course was unique to the Defendants' Centre, the experience and education gained by the Claimant

in the first year thereof was, and would be invaluable in assisting him in his proposed career in antique furniture restoration.

(2)   In about September 2005, in an attempt to assist the Claimant either to complete the said course, or to mitigate his loss, the Defendants made arrangements whereby:

(a)   they would continue to provide theoretical tuition to the Claimant for the second year of the course;

(b)   the Claimant would complete the practical side of the course by attending for 3 days per week at a well-known restoration centre in London, which would have been especially advantageous to him, in that the said centre specialised in restoration of important and high quality furniture, and would have introduced the Claimant to a greater variety of work and personnel in the trade, than would have been the case had he carried out practical work at the Defendants' premises;

(c)   the Claimant would have taken the Diploma examination set by the Defendants, at the end of the said course;

(d)   the Defendants would have made an appropriate financial adjustment with the Claimant to compensate him for any increased expenditure and/or inconvenience in the light of the above.

(3)   In a letter to the Claimant, dated 20th September 2005, the Defendants made the above proposals, and invited the Claimant to meet with them to discuss the same, but the Claimant at all times thereafter refused to do so.

4.   In the circumstances, it is denied that the Claimant is entitled to the relief claimed, or any relief, for the reasons alleged or at all.

5.   Further or alternatively, the Defendants will seek to set off against the Claimant's claim the matters set out in the Counterclaim below, so as to reduce it or extinguish it altogether.

COUNTERCLAIM

6.   The Defendants repeat paragraph 1 of their Defence above.

7.   On a date unknown, but after the commencement of the said course, the First named Defendant lent the Claimant a textbook entitled *Barnacle's Restoration*, together with a travelling case of specialist wood dyes, both belonging to the Defendants.

8. In about early September 2005, the First named Defendant orally requested the Claimant to return the said property, notwithstanding which the Claimant at all times thereafter failed and/or refused to do so.

9. In the circumstances, the Claimant has unlawfully detained the said property, and converted the same to his own use.

10. The said book is valued at £50, and the said case and dyes are valued at £750. The value of this Counterclaim does not exceed £5,000.

11. The Defendants further claim interest on such amount as they may be awarded under this Counterclaim, (etc.), pursuant to section 69, County Courts Act 1984.

AND the Defendants Counterclaim:

1. An Order that the Claimant do specifically deliver the said property to the Defendants, together with damages for its detention, and interest as aforesaid.

Further or alternatively:

2. Delivery up of the said property, or the said value thereof, together with damages for its detention, and interest as aforesaid.

Further or alternatively:

3. Damages for conversion, together with interest as aforesaid.

IVAN EDEK

Statement of Truth (etc.)

I hope that this chapter has given you some insight into the various thought processes which should be employed when dealing with the drafting of a Defence. As in the previous chapter, I make no claim that the above discussion is exhaustive, or that the above examples are paragons of their type. It is enough, for the purposes of this work, if you feel that you can, in future, approach the drafting of a Defence and Counterclaim with greater confidence, flexibility and accuracy. Your clients will feel better too!

In the next chapter, I will examine the use and abuse of the Reply.

Chapter Four

The Right to Reply
(The Reply)

> 'It's time for you to answer now', the
> Queen said, looking at her watch: 'open
> your mouth a little wider when you
> speak, and always say "your Majesty".'

Once you have issued proceedings, there is always the chance that the
other side may not file a Defence. As the days roll on without any sign
of response, you may perhaps experience a heightening of the delicious
feeling that perhaps they're not going to bother after all. The wonderful
prospect of 'default judgment' becomes increasingly possible, and it is
often quite a disappointment when the Defence ultimately plops through
the letter-box, and you realise that the matter is being taken reasonably
seriously after all.

It is at this stage that you must resist the understandable instinct to 'have
another go' and file a Reply, unless there are proper legal grounds for so
doing. To do otherwise is not only to break the rules, but also to detract from
the integrity of your case. A good cause of action does not get any better by
repetition — indeed repetition itself sows the seeds of doubt, from a tactical
point of view. Thus, unless you have to do so, do **not** draft a Reply, and
certainly do not consider that you have to do so as a matter of course.

It is of course necessary to draft a Reply if the Defendant has served a Counterclaim. Although there is an implied joinder of issue to a Defence, so that no further statements of case are necessary, the same does not apply to a Counterclaim. The conventional manner of dealing with a Counterclaim is to append a Defence to Counterclaim after a Reply, which may itself only be a formal joinder of issue in the absence of any other compelling circumstances. So when do we need a Reply, and what should it contain?

A Reply is used where it is felt necessary further to define the issues between the parties. This should normally only arise as a result of the contents of the Defence, which may have raised issues which require an answer. These can be of three types:

1.   where the Defence has raised a point for the first time, which requires some clarification or answer from the Claimant; or
2.   where some new matter may have arisen as a direct and relevant result of something that has been pleaded in the Defence; or
3.   where there may be certain issues to which admissions can be made in order to delimit the extent of contention at the trial.

Very often, the need for a Reply may rise by virtue of the above when the Particulars of Claim has been extremely short, and the Defence has 'narrated' a sequence of events which ought properly to have been set out in the original claim. In such an event, one is left with no alternative but to deal with the matters raised by way of a Reply. There may be a lesson to be learnt from this. Let us take a short and straightforward example:

IN THE HIGH COURT OF JUSTICE   2006 S No. 0000
QUEEN'S BENCH DIVISION

BETWEEN:

SELLAROLL LIMITED

Claimants

— and —

PASSION GARMENTS LIMITED

Defendants

PARTICULARS OF CLAIM

1. The Claimants' claim is for £90,765 due and owing for goods ordered by the Defendants and uncollected by them on the Claimants' invoices scheduled hereafter copies of which are attached hereto:

26th June 2005	Invoice 245368	£1,325.47
28th June 2005	Invoice 245389	£50,321.53
6th July 2005	Invoice 245411	£6,730.12
14th Aug. 2005	Invoice 245475	£22,771.23
3rd Sept. 2005	Invoice 245398	£9,616.65
Total		£90,765.00

2. The value of this claim exceeds £15,000.

3. The Claimants further claim interest on the sum of £90,765.00 (etc. ...) pursuant to section 35A, Supreme Court Act 1981.

AND the Claimants claim:

1. £90,765.00 alternatively damages.

2. Interest as aforesaid.

Statement of Truth (etc.)

Served this 6th day of March 2006 by Rottweiler and Dogg, Solicitors for the Claimant, whose address for service is Kerr House, Kennel Lane, Barking.

This is the type of short claim which is frequently employed when costs are to be kept to a minimum, everything seems straightforward, and where no substantive defence is anticipated. Whatever excuse **is** raised, the real reason for non-payment is probably lack of funds.

This form of statement of case is normally successful in 9 cases out of 10. Either the money is paid, there is some form of compromise, or a judgment is obtained which may or may not be worthless. However, on that 10th occasion, one is likely to be on the receiving end of a Defence which, of necessity, has to be in narrative form:

IN THE HIGH COURT OF JUSTICE   2006 S No. 0000
QUEEN'S BENCH DIVISION

BETWEEN:

SELLAROLL LIMITED
<u>Claimants</u>

— and —

PASSION GARMENTS LIMITED
<u>Defendants</u>

DEFENCE

---

1. The Defendants are and were at all relevant times, a limited company carrying on business as manufacturers of fashion clothing. The Claimants are and were at all relevant times a limited company carrying on business as wholesale suppliers of fashion materials.

2. In the course of a series of agreements between the Claimants and the Defendants, commencing in about January 2005, the Defendants ordered quantities of cloth from the Claimants to be drawn from their stocks as and when required.

3. Prior to the first of the said agreements, in about January 2005, it was orally agreed between Mr Bolt of the Claimants, and Mr Love of the Defendants, that the Defendants would be entitled to be released from any obligation to purchase cloth ordered, provided that notice of the same was given within 10 days of the Claimants' invoice in respect of such order.

4. By various written notices, in each case given within 10 days of the respective invoices set out in the Particulars of Claim, the Defendants duly informed the Claimants of their intention to be released from the said orders, and the Defendants are consequently not liable thereon.

5. In the circumstances it is denied that the Claimants are entitled to the relief claimed or any relief for the reasons alleged or at all.

PADDY REVSKI

Statement of Truth (etc.)

As it happens, your case is that the agreements were made in writing, and were expressed to be on the Claimants' standard terms and conditions of business, which expressly prohibit the cancellation of orders once made, save on the grounds of imperfections etc. in the goods. Trading went perfectly normally with the Defendants for nearly 18 months, whereafter purported 'notices of cancellation' were received in respect of the last few orders. There was never any agreement with the Defendants along the lines suggested.

Now it may be argued that this should have been set out in the first instance, as the CPR require that a party relying on the terms of a written agreement should set it out and attach a copy to the claim. However, I am doubtful as to whether the rule was intended to prohibit a Claimant from using the 'short-form' type of claim that has been so successful in the past. In this case, I consider that the Claimants did enough originally — they relied on the invoices, which were attached, and did not 'jump the stile' by anticipating the Defence. However, from a tactical point of view, we may be faced with some disadvantage.

I do not propose here to set out the Reply in the above case. Essentially it will have to be along the lines of a 'Defence to the Defence', and will thus lose some of the tactical advantages of having been expressed in the Particulars of Claim. Although the situation is far from being disastrous, we are now being forced to set out the entirety of our claim, but at the behest of, and in the format of, the Defence. This is not a 'Good Thing'. Furthermore, our Reply must necessarily consist of the exposition of our case — and for the first time. We thus lose some, if not all, of the tactical advantages of the use of the Reply, had we properly set out our case in the first place. These advantages will, I hope, be evident in the full example later in this chapter.

Another way of examining when and how to use a Reply, is to look at things from the other way around, and state what one should **not** do:

(a) As said before, it should not be used merely to reiterate matters which have been set out in the claim, although there are certain instances in which this can 'formally' be done, as will be explained in a moment.

(b) Also, the Reply must not be used in order to raise new issues which should have been set out in the claim in the first place. The proper process in such an event is to amend the claim (if this is still permissible). The rationale for this is that to insert new matters would not assist clarification or definition of the issues, and would have to give the Defendant a right in turn to meet these new matters. This would inevitably lead to a proliferation of documentation which would not read logically and which would add considerably to the expense of the trial.

The Reply is also different from previous statements of case, in that it is not an 'entire' document. In other words, although it refers to specific paragraphs in the Defence, it is not required to be, nor should it be, a comprehensive statement or restatement of your case. Thus, read on its own, it may not mean very much to anyone, but as part of the body of statements of case, it should be very significant.

From a tactical point of view, the Reply can be most effective. If the Defence is weak, or poorly drafted, the format of the Reply can give you an excellent opportunity to consolidate your position, demonstrate the weaknesses of your opponent's case, and gain you the psychological ascendancy. However, the inherent format of the Reply can, if not approached from the correct standpoint, lead to the opposite effect, by making you appear on the defensive. One example of this has already been illustrated above, when the claim has not been fully set out in the first place.

Therefore, in order to gain most effective use of the Reply, we have to adopt the tactically 'correct' style, which itself is only possible if we are quite certain what it is we are doing, and trying to achieve. It always boils down to the same thing in the end!

Because the Reply is not an 'entire' document, we traditionally use a layout which relates to the particular paragraph of the Defence to which we are replying. It is often unnecessary to depart from this at all during the course of the Reply, although as in all drafting, inflexible rules lead to inflexible minds, and thus to a stultification of creative and effective objects.[1]

The Reply traditionally contained a form of the good old general traverse. This is probably because, although a joinder of issue with a Defence is considered 'as read' in the absence of a Reply, this was, under the old rules, technically not the case once a Reply was filed. In other words, if you did file a Reply, no one thereafter technically assumed anything! This is now no longer the case — the CPR specifically provide that a Reply that fails to deal with a matter raised in the Defence,

---

[1] A translation of the above sentence will be provided on request.

shall nevertheless be taken to require that matter to be proved. However, I have no doubt that, out of an abundance of caution, the profession will continue to use the general traverse, and there seems to be no disadvantage in so doing. Old habits die hard! Thus, to make the situation clear, we normally insert the following words at some stage in the text:

> Save in so far as the same consists of admissions, the Claimant joins issue with the Defendant upon the Defence (and Counterclaim).

Translated into basic English, this means that we do not agree with any part of the Defence unless and in so far as it has conceded any part of the claim.

Opinions vary as to where the above paragraph should appear. Some people prefer to insert it at the end of the Reply as a final 'catch-all'. I prefer to make it the first paragraph. This is because I consider that the joining of issue with the Defence is of primary importance, and a statement at the beginning reminds everyone that the remainder of the Reply is incidental to this joinder. I also feel that it has an advantageous psychological effect — 'I dispute the entire Defence, and additionally I wish to add this ...'. To place the general traverse at the end is also to make the Reply more akin to a Defence, and for reasons which I am just about to explain, I consider that to be bad tactics.

It will be inevitable that much of the Reply will be taken up with disputing matters raised in the Defence. Often there will be no alternative to a simple denial of matters which have been alleged therein. However, as a general rule, I would suggest that you never use the word 'deny' if there is any possibility of the matter being expressed in a more positive form. This is because the 'denying' of matters raised in the Defence makes the Reply more of a 'Defence to the Defence', which by implication dignifies the Defence with a degree of authority and importance which is tactically counter-productive.

Often this can be easily avoided by making averments to the contrary of those set out in the Defence. For example, where there is a dispute as to the time and place of coming to an agreement, the claim may state:

> 2. By an oral agreement made on 4th July 2005, the Defendant, in the course of his said business ...

The Defence may contend:

> 2. Paragraph 2 is denied. The said agreement was contained in a written letter of agreement signed by the Claimant and the Defendant and dated 8th July 2005.

Now your instructions are that the written letter was no more than a confirmation of the agreement, and was written at the request of the Defendant, some 3 days later. Thus, your reply could read:

> 2. As to paragraph 2 thereof, it is denied that the said agreement was made in writing and/or was dated 8th July 2005. The said letter was written at the request of the Defendant, and contained a written confirmation of the oral agreement set out in paragraph 2 of the Particulars of Claim, together with evidence of the terms thereof.

Alternatively, you could state:

> 2. As to paragraph 2 thereof, the Claimant repeats paragraph 2 of the Particulars of Claim. The letter dated 8th July 2005 was written at the request of the Defendant, to confirm the said oral agreement and evidence the terms thereof.

I very much prefer the latter version. For a start, it rejects the defensive attitude of the first draft. Secondly, its main thrust is not directed at a refutation of the Defence, but comprises a re-affirmation of the Particulars of Claim. The formal repetition of the relevant paragraph of the Particulars of Claim implies, 'I'm not resiling one inch from what I have previously said.' The use of the words 'confirm the said oral agreement and evidence the terms thereof' also carry a quiet insistence that the whole starting point of the legal relationship was as set out in the original claim. The Defence is implied to be an attempt to deviate from the true facts of the case. It's not an overwhelming point, but in my view it's a wholly more satisfactory way of dealing with the matter.

However, as I have said, sometimes there is no alternative but to issue a straight denial. You will see this in the main example below. If this has to be done, remember, never let the Reply appear more defensive than absolutely necessary. If a denial is necessary, see if you can qualify the point with some assertion backing up the matters in the claim.

You may have noticed that I commenced the paragraph 'As to paragraph 2 thereof...'. This is a conventional (but by no means the only) way of referencing the Reply to the Defence. The advantage of this form of words is that concise and direct reference is made to the paragraph under fire. The disadvantage can be that the layout may be boring if repeated many times. On the other hand, the Reply should not be a long document. I advocate the use of the conventional words if possible, in order to distinguish the Reply from other statements of case, and to prevent it from adopting the format of the Defence and thus giving the wrong impression. However, as always, it is a matter of taste and style. Suit yourself!

In order to demonstrate the drafting of a Reply, I am going to use an example which will set out both Particulars of Claim and a Defence. I have not used any of the examples in the earlier chapters, as I have deliberately made the next set of facts rather more complex. This has been done, first, to demonstrate statements of case containing a little more substance than hitherto, secondly, to provoke a suitable opportunity for us to examine when and when not to include various matters in a Reply, and lastly to enable the same example to be used in our examination of the Request for Further Information, and the information itself, in later chapters. So, in getting to grips with the following example, take the opportunity as you do so, to review the principles of drafting the claim and Defence. The example concerns a dispute over the nature and quality of engineering services rendered.

EXAMPLE

The claim has been drafted on the basis of our instructions which are as follows:

> The Defendants were installing mechanical services (essentially air-conditioning and central heating systems) at the World of Wonder Leisure Centre, Neasden, Kent. Once these were *in situ*, they required commissioning; essentially switching on, balancing, and ensuring that they worked to the maximum possible efficiency. This is a highly specialised and technical task, which requires many days'

work to complete. By an oral agreement on 3rd September 2004, between Alan Tapp of the Claimants and Richard Thunder of the Defendants, the Claimants (who are commissioning specialists) agreed to commission these particular installations. They originally quoted just over £102,000, which would have involved them in giving advice all the way along the line, supervising the installations and performing certain pre-commissioning works. However, the Defendants considered that to be too expensive, and asked for a further quotation based on all preliminary works of advice, installation and pre-commissioning being done by themselves. Thus our clients quoted £78,450 on that basis.

As the works had not been completed, it was agreed that the Defendants would contact the Claimants nearer the time, to arrange a suitable starting date. It was envisaged that the total time required for the commissioning of the installation (provided it had been competently installed) would be 8 weeks.

On 17th May 2005 the Defendants informed the Claimants that the commissioning works could start on 4th July. The works were to be completed by 1st September so that final preparations could then be made for the Defendants to hand the building over. By their letter of 18th May, the Claimants wrote:

'We confirm that we will be attending at the site to commence the agreed commissioning works on 4th July, and that we envisage completion by 1st September as discussed. Please ensure that all systems are fully installed, flushed, checked and pre-commissioned prior to that date, or else we will be unable to commence the works. To assist you, we will send you a copy of our standard pre-commissioning checklist in due course.'

On 19th May 2005 the Defendants replied:

'Thank you for your letter of 18th May. We look forward to receiving your checklist as soon as possible, and preferably about two weeks prior to the commencement of your works.'

To this effect, on 22nd June, the Claimants supplied the Defendants with a copy of their standard 'air and water installation completion check sheet' in order to assist them in ensuring that the installations would be ready for commissioning. This form would normally have been used by the Claimants themselves had they been carrying out the full £102,000 contract, but was supplied merely to assist the Defendants.

However, the day before the works were due to commence, the Claimants received a telephone call from the Defendants informing them that matters had been delayed, and that they would not be able to start until 26th July. When the Claimants did attend on 26th July, they found that some of the power supplies were not available to switch on the installations, and that the installations had not been properly prepared for commissioning, and that the heating system had not been filled, flushed or cleaned. The commissioning was therefore put off until 2nd August.

A whole chapter of disasters occurred once the Claimants started commissioning. They discovered that the systems had not been properly cleansed, parts of the machinery had not been properly installed, and that as a result there were delays both in getting the machinery started, and then in testing and retesting once the various defects had been discovered and eliminated. The various defects were noted in engineers' site reports, which have been supplied to the Defendants. As a result of the above, the job took a total of 17 weeks to complete, and the Claimants have calculated that they have incurred additional expenses in time, material and labour, amounting to £33,996.78. The Defendants have refused to pay any sum greater than the £78,450 originally agreed. The Claimants wish to commence proceedings to recover their loss.

The Particulars of Claim reads as follows:

THE HIGH COURT OF JUSTICE   2006 T No. 0000
QUEEN'S BENCH DIVISION

BETWEEN:

TURNONN LIMITED
                                                              Claimants
— and —

THUNDER ENGINEERING LIMITED
                                                              Defendants

---

PARTICULARS OF CLAIM

---

1. The Claimants are and were at all relevant times a limited
company carrying on business as experts in the commissioning of
mechanical services installations. The Defendants are and were at all
relevant times a limited company carrying on business as engineers and
as installers of such mechanical services.

2. By an oral agreement made on 3rd September 2004, the Claimants,
in the course of their said business, agreed with the Defendants that
they would commission the mechanical services installations at the
World of Wonder Leisure Centre ('The Centre'), Neasden, Kent, for the
sum of £78,450. At all relevant times the Defendant company were
sub-contractors at the said site, responsible, amongst other matters, for
the installation of the said mechanical services. The agreement took
place in a telephone conversation between Alan Tapp of the Claimants
and Richard Thunder of the Defendants, in which the terms set out
above were agreed.

3. There were, amongst others, the following express or implied
terms of the said agreement:
    (a) That the said commissioning works would be carried out on a
date to be agreed between the parties;
    (b) That the systems to be commissioned would be fully and
competently installed by the Defendants prior to the Claimants commencing the said commissioning works;

(c)   That the Defendants would ensure that all water systems were totally free from all foreign matter prior to the start of commissioning works;

(d)   That the Defendants would conduct all necessary pre-commissioning checks on all systems to ensure their readiness for commissioning.

4.   Further, it was an implied term of the said agreement that the price quoted by the Claimants would only hold good in so far as the said commissioning works could be carried out by them within a reasonable time and without unreasonable delay or additional works caused to them as a result of any failure by the Defendants properly to complete the said installation or to ensure the readiness of the same for commissioning on the agreed date. The Claimants will aver that a reasonable time was, and/or was agreed to be, just over 8 weeks from commencement of the said commissioning.

5.   Pursuant to the said agreement, on or about 17th May 2005 the Defendants informed the Claimants that they could commence the said commissioning works on 4th July 2005, and by their letter dated 18th May 2005 the Claimants duly agreed to do so and to complete the same by 1st September 2005.

6.   In order to assist the Defendants to conduct the necessary pre-commissioning checks, on or about 22nd June 2005 the Claimants provided the Defendants with their standard 'air and water installation completion check sheets' and requested that the appropriate checks should be made prior to commissioning works being undertaken on any system.

7.   In breach of the said agreement, the Defendants, their employees or agents:

(a)   Caused the Claimants to suffer excessive and unreasonable delay in commencing, and thereafter carrying out the said works of commissioning;

(b)   Failed on repeated occasions to ensure that the said systems were completely installed in time for the said works of commissioning to be carried out;

(c)   Failed adequately or at all on numerous occasions properly to conduct the necessary pre-commissioning checks as set out in the Claimants' said check sheet, or at all;

(d)   Failed on repeated occasions to ensure that the said systems were in a proper state for works of commissioning to be carried out.

PARTICULARS

(1)   On or about 2nd July 2005 the Defendants informed the Claimants by telephone that the said systems were not ready, and that the commissioning works could not start until 26th July 2005.

(2)   On 26th July 2005 the Claimants duly attended at the said site to perform the said works and found:

   (a)   power was not available;

   (b)   the said equipment had not been prepared for commissioning;

   (c)   the heating system had not been filled, flushed or cleaned; whereafter the said commencement date was again put off until 2nd August 2005.

(3)   The various defects in the said works of installation and preparation, and the resultant delays caused to the Claimants are set out in the Claimants' various site reports dated between 2nd August and 27th October 2005, copies whereof were supplied to the Defendants on site.

8.   By reason of the matters hereinbefore set out, the Claimant company was caused additional work, delay and expense:

PARTICULARS

(1)   The Claimants had agreed to perform the said works between 4th July 2005 and 1st September 2005, a period of just over 8 weeks. By reason of the Defendants' said breaches of contract, the said works took 17 weeks to carry out;

(2)   The failure of the Defendants adequately or at all to ensure that the said systems were totally free of all foreign matter prior to commissioning, meant that the Claimants became involved in repeated testing of the systems as a result of problems associated with blockages thereof, causing additional work, expense and delay;

(3)   A schedule of hours lost and losses incurred by the Claimants has been supplied to the Defendants, and amounts to £33,996.78.

9.   The Defendants have paid the Claimants the sum of £78,450.00 but have failed and/or refused to pay the additional loss and damage

incurred or any part thereof, and there is presently due and owing to the Claimants the sum of £33,996.78.

10.   The Claimants further claim interest (etc.) pursuant to section 35A of the Supreme Court Act 1981.

11.   The value of this claim exceeds £15,000.

AND the Claimants claim:

1.   Damages;

2.   Interest as aforesaid.

ANNA KLEINE-NACHTMUSIK

Statement of Truth (etc.)

Some weeks after the despatch of this *tour de force*, we are served with a Defence as follows:

IN THE HIGH COURT OF JUSTICE   2006 T No. 0000
QUEEN'S BENCH DIVISION

BETWEEN:

TURNONN LIMITED

Claimants

— and —

THUNDER ENGINEERING LIMITED

Defendants

DEFENCE

1.   Paragraph 1 of the Particulars of Claim is admitted.

2.   By a contract contained in or evidenced by a letter from the Defendants to the Claimants dated 22nd September 2004, a copy of

which is attached to this Defence, the Claimants agreed to commission the said mechanical services installations for the sum of £78,450. The said agreement was expressed to be subject to the Defendants' standard terms and conditions. Save as aforesaid, paragraph 2 of the Particulars of Claim is admitted.

3.   Save that no admissions are made as to sub-paragraph (a) thereof, paragraph 3 is denied. The Defendants aver that it was an implied term of the said agreement that the Claimants would commence the said commissioning works when mechanical services capable of commissioning had been installed.

4.   Paragraph 4 is denied.

5.   Save that it is admitted that on 17th May 2005 the Defendants informed the Claimants that they could commence the said works on 4th July 2005, and that in the course of their letter dated 18th May 2005 the Claimants agreed to do so, paragraph 5 is denied. The Defendants aver that the Claimants, by their letter dated 18th May 2005 purported to vary the said agreement between the parties by imposing a condition precedent to commencing the said commissioning works, which said condition was not accepted by the Defendant. A copy of this letter is attached hereto.

6.   Paragraph 6 is denied. It is admitted that by a letter dated 22nd June 2005 the Claimants forwarded to the Defendants their standard 'Air and Water Installation Completion Check Sheets', but it is denied that the same had any contractual effect, or that the Defendants were contractually obliged to complete the same.

7.   It is denied that the Defendants committed the breaches alleged in paragraph 7 or any breaches.

8.   No admissions are made as to the matters alleged in paragraph 8, save that if, which is not admitted, the Claimants suffered the said or any additional work, delay and expense, the same was in no way due to any breach of contract and/or default of the Defendants, as alleged or at all.

9.   Save that it is admitted that the Defendants paid the Claimants the sum of £78,450, paragraph 9 is denied. It is further denied that the

Claimants are entitled to the relief claimed in paragraphs 9 and/or 10, or any relief, for the reasons alleged or at all.

DOLLY INCAPAX

Statement of Truth (etc.)

The principal issues between the parties thus appear to be:

1.   The Claimants say that the contract was oral. The Defendants aver that it was contained or evidenced in a letter, and was expressed to be subject to the Defendants' standard terms and conditions. The Defendants have properly attached the relevant letters to the Defence.

2.   There is a fundamental disagreement as to the respective works to be performed by the parties. The Claimants' case is that they were merely to commission the installations once they had been properly installed, cleaned and pre-commissioned by the Defendants. The Defendants clearly do not accept that they were to have installed and checked the installations to a certain minimum standard prior to the Claimants commencing their works.

3.   Although the Defendants have been somewhat coy as to the various delays and defects alleged by the Claimants, they do not accept any responsibility for any increase in the contract time or the amount of additional works alleged to have been occasioned.

Of course, at this point we must take additional instructions from our clients in relation to the matters raised in the Defence. Having done so, we discover as follows:

> The agreement in September 2004 was prefaced by con-
> siderable negotiations, including the Claimants' original
> quotation of over £102,000 for performing the full com-
> missioning procedure. However, on 3rd September 2004
> an oral agreement had been concluded between Mr Tapp
> of the Claimants and Mr Thunder of the Defendants. It
> is true that the Defendants sent a letter dated 22nd
> September 2004, which letter simply read:

'We are pleased to confirm our agreement that you will commence commissioning works at a date to be agreed, for £78,450 inclusive of VAT. We will send you the standard site sub-contract in due course.'

Nothing was said or ever discussed about the Defendants' standard terms and conditions, and in fact the sub-contract was never sent, nor ever mentioned again.

Mr Tapp is quite certain that it was specifically agreed with Mr Thunder that the Claimants were to carry out only the final commissioning process, in view of the greatly reduced price, and that the Defendants would ensure that the systems were properly installed and pre-commissioned. The amount of time needed to perform this commissioning was specifically discussed between the parties, in the context of the price that the Claimants were to charge.

The letter of 18th May 2005 did not impose any new pre-conditions but was merely a reminder of what had already been agreed.

As a result, the Claimants consider that the various delays and unsatisfactory workmanship constituted a breach of contract, and that the Defendants are liable for the consequences.

Now, the length and complexity of the above problem should provide us with a useful exercise in fact management, particularly when it comes to deciding what, if anything, should be included in the Reply. I have deliberately left several areas of ambiguity in the statements of case (at least that's my excuse!) which may be considered when we come to any Request for Further Information. Let us therefore take stock of our position:

The Defence does raise certain issues with which it would be appropriate to deal by way of Reply. (Well, you guessed that, didn't you, otherwise the whole example's been a waste of time!) The principal points which we will have to cover will be those areas of dispute set out above, particularly where issues have been raised by the Defence which are not fully set out in the Particulars of Claim.

We should deal with these matters in a way which will put our client's case to the maximum advantage, and, if possible, put the Defence to the maximum discomfort. This latter may not be possible through the sole medium of the Reply, but may be achieved through judicious use of an associated Request for Further Information.

Let us now examine the Defence paragraph by paragraph in order to ascertain whether, and if so how, we should deal with it in the Reply, always remembering that we should not fall into the trap of restating the claim, nor should we adopt too detailed and defensive an approach. Our aim should be to define and clarify the issues (preferably to our best advantage), and we will do this more by way of a 'gloss' on the relevant paragraphs of the Defence, than by way of a point by point refutation.

For the reasons advanced earlier, I propose to commence with the general joinder of issue thus:

> 1. Save in so far as the same consists of admissions, the Claimants join issue with the Defendants upon their Defence.

No surprises there! The above wording is not sacrosanct — there are some individuals even more pedantic than myself who prefer to put:

> Save in so far as the same consists of admissions, or save as hereinafter appears, the Claimants join issue with the Defendants upon their Defence.

Nothing wrong with that if you've plenty of ink in your pen, and no shortage of time and paper. Technically it is more correct, in that it covers the situation where you may wish to make admissions in the Reply in order to abbreviate the issues before the Court, thus saving time and expense. However, if you do not propose to make any admissions or concessions in your Reply, the additional wording does not seem to me to be necessary. I propose to leave it out in the present case.

Paragraph 2

The principal differences between this paragraph of the Defence and paragraph 2 of the claim, are:

(a) The Defendants claim that the contract was contained or evidenced in writing, whilst the Claimants say it was oral.

(b) The Defendants state that the contract was expressed to be subject to their standard terms and conditions, whereas the Claimants' case is that not only was the contract **not** subject to such conditions, but the letter from the Defendants (even if containing or forming the basis of the contract) did not make any reference to them.

As to the first difference, what could we put in the Reply?

> 2. As to paragraph 2 thereof, the Claimants repeat paragraph 2 of the Particulars of Claim and aver that the said agreement was made orally.

The above is a fine example of the way **not** to formulate a Reply. It is response for the sake of response. It adds nothing new to what has already been said. Issue has already been joined, and the above paragraph is mere repetition. So, nothing needs to or should be done here.

However, the second difference is very important. A very substantial line of defence has been raised. After all, it matters not whether the contract was made orally or in writing, if there is no serious dispute as to the substance of the main terms. However, were the contract to have been made on (so far undisclosed) standard terms and conditions, the whole character of the legal relationship between the parties may have been changed. Further, you can bet your sweet life that the Defendants' standard terms and conditions would not have been drafted with the Claimants' comfort and well-being as the principal objective!

By the sheerest coincidence the above illustration epitomises an example of the way in which the Reply can be used to impugn the credibility of the Defence. Let us remind ourselves of the pertinent words actually contained in the Defendants' letter of 22nd September 2004:

> 'We are pleased to confirm our agreement ... We will send you the standard site sub-contract in due course.'

On the basis of that letter, the Defendants are alleging that the contract was subject to their Standard Terms and Conditions. Now of course, it may be that the evidence will show that it was **orally** agreed that the contract was to be in the form of the standard site sub-contract, and that that contract contained standard terms and conditions etc. However, that is **not** what is set out in the Defence, which alleges:

(a)   that the contract was contained in or evidenced by the above letter; and

(b)   that the agreement was **expressed** to be subject to the standard terms and conditions.

So, the devilish ingenuity of our example gives us an opportunity not merely to deal with our denial that the standard terms and conditions were incorporated into the contract, but also ever so gently to point out that the particulars provided by the Defendants in support, do not bear out their point.

'... ever so gently to point out ...'

So we commence:

 2.   As to paragraph 2 thereof ...

and then must decide whether to adopt the rather predictable and defensive:

... the Claimants deny that the said agreement was subject to the Defendants' standard terms and conditions ...

or to put it the other way around:

> ... the Claimants aver that the said agreement was not sub-
> ject to the Defendants' standard terms and conditions ...

Were that to be the only matter dealt with in this paragraph, it may well be that neither form has any significant advantage or disadvantage over the other.

However, we are not finished yet! Notice how carefully I have so far avoided the use of the words 'expressed to be' in either of the above alternatives. Although the Defence alleges that the agreement was 'expressed to be' subject to the terms etc., the Reply starts off by making it quite clear (by implication) that the agreement was **not** subject to those terms, whatever may have been set out in the letter. To back that up, we will now rub salt in the wound by pointing out that the letter itself doesn't say that which is alleged by the Defendants. If we now take the above alternatives, I would suggest that a winner begins to emerge:

> 2.   As to paragraph 2 thereof, the Claimants deny that the
> said agreement was subject to the Defendants' standard terms
> and conditions, or that the same was expressed to be the case
> in the Defendants' said letter dated 22nd September 2004.

> Or

> 2.   As to paragraph 2 thereof, the Claimants aver that the
> said agreement was not subject to the Defendants' standard
> terms and conditions, nor was it expressed to be so in the
> Defendants' said letter dated 22nd September 2004.

The second version is to me a far more confident and assertive statement of our case than the first. It flows better and has a consistency of purpose, making the first appear rather pedestrian and self-effacing.

Paragraph 3
Once again, the necessity for and contents of the Reply should become clear once we have analysed the respective differences between the Particulars of Claim and the Defence:

(a)   The claim is that the works would be carried out on a date to be agreed. Prior to such date, the systems were to have been fully installed and cleaned by the Defendants.

(b) The Defence does not admit anything to do with a commencement date to be agreed, but contends only that the works were to be commenced once systems capable of being commissioned had been installed.

These areas of contention are of great importance, in that our case is, of course, that the reduced price was due to the fact that the Defendants were to take responsibility for the installation, cleansing and pre-commissioning of the systems prior to our becoming involved. We should notice that the Defendants have been a little coy about their position, in that it would not have hurt them to have admitted that the works were to start on a date to be agreed, and they are perhaps being rather less than forthright about the conditions that were to prevail prior to the Claimants commencing commissioning.

Your ingenious author has devised this particular paragraph to illustrate when it may be necessary to take a decision between dealing with matters raised, by use of the Reply, or by making a Request for Further Information. Occasionally the line between the two becomes a little blurred, if all that we are trying to achieve is to score one or two points off the other side. This, of course, is **not** the object of the exercise — officially. Nevertheless, bearing in mind that we must **not** abuse the rules, if we can legitimately score the odd point in the course of properly putting our case, we'd be stupid not to!

Looking at the paragraph in question, however, it must be apparent that the nature of the dispute is clearly set out.We say that there were terms as we have alleged, and the Defendants say that there were not. In the context of setting out our case, it seems to me that we have little or nothing to add, and that therefore we should avoid falling into the trap of trying to argue the case at this stage.Were we to do so, we would have to resort to repetition, or putting in evidence, which is yet another indication that we should hold our peace for the time being. The vagaries of the Defendants' case can be exploited in a Request for Further Information, which should be sufficient to force their hand.

Paragraph 4
This illustrates a simple point — where the Defence consists of a simple admission or denial, there will almost inevitably be no necessity for a Reply. Where the Defence merely makes no admissions, there are circumstances where a Reply can amplify matters, but these are very rare, and you should avoid Replying in such circumstances unless you are absolutely convinced that your case would suffer by not so doing.

Paragraph 5
This paragraph clearly raises serious and substantial issues. However, what would you do? Using the principles set out above, decide first if you need to deal with the matter in the Reply and then, if so, how you would do so to maximum advantage. Having done that, compare your masterpiece with the following humble effort.

The dispute can be summarised thus:

> Our case is that on 17th May 2005 we were given the go-ahead by the Defendants to commence works on 4th July. We agreed to complete them by 1st September, and in accordance with the basis upon which we had agreed to perform the works, reminded the Defendants that they were responsible for installing and checking the systems prior to our going onto site.
> The Defendants' version is that they do not accept that they had agreed to install and check the systems to the extent and standard claimed by the Claimants, so that the requirements in the letter of 18th May amounted to unlawful preconditions and/or a variation of the contract terms. To remind ourselves of the letter, it read:
>
>> 'Please ensure that all systems are fully installed, flushed, checked and pre-commissioned prior to that date, or else we will be unable to commence the works. To assist you, we will send you a copy of our standard pre-commissioning checklist in due course.'

An interesting and important matter which should be raised at some point is that the Defendants did not appear to consider the Claimants' letter to be in any way untoward at the time that it was written. Their response dated 19th May 2005 expressed no surprise at the preconditions about which they are now complaining. This last letter was not attached to the Particulars of Claim, as it did not appear (then) to be relevant to the issues.

It is also noteworthy that the Defence states that the condition was not accepted by the Defendants. This is not evident in their letter of 19th May, although of course silence would not signify consent if there **had** been a unilateral attempt at variation by the Claimants. However, this failure to take objection at the time certainly qualifies for inclusion in the Reply, as the Defence has, for the first time, raised an issue as to alleged variation of contractual terms, or unlawful preconditions. This allegation is deserving of an answer, and once again we have the potential to deal the Defendants a sideswipe on the way.

Our paragraph must thus contain our refutation of the allegations made in paragraph 5 of the Defence. We can also reinforce our case by pointing out that the Defendants did not make these allegations at the time when they had an opportunity to do so. It is even possible to express the paragraph in exactly these terms:

> 3. As to paragraph 5 thereof, the Claimants deny that their letter dated 18th May 2005 purported to vary the said agreement as alleged or at all. Further, in their letter of reply dated 19th May 2005, the Defendants did not make the said or any allegations of variation.

Personally, I consider that last paragraph to be perfectly horrible. The style is that of a Defence, it is badly worded, and it does not take advantage of the golden opportunity presented to administer a dose of the Wellington Boot. What we need is a positive statement of the Claimants' position, supported by the Defendants' failure to take objection at the time. I suggest:

> 3. As to paragraph 5 thereof, the Claimants repeat paragraph 3 of the Particulars of Claim, and aver that their letter of 18th May 2005 was written in pursuance of the terms of the said agreement, and did not amount to a variation of the same. The Claimants will further rely on a letter in reply from the Defendants dated 19th May 2005, which took no objection to the terms of their said letter, and which requested the Claimants to forward their checklist referred to in paragraph 6 of the Particulars of Claim.

The above draft seems to me to have the advantage of being a positive and logical retort to the Defence. It starts by uncompromisingly standing by the Claimants' version of the contract as previously set out in the Particulars of Claim. Note that I have not repeated the paragraph in dispute, but have, without repetition of the content, reaffirmed the paragraph which is the basis of the Claimants' case.

Thereafter, note the use of the word 'aver', which is preceded by a conjunction. In order not to fall into the trap of defensive drafting, I have followed on from the reaffirmation of the contract with a confident assertion that the letter of 18th May was written in consequence of what we understood to be its terms. The subsequent words 'and did not amount to a variation of the same' are almost otiose, but are used as a final 'put down' to the Defence as pleaded.

The next few lines are little short of arrogant, in that the Claimants place sufficient confidence in their case, such as to be content to rely on the **Defendants'** documents to support their version of events.

Although there may be several alternative ways of expressing the above, the differences between the illustrated versions should be sufficient to demonstrate the manner in which the Reply can be tuned to convey the required emphasis.

Paragraph 6

This paragraph follows on naturally from that preceding. There is no dispute between the parties that the checklists were provided, but the Defendants claim that they had no contractual obligation to fill them out. As it happens, that is correct. In fact, such a contractual obligation was never alleged. The Defendants have, by virtue of their general denial of the paragraph, also denied that the pre-commissioning checks were 'necessary' as alleged. This is obviously consistent with their case.

In my opinion, this paragraph does not demand a Reply, in that the issues between the parties are quite clear. Certainly, I would not draft a Reply to the Defence were this to be the only paragraph in which a Reply was to be considered. However, the Reply is to be drafted in any event, and this paragraph has been included to illustrate the way in which we can use the medium to weaken the authority of the Defence, by exposing weaknesses in its drafting. However, I do not recommend that this is done except as a by-product of a more substantial Reply, as it will do one's case no good merely to be seen as a 'smart aleck'.

Thus, the object of the paragraph will be to tie in the sending of the checklists with the Defendants' obligation to perform the pre-commissioning checks, and to make it quite clear that it has never been asserted that the completion of the form was a contractual requirement.

This last objective has to be done carefully, in that we must not appear too condescending — (just a little!):

> 4. As to paragraph 6 thereof, the Claimants aver that they forwarded the said check sheets to the Defendants in order to assist them in performing their said contractual obligations to pre-commission the said installations. At no time have the Claimants alleged that the said check sheets were of any contractual effect, or that the Defendants were contractually obliged to complete the same.

This paragraph does not actually repeat paragraph 6 of the Particulars of Claim, whatever the initial impressions. The original paragraph refers to 'the necessary pre-commissioning checks', and although this can be referred back to the contractual obligations expressed in paragraph 3, the Reply leaves the Defendants in no doubt that it is alleged that they had certain contractual obligations, and that the Claimants were doing their best to help. The remainder of the paragraph effectively crushes the *faux pas* in the Defence. Notice that I have refrained from using the word 'admits' or 'agrees' with reference to what is effectively our agreement with the Defendants' construction of the legal status of the check sheets. After all, we do not want to seem too accommodating! The paragraph does not actually make any direct reference to the offending passage in paragraph 6 of the Defence, and the rebuff is made to follow on as a logical consequence from the first sentence of the paragraph.

The remainder of the Defence consists of formal denials which clearly do not require any further reply. Our final document therefore reads as follows:

IN THE HIGH COURT OF JUSTICE   2006 T No. 0000
QUEEN'S BENCH DIVISION

BETWEEN:

TURNONN LIMITED

Claimants

— and —

THUNDER ENGINEERING LIMITED

Defendants

REPLY

---

1. Save in so far as the same consists of admissions, the Claimants join issue with the Defendants upon their Defence.

2. As to paragraph 2 thereof, the Claimants aver that the said agreement was not subject to the Defendants' standard terms and conditions, nor was it expressed to be so in the Defendants' said letter dated 22nd September 2004.

3. As to paragraph 5 thereof, the Claimants repeat paragraph 3 of the Particulars of Claim, and aver that their letter of 18th May 2005 was written in pursuance of the terms of the said agreement, and did not amount to a variation of the same. The Claimants will further rely on a letter in reply from the Defendants dated 19th May 2005, which took no objection to the terms of their said letter, and which requested the Claimants to forward their checklist referred to in paragraph 6 of the Particulars of Claim.

4. As to paragraph 6 thereof, the Claimants aver that they forwarded the said check sheets to the Defendants in order to assist them in performing their said contractual obligations to pre-commission the said installations. At no time have the Claimants alleged that the said check sheets were of any contractual effect, or that the Defendants were contractually obliged to complete the same.

ANNA KLEINE-NACHTMUSIK

Statement of Truth (etc.)

A final word. The example above does not, of course, illustrate a Defence to Counterclaim. I do not consider this to be necessary, as the form is precisely the same as the Defence. The tactical and stylistic approaches to be considered are also identical. At the conclusion of the Reply, simply commence the new heading, 'DEFENCE TO COUNTERCLAIM', continue with the paragraph numbering, and recommence as if you were drafting a Defence from the beginning. The only difference is that if the Defence to Counterclaim relies on matters pleaded in the Claim or Reply, you can formally 'repeat' those in the Defence to Counterclaim, rather than map the whole thing out again. I don't feel it necessary to give an example of this — I hope you have got the idea by now.

The aim of this chapter has been to give you some insight into the mysteries of the Reply. Remember always, that it is far better to think twice, and then decide **not** to use the Reply, rather than to pitch in as a matter of course. The Reply has a specific purpose, and can achieve a significant enhancement of your case — if used correctly! If it is not, it weakens your authority, if not your case.

Chapter Five

Don't Answer Back
(Rejoinder, etc.)

'Hold your tongue!' said the Queen,
turning purple.
'I won't!', said Alice.
'Off with her head!' the Queen shouted
at the top of her voice.

Technically, there exist further statements of case after the Reply. They used to be, in order, the:

Rejoinder,
Surrejoinder,
Rebutter, and
Surrebutter.

I have never had to use any of them, and hope never to have to do so. Come to that, I've never even **seen** an example of any of them, although I dare say there's an odd precedent or two in the leading works.

You have to apply for permission to file any of them. In almost every circumstance the difficulties (real or imagined) could probably best be dealt with by amendment of an earlier statement of case, or will have already been covered in the Reply, or in the Defence to Counterclaim. The CPR do not even provide a name for subsequent statements of case, and if that isn't a broad hint I don't know what is!

Frankly, save in the most complex and technical of cases, if you are considering applying for leave to file an additional statement of case, think:

(a)   whether it is necessary — are you over-drafting? **or**

(b)   have you made a mess of your earlier statement(s) of case, and if so, are you better off seeking leave to amend?

If you still feel it essential to make the application, good luck to you! You're on your own here, and that's my last word on the subject.

Chapter Six

Pray — Tell Me (The Request for Further Information)

> *'What do you mean by that?'* said the Caterpillar, sternly. *'Explain yourself!'*
>
> ...
>
> *'I should like to have it explained'*, said the Mock Turtle.
> *'She can't explain it'*, said the Gryphon hastily. *'Go on with the next verse.'*

Before the CPR, a party wanting to obtain further information from another had to make a decision as to whether the information required was necessary in order for him to be able properly to plead his case, or whether he was seeking the discovery of **facts** which related to matters in issue between the parties but which were not disclosed on the face of the pleadings. If it was the former then the proper means was by way of a Request for Further and Better Particulars (or Request for F&BP as it was invariably called), which was technically part of the pleadings process. If it was the latter then you had to administer **interrogatories**, which were (or at least should have been) questions of fact which you wanted the other side to answer. Such answers were usually given by affidavit, with the other side having an opportunity to apply to the Court for some or all of the interrogatories to be varied or withdrawn. Interrogatories were technically not part of the pleadings process, but were a part of discovery — the questions being usually (but not invariably) administered after close of pleadings.

The distinction between the two has now been abolished, and the new procedure, called a 'Request for Further Information' (whether or not it will be known as an 'RFI' will doubtless soon become clear), is set out in CPR Part 18, which I will leave you to read. Subject to the criteria of relevance and proportionality, you can now use the single procedure either to obtain information about the other side's case, or to ask questions which you hope will expose the shortcomings in their case (although your excuse will of course be that you are attempting to clarify the issues between the parties).

There is no requirement that the Request should be in a particular form. If the text is brief, and the reply likely to be so as well, it may be made by letter. However, for the purposes of this work, I shall assume that you will be making your Request in a separate document in a formal manner, so that your drafting techniques will be fully utilised to the ultimate benefit of your client! After all, this is a book about drafting, and I intend here to show some of the 'tricks of the trade' which I consider still apply to this discipline.

The Request for Further Information is capable of being possibly the most satisfyingly ruthless, vicious and successful means that you have at your command of exploiting the weaknesses in your opponent's case. As in so many other instances of drafting, the converse is also true. A badly drafted Request can lead to all sorts of faintly (!) concealed rudery in reply, and can leave your case, if not in tatters, certainly smelling of something less socially acceptable than attar of roses! A Request should be concise, and strictly confined to matters which are reasonably necessary and proportionate to enable the party requesting the information to prepare his own case, or to understand the case he has to meet. The requirement of proportionality is, of course, to ensure compliance with the overriding objective in CPR Part 1, and provides the recipient with a new ground for refusing to give further information (although I suggest this argument will not extend to a genuine request for clarification), even though the request might otherwise be legitimate.

You must unfortunately appreciate that the Courts have done a great deal to ensure that much of the potential fun is taken out of a Request for Further Information. You are not allowed to ask questions going to the credibility of witnesses, 'fishing expeditions' are rigorously discouraged, scandalous questions are prohibited, they must be relevant only to the present action, and must not be oppressive or disproportionate. However, the old principles are not entirely dead. If you think that there is no scope left for creative thought, in a case in 1886, Lord Esher MR stated that interrogatories (as they were then) need not be confined

> to the facts directly in issue, but [can extend] to any facts the existence or non-existence of which is relevant to the existence or non-existence of the facts directly in issue.

So now you know! For those of you who consider the above to be not far removed from trying to describe a circular staircase without using one's hands, I confess that my intellect went into terminal overload at that point as well!

In 1882 Cotton LJ said that interrogatories were

> not limited to giving the [claimant] a knowledge of that which he does not already know, but include the getting an admission of anything which he has to prove on any issue which is raised between him and the defendant.

In 1917 Lord Finlay LC said that it was not necessary that answers to interrogatories should be conclusive on the question at issue. It was enough that they should have some bearing on the question and that they might form a step in establishing liability.

So it is to be hoped that the position is relatively clear!

It is almost certain that the ethos of the CPR will militate against excessive use of the Request for Further Information, and it must therefore be approached with some caution. Certainly, in my view, some of the more advanced tactical considerations examined in this chapter should be reserved for fairly complex cases, usually in the High Court. Experience over the past few years has shown that the Request for Further Information is now rarely, if ever, used in the County Court.

Despite the standardisation of approach, I still consider that there are different techniques and considerations that apply depending on the type of information that you are seeking, and I will therefore give separate consideration to requests for information about the other party's statement of case, and requests for information about their case itself.

As in all matters pertaining to case preparation and drafting skills, there are two fundamental matters to ask yourself before you set out to draft a Request for Further Information:

1.   'Do I fully understand my case, and what it is I am trying to achieve?'

2.   'Am I about to go over the top?'

'Am I about to go over the top?'

Often you will find that a positive answer to the first will lead to the answer to the second!

The majority of mistakes made in a Request for Further Information concern asking for information to which you are not entitled. This is often born of a not unnatural enthusiasm to argue the entire case on the papers, rather than to do so in the proper place, which is before the Court. The criterion for deciding whether to ask for Further Information should be whether you can reasonably be expected to prepare your case properly on the basis of what has been alleged against you. If you can, you may wish to consider **not** making a Request for Further Information, and to point out the shortcomings of your opponent's case at the trial, thus impugning the credibility of his or her evidence. Above all things, remember the golden rule:

THERE IS A SERIOUS RISK THAT IF YOU ASK THE OTHER SIDE A QUESTION, THEY MIGHT ANSWER IT!

Obviously, there are many cases in which that is precisely what you want. It may be that you simply cannot understand the nature of the opposing case without Further Information, or that without it, you are seriously prejudiced in the drafting or preparation of your own case. You are, after all, entitled to know the case (Claim or Defence) that you have to meet in Court.

On the other hand, there may be instances in which you consider your case clear enough, but the opposing allegations are vague, and you wish them to 'nail their colours to the mast', so that they cannot change course in mid-stream.

If in those circumstances, you are supremely confident that Further Information can only benefit your case, or will only push them further and further into a tight corner, then there may be little risk in going ahead and making the Request. It may also serve as a warning that you are prepared to harry them up hill and down dale, and that there is no question of your client being prepared to let the whole thing die down and go to sleep. Sometimes that will have the desired effect, and stop any further 'messing around', leading to some serious talking, and a prompt settlement of the dispute.

There is, however, another side to the coin. First, it may be that the other side can give a good answer, and that it will not be beneficial to your case. Possibly you may have misread the mood of the opposition, or have become too convinced of your interpretation of the facts. Secondly, it is possible that as a result of being forced to research the answers to your Request, the other side will be jolted into a better pre-paration of their case — not, I suggest, what you intended! Thirdly, and as a consequence of the above, in the course of such better preparation, facts might emerge which may assist your opponent and redound to your disadvantage. Bear all the above in mind.

Therefore, in deciding whether or not to make a Request for Further Information, you will have to weigh up both the legitimate requirement for particulars that are missing from the relevant statement of case, and the tactical pros and cons of provoking the other side into action.

As I have said, you have a legitimate right to relevant Further Information concerning matters which have been inadequately raised in the offending statement of case. These particulars will arise in one of two basic ways:

1.   Where there is vagueness or ambiguity in the offending document;
or
2.   Where particulars are required by Rules of Court, see in particular, CPR Part 16 and its associated Practice Direction.

This brings me to certain matters which we should consider, but which are not to be found in any of the official rule books.

Of course, the Request for Further Information has to be used to help in the preparation of the case, to clarify issues, and thus, one hopes, to save time and costs. It is not a vehicle for exposing the bad drafting of the other side's case! Having said that, if the latter would occur as a by-product of the former, we are hardly going to fail to make a Request as a result! We are not to know whether bad drafting is a result of incompetence by the lawyers, or is due to the inherent weaknesses of our opponent's case. If we can force the other side to alter their position, or amend their statement of case, or to resile from something originally alleged, or to aver something at variance with some other part of their case, so much the better. If this is due to the fault of their lawyers, well, that's unfortunately their concern. We have to take such legitimate advantage of weaknesses in their case as are open to us. In other words, if, at the end of the day, we have a legitimate and realistic opportunity to use a Request to impugn the credibility of the other side's case, then we should not hesitate to do so.

The degree and extent to which we are successful in achieving our desired objective in a Request for Further Information will depend very much on the accuracy and style with which we ask our questions. A flabby question will enable the other side to avoid giving an answer with the precision that we may have wanted. As we will see when examining the way to reply to a Request for Further Information, our opponent will (if 'on the ball') do his or her best to limit the answers to the minimum required. Likewise, a question which, although incisive, is phrased in a bland or ineffectual manner, may not make the most of the opportunity presented by the lack of particularity of the other side. This will, I hope, become apparent when we examine the examples set out in this chapter.

Although, as I have said, a Request need be in no particular format, where clarification of a statement of case is requested, there seems to be little reason to depart from the 'tried and tested' formula used in the old Request for Further and Better Particulars. Here, one first identifies the 'offending' paragraph, then indicates precisely the words or passage of which further information is required, and then the Request itself is set out with great precision. The question(s) should be formulated in such a way as to enable a clear and precise answer to be given, particularly as such answers are required to be given after each appropriate question, and specifically referred thereto. Let us take a very simple example, where the Particulars of Claim (obviously not drafted by someone who has read this book) reads as follows:

IN THE WHALES COUNTY COURT   Case No. WH990000

BETWEEN:

Mr HUBERT WHITING

Claimant

— and —

Mr ANGUS SNAIL

Defendant

PARTICULARS OF CLAIM

---

1. By an agreement made in about March 2006, the Defendant agreed to supply the Claimant with a quantity of mixed fish at a price of £300 per box.

2. Notwithstanding several requests to do so, the Defendant has failed and/or refused to deliver the said fish or any part thereof, as a result of which the Claimant had to purchase the same elsewhere at a greater cost.

3. The Claimant further claims to be entitled to interest on such damages as may be awarded to him, at such rate and for such period as the Court shall deem fit, pursuant to section 69, County Courts Act 1984.

4.   The value of this claim does not exceed £15,000.

AND the Claimant claims:

1.   Damages.

2.   Interest as aforesaid.

GRAHAM PORPOISE

Statement of Truth (etc.)

Obviously, I have deliberately left the above example begging for a Request for Further Information, and we will now happily oblige. Our instructions are briefly as follows:

> The Defendant is a wholesale supplier of seafood, particularly shellfish. He does not deal in what is commonly described as 'wet fish', but in whelks, cockles, mussels, and lobsters (for those who can afford it).
>
> In late February 2006, the Defendant recalls meeting Mr Whiting, who said that he was opening a fish restaurant and was looking for a regular supplier of fish, and in particular Dover Sole. He seemed rather vague and unbusinesslike.
>
> Mr Snail told him that he would be unable to supply the wet fish, but would be delighted to supply shellfish to order. He sold the same either by the pint (in the case of the smaller crustaceans) or in boxes by weight.
>
> Mr Whiting asked him about the price, and in particular about lobster. He was told that the average price at the present time was about £20 per kilo, and that a box of 10 lobsters of average weight would work out at about £300. However, the price varied almost from day to day, according to the catch.
>
> Nothing more transpired that day, save that about 2 weeks later the Claimant approached the Defendant and asked him if he could buy a box of lobster at £300. He was told that the price had unfortunately risen and was now £365. The Claimant walked off in a huff.
>
> Save for the fact that it appears that the Claimant has been mouthing off about the Defendant in the local market, nothing has been heard from him since. Mr Snail has never

offered to sell mixed fish for £300, by the box, or at all.
He has never heard of any alleged breach of contract prior to
receiving the summons. He considers that Mr Whiting is a
bit 'doolally', and that the whole thing is a bit fishy.

It is of course, perfectly possible in the present instance to draft a
Defence, denying the contract and its breach. You may even wish to have
a try at this yourself, by way of revision. However, such a Defence will
amount to little more than a denial, coupled with an assertion that
the Defendant does not deal in 'mixed fish' (whatever that may be). The
Particulars of Claim are vague, and even if a Defence can be filed, the
Defendant will not have any real means of knowing precisely what
the Claimant is alleging until possibly as late as the trial. (I am assuming, for the purposes of this example, that no attempt has been made to
strike the case out — after all, this is a book on drafting techniques!) He
will therefore be genuinely hindered in his Defence.

In addition, by knowing precisely what the Claimant is alleging, the
Defence may be able to show that certain aspects of the claim were not
capable of being true. For example, if the Claimant was to allege that
'mixed fish' contained Dover Sole, evidence may be brought at the trial
to show that the Defendant never dealt with this fish. The nature of the
fish may be highly relevant in view of the somewhat specialised nature
of the Defendant's business. Mr Snail might be prejudiced in his
Defence were he to have to wait until trial to discover whether or not the
Claimant was alleging that he had agreed to sell fish not ordinarily sold
in the course of his business.

Additionally there is vagueness as to dates, times and places, with
which we will deal when we examine our potential Request, paragraph
by paragraph.

Finally, in the present case, our instructions are quite firm. There is
reason to believe that the Claimant will not be able to justify his claim,
and there is therefore every motive for pushing him as hard as possible
into giving firm particulars of his allegations, so that he cannot alter his
position in the future.

Note, however, that whereas there are many instances here in which
we will be able to ask for Further Information of facts alleged, we will
not be able to ask questions such as 'stating why it is alleged that the
Defendant agreed to supply the said fish', or any other question the
answer to which will involve the giving of evidence as to what allegedly
transpired between the parties. Let us therefore look at the individual
paragraphs, and begin to formulate our Request.

Paragraph 1
Our case is, of course, that there never was any agreement, as alleged or
at all. However, we are entitled to know when it is alleged that this
agreement took place, and so far the Claimant has been very vague.
A question to this effect will either tie the Claimant down to a particular
date (which may assist us when it comes to collating evidence), or will
produce an admission that the Claimant cannot be more precise, which
will not exactly add to his credibility! So we can safely ask for Further
Information of the date.

Another area in which we will be interested, is whether this alleged
agreement was oral or written. From our instructions, we cannot believe
that the latter will be alleged, but it will nevertheless be interesting to
find out. If the agreement is alleged to be oral, the Particulars of Claim
does not actually state that it was made between the Claimant and
the Defendant (even if there is a strong implication to this effect).
Statements of case are not made of implications, so we should ask for
this information as well, particularly as the Rules require particulars of
an oral agreement to be set out in full.

The next area in which there has been a surprising lack of particularity is in setting out the terms of the agreement. You may care at this stage
to make a list of the relevant particulars (not evidence) which you feel
are missing, and which can properly be requested. Compare them with
the following, to see if you are on the right track.

You may have noticed that the Particulars of Claim does not identify
the Defendant, particularly as a wholesale supplier of seafood. However,
it cannot be said that this is such a vital omission from the Particulars
that we could request the status or capacity of the Defendant to enter into
such an agreement. To ask:

> Please state the capacity in which it is alleged that the
> Defendant entered into the said agreement...

comes very close to asking the Claimant to state why it is alleged that
the Defendant entered into the agreement, which transgresses the rule
about requesting evidence.

On the other hand, it would be helpful were we to be able to induce
the Claimant to commit himself to a version of events which is incompatible with what we know to be the Defendant's business. In other
words, were the Claimant to allege that the contract was for the supply
of fish which it was not in the course of our usual business to provide,
this may be used at the trial, to sow doubts as to his credibility.

From our instructions, two other matters may be relevant. First, there is no mention in the Particulars of Claim as to when this mixed fish is supposed to have been supplied. Secondly, in view of the way in which we package our fish, the size and nature of the alleged 'box' is also a matter on which it would be proper to press the Claimant.

Our requests therefore will be for:

1. The date of the agreement.
2. The nature thereof.
3. The parties thereto.
4. The amount of the consignment.
5. The nature of the consignment.
6. The date of delivery.
7. The meaning of 'box'.

Let us now look at the most advantageous method of setting out the above Request. The first essential is to identify the paragraph containing the matters in respect of which the Request will be made. Thus we put:

> Under paragraph 1

or

> Under paragraph 2(b)

or

> Under paragraph 3 — Particulars

etc.

Then the 'offending words'. There are a number of different ways of doing this, all of which have something in their favour. One conventional method is to set out the words relevant to the question which is immediately following. The process is then repeated for questions relating to other words in the paragraph. So, in the present example we might put:

> Under paragraph 1
> Of: 'By an agreement ...'

> Stating: (question)

Of: '... made in about March 2006 ...'
Stating: (a) (question)
Stating: (b) (further question)

Of: '... the Defendant agreed ...'
Stating: (question)
etc.

The CPR now require that each request for information or clarification should be set out in a separate numbered paragraph.

The above layout is particularly useful where the paragraph itself is long or complex, and where it would not greatly assist comprehension by setting out its entire length at the beginning. However, it becomes a little unwieldy when the paragraph is short and the questions, although attacking different parts, are easily referred to their context. Thus in the present case I would opt for setting out the paragraph at length:

Under paragraph 1
Of: 'By an agreement made in about March 2006, the Defendant agreed to supply the Claimant with a quantity of mixed fish at a price of £300 per box.'
Stating:

(1)   (question)
(2)   (question)
etc.

There are some who do not even bother to set out the whole paragraph, but who simply put:

Under paragraph 1
Of: The whole paragraph

but what this gains in brevity, it lacks in clarity, as one then has to refer to the original document in order to make head or tail of the Request. I confess to having done it once or twice myself during my misspent past, but I've gone straight now, M'Lud.

Your question should be prefaced with the title 'Request'. You will doubtless be amazed to discover that, in order to provide clarity to a document which could otherwise be confusing, the reponses should set out the original question and then clearly identify the answer. Would that everything else in the law ...!!

Whichever of the above examples you choose (and I do not recommend the third), it is essential that the questions are set out in such a way as to be capable of logical answer.

Back to our case. As I have said, I have elected to set out the whole paragraph, and now wish to formulate my Requests. Some conventional formats are:

Stating:

Or

Give full particulars of

Or

State with particularity:

I think you get the message! The precise nature of the request will, of course, depend on the information required, and the format will also depend on the number of requests to be made of a particular paragraph, and the stylistically appropriate way of setting them out. For many years I contented myself with putting simply: 'State ...', but in my old age, became a little more polite: 'Please state ...', or 'please give full particulars ...' etc. I find a little courtesy does not upset the balance of the document, does no one any harm at all, and certainly does not indicate timidity or weakness.

Please state:
1.   The alleged date of the said agreement.

Note the use of the word 'alleged'. Although we have not yet drafted our Defence, we are going to deny the agreement, and this is as good a warning of our intentions as any. In any event, the tone of the request does not imply any acceptance whatsoever of the allegation — at best it is neutral, at worst, frankly dismissive.

The next question concerns the nature of the agreement. Before drafting the Request, let us examine carefully what it is we would like to know. Once we have done this, we will find that we have formulated the Request itself. It's as straightforward as that!

The alleged agreement will be either oral or written, or partly oral and partly written. If it was oral, we would like to know the parties to that agreement, as although it is strongly implied that this was between the Claimant and the Defendant, the Particulars of Claim does not actually say that. Further, the claim is vague as to the terms of the agreement, and we are entitled to be made aware of what is being alleged in this regard, and in particular to the words used by and to whom, which are alleged to have given rise to the agreement. A Request is often made for the 'gist' of all words spoken. It's not a particularly attractive word, but is nevertheless an accurate description of what is required.

Finally, under this aspect of the Request, we would like to know the position if it is alleged that the agreement was not oral but written. In such an event, we would be entitled to identification of the document alleged to contain the agreement, as well as particulars of the parties to and nature of the contract. Additionally, we are entitled to have a copy of any written agreement attached to the Particulars of Claim, or, as would have to be the case, attached to the Further Information.

It now remains to put this into Request form. As you can imagine, this particular type of Request is very common, and a conventional form of words evolved over the years. The finished product was a Gothic Horror of English literature, but did the job. In typical form, it went as follows:

> State whether it is alleged that the said agreement was made orally or in writing. If made orally, state the date thereof, the parties thereto and the gist of all words spoken. If made in writing, give the like particulars *mutatis mutandis* together with full particulars of any document or documents relied upon in support.

This little jewel of a paragraph made up in conciseness what it lacked in elegance, and, at the time, encapsulated a request for all the information that we were reasonably entitled to require. The use of the phrase '*mutatis mutandis*' means 'with the necessary changes' and essentially requires the same particulars as previously requested, but adapted to meet the peculiar circumstances of the new situation. Today, however, we will have to adapt this paragraph, first to omit the Latin, which is totally unacceptable in modern comprehensible drafting, and secondly to ensure that a copy of any written contractual documents is attached to the Further Information supplied. Thus, if we are going to use any form of standard format paragraph, I suggest it goes along the lines of:

> State whether it is alleged that the said agreement was made orally or in writing. If made orally, state the date on which

it took place, the parties to the agreement, and the gist of all words spoken. If it is alleged that the agreement was made in writing, give the same particulars with the necessary changes, identify the documents which it is alleged formed or evidenced the agreement, and attach a copy of such documents to the answer.

(I have deliberately used the word 'answer' rather than 'reply' in order to avoid confusion.)

In any event, some attempt could be made to mitigate the brontosaurian propensities of the above paragraph, by splitting it into its constituent elements. Thus, we have already asked for the alleged date of the agreement in our first question. We could therefore continue:

2.   Whether it is alleged that the said agreement was made orally or in writing;

3.   (If an oral agreement is alleged) the parties to the agreement, and the gist of all words spoken;

4.   (If a written agreement is alleged) give the same particulars with the necessary changes, identifying the documents which it is alleged formed or evidenced the agreement, and attach a copy of such documents to the answer.

If you really wanted to be clever, you could eliminate question 4, and subdivide question 3 into (a) and (b), thus ensuring that a relevant answer was given to each question. That is what I shall do.

Unfortunately, however, that does not conclude our Request in respect of the first paragraph. We should be able to polish this off fairly rapidly, using the same thought processes as hitherto. We wish to obtain Further Information of the date upon which the supply was to take place, the quantity of mixed fish to be supplied, what is meant by 'mixed fish', and the size or description of the box. Additionally, there may be some confusion as to whether it is being alleged that the Defendant agreed to supply one consignment of mixed fish, or whether the agreement was for a continuing supply. So we proceed:

4.   The date or dates upon which it is alleged the Defendant agreed to supply mixed fish to the Claimant;

5.   The quantity of mixed fish to be supplied;

6.   Whether it is being alleged that the Defendant agreed to supply the Claimant with one or more than one consignment of fish, and if the latter, the number of consignments allegedly so agreed;

7.   What it is alleged was understood and agreed by the parties to comprise 'mixed fish';

8.   What it is alleged was understood and agreed by the parties to comprise 'a box of mixed fish'.

Paragraph 2
See if you can identify the areas in which we are entitled to Further Information.

Clearly, we should be given particulars of the nature and form of the various alleged requests to deliver the fish. We should also ask for details of the Claimant's alternative purchase, at least to the extent of knowing the extra cost allegedly paid.

However, I hope you have not asked for Further Information of why it is alleged the Defendant failed and/or refused to deliver the fish! Likewise, there may be some argument for saying that we should not strictly be entitled to particulars of the party from whom the Claimant eventually purchased the fish. On the other hand, we may wish to have this information in order to conduct our own investigations, or to test the veracity of the Claimant's case. On balance, it may be that the proper place for such information is upon disclosure, although that would not prevent me from asking the question, in the hope that I would get an answer!

Under paragraph 2
Of: 'Notwithstanding several requests to do so ...'

Please give full particulars of the date or dates of every such alleged request, whether it is alleged the same were made orally or in writing; if orally, stating by and to whom the said requests were made, the nature of the said request and the answer thereto; if in writing, giving the like particulars with the necessary changes together with particulars of any document or documents relied upon in support.

Of: '... the Claimant had to purchase the same elsewhere at a greater cost.'

Please state from where it is alleged the Claimant purchased the said fish, the quantity so purchased, and the price paid.

In the above example, I have pleaded the Requests without paragraph numbers, and in unbroken form. I will now put the entire Request together in two ways — one using numbered paragraphs, and one without:

IN THE WHALES COUNTY COURT   Case No. WH990000

BETWEEN:

Mr HUBERT WHITING

Claimant

— and —

Mr ANGUS SNAIL

Defendant

REQUEST FOR FURTHER INFORMATION ABOUT
THE PARTICULARS OF CLAIM

Under paragraph 1
Of: 'By an agreement made in about March 2006, the Defendant agreed to supply the Claimant with a quantity of mixed fish at a price of £300 per box.'

Please state:

1.   The alleged date of the said agreement;

2.   Whether it is alleged that the said agreement was made orally or in writing;

3. (a)   (If an oral agreement is alleged), the parties to the agreement and the gist of all words spoken;

3. (b)   (If a written agreement is alleged), give the same particulars with the necessary changes, identifying the documents which it is alleged

formed or evidenced the agreement, and attach a copy of such documents to the answer;

4.   The date or dates upon which it is alleged the Defendant agreed to supply mixed fish to the Claimant;

5.   The quantity of mixed fish to be supplied;

6.   Whether it is being alleged that the Defendant agreed to supply the Claimant with one or more than one consignment of fish, and if the latter, the number of consignments allegedly so agreed;

7.   What it is alleged was understood and agreed by the parties to comprise 'mixed fish';

8.   What it is alleged was understood and agreed by the parties to comprise 'a box of mixed fish'.

Under paragraph 2

Of: 'Notwithstanding several requests to do so ...'

Please give full particulars of:

9.   The date or dates of every such alleged request;

10.   Whether it is alleged that the same were made orally or in writing;

11. (a)   (If oral requests are alleged), by and to whom the said requests were made, the nature of the said requests and the answer thereto;

11. (b)   (If written requests are alleged), give the same particulars with the necessary changes, together with particulars of any document or documents relied upon in support.

Of: '... the Claimant had to purchase the same elsewhere at a greater cost.'

Please state:

12.   From where it is alleged the Claimant purchased the said fish;

13. The quantity of fish allegedly purchased;

14. The price allegedly paid.

TITUS CLAM

Alternatively:

Under paragraph 1

Of: 'By an agreement made in about March 2006, the Defendant agreed to supply the Claimant with a quantity of mixed fish at a price of £300 per box.'

1. Please state whether it is alleged that the said agreement was made orally or in writing; if orally, giving the alleged date thereof, the parties thereto and the gist of all words spoken; if in writing, giving the like particulars with the necessary changes, identifying the document which it is alleged formed or evidenced the agreement, and attaching a copy of such document to the answer.

2. Please give full particulars of:
   (a) The date or dates upon which it is alleged the Defendant agreed to supply mixed fish to the Claimant;
   (b) The quantity of mixed fish to be supplied;
   (c) Whether it is being alleged that the Defendant agreed to supply the Claimant with one or more than one consignment of fish, and if the latter, the number of consignments allegedly so agreed;
   (d) What it is alleged was understood and agreed by the parties to comprise:
      (i) 'mixed fish'
      (ii) a 'box' of mixed fish.

Under paragraph 2

Of: 'Notwithstanding several requests to do so ...'

Please give full particulars of the date or dates of every such alleged request; whether it is alleged that the same were made orally or in writing; if orally, stating by and to whom the same were allegedly made, the nature of the said requests and the answers thereto; if in writing, giving the like particulars with the necessary changes together with particulars of any document or documents relied upon in support.

Of: '… the Claimant had to purchase the same elsewhere at a greater cost.'

Please state:

1. From where it is alleged the Claimant purchased the said fish;

2. The quantity allegedly purchased;

3. The price allegedly paid.

C. WEED

As you can see, there is not a lot to choose between the two styles, each of which complies with the Rules, and you may wish to adopt (or adapt) either depending on the situation with which you are faced. The above example is obviously somewhat artificial, as it was designed with a Request for Further Information in mind, showing a degree of ineptitude which I hope would not be manifest in a real case.

   For what is perhaps a rather more realistic example, let us turn again to the case of *Turnonn Ltd* v *Thunder Engineering Ltd*, which first reared its ugly head in Chapter 4. We are acting for the Defendants. Here are the Particulars of Claim, and a reminder of the instructions we have taken as a result:

IN THE HIGH COURT OF JUSTICE   2006 T No. 0000
QUEEN'S BENCH DIVISION

BETWEEN:

TURNONN LIMITED

Claimants

— and —

THUNDER ENGINEERING LIMITED

Defendants

PARTICULARS OF CLAIM

---

1. The Claimants are and were at all relevant times a limited company carrying on business as experts in the commissioning of mechanical services installations. The Defendants are and were at all relevant times

a limited company carrying on business as engineers and as installers of such mechanical services.

2.   By an oral agreement made on 3rd September 2004, the Claimants, in the course of their said business, agreed with the Defendants that they would commission the mechanical services installations at the World of Wonder Leisure Centre ('The Centre'), Neasden, Kent, for the sum of £78,450. At all relevant times the Defendants were sub-contractors at the said site, responsible, amongst other matters, for the installation of the said mechanical services. The agreement took place in a telephone conversation between Alan Tapp of the Claimants and Richard Thunder of the Defendants, in which the terms set out above were agreed.

3.   There were, amongst others, the following express or implied terms of the said agreement:
    (a)   That the said commissioning works would be carried out on a date to be agreed between the parties;
    (b)   That the systems to be commissioned would be fully and competently installed by the Defendants prior to the Claimants commencing the said commissioning works;
    (c)   That the Defendants would ensure that all water systems were totally free from all foreign matter prior to the start of commissioning works;
    (d)   That the Defendants would conduct all necessary pre-commissioning checks on all systems to ensure their readiness for commissioning.

4.   Further, it was an implied term of the said agreement that the price quoted by the Claimants would only hold good in so far as the said commissioning works could be carried out by them within a reasonable time and without unreasonable delay or additional works caused to them as a result of any failure by the Defendants properly to complete the said installation or to ensure the readiness of the same for commissioning on the agreed date. The Claimants will aver that a reasonable time was, and/or was agreed to be, just over 8 weeks from commencement of the said commissioning.

5.   Pursuant to the said agreement, on or about 17th May 2005 the Defendants informed the Claimants, that they could commence the said commissioning works on 4th July 2005, and by their letter dated 18th May 2005 the Claimants duly agreed to do so and to complete the same by 1st September 2005.

6.   In order to assist the Defendants to conduct the necessary pre-commissioning checks, on or about 22nd June 2005 the Claimants provided

the Defendants with their standard 'air and water installation completion check sheets' and requested that the appropriate checks should be made prior to commissioning works being undertaken on any system.

7.   In breach of the said agreement, the Defendants, their employees or agents:
    (a)   Caused the Claimants to suffer excessive and unreasonable delay in commencing, and thereafter carrying out the said works of commissioning;
    (b)   Failed on repeated occasions to ensure that the said systems were completely installed in time for the said works of commissioning to be carried out;
    (c)   Failed adequately or at all on numerous occasions properly to conduct the necessary pre-commissioning checks as set out in the Claimants' said check sheet, or at all;
    (d)   Failed on repeated occasions to ensure that the said systems were in a proper state for works of commissioning to be carried out.

PARTICULARS

(1)   On or about 2nd July 2005 the Defendants informed the Claimants by telephone that the said systems were not ready, and that the commissioning works could not start until 26th July 2005.

(2)   On 26th July 2005 the Claimants duly attended at the said site to perform the said works and found:
    (a)   power was not available;
    (b)   the said equipment had not been prepared for commissioning;
    (c)   the heating system had not been filled, flushed or cleaned;
whereafter the said commencement date was again put off until 2nd August 2005.

(3)   The various defects in the said works of installation and preparation, and the resultant delays caused to the Claimants are set out in the Claimants' various site reports dated between 2nd August and 27th October 2005, copies whereof were supplied to the Defendants on site.

8.   By reason of the matters hereinbefore set out, the Claimant company was caused additional work, delay and expense:

PARTICULARS

(1)   The Claimants had agreed to perform the said works between 4th July 2005 and 1st September 2005, a period of just over 8 weeks.

By reason of the Defendants' said breaches of contract, the said works took 17 weeks to carry out;

(2)   The failure of the Defendants adequately or at all to ensure that the said systems were totally free of all foreign matter prior to commissioning, meant that the Claimants became involved in repeated testing of the systems as a result of problems associated with blockages thereof, causing additional work, expense and delay;

(3)   A schedule of hours lost and losses incurred by the Claimants has been supplied to the Defendants, and amounts to £33,996.78.

9.   The Defendants have paid the Claimants the sum of £78,450.00 but have failed and/or refused to pay the additional loss and damage incurred or any part thereof, and there is presently due and owing to the Claimant the sum of £33,996.78.

10.   The Claimants further claim interest (etc.) pursuant to section 35A of the Supreme Court Act 1981.

11.   The value of this claim exceeds £15,000.

AND the Claimants claim:

1.   Damages;

2.   Interest as aforesaid.

ANNA KLEINE-NACHTMUSIK

Statement of Truth (etc.)

In deciding whether, and to what extent, to serve a Request for Further Information, we must look at two factors:

1.   Are there defects in the statement of case such as to warrant such a Request being made?

2.   In the light of our instructions, would the making of a proper Request for Further Information of certain matters in the statement of case materially assist our case?

It is only if one or both of the above questions are answered in the affirmative, that we then bring into issue the tactical considerations with which I have dealt earlier in this chapter.

In so far as our instructions are concerned, I shall do no more than set out, once again, the points of difference between the parties:

> 1. The Claimants say that the contract was oral. We aver that it was contained or evidenced in a letter, and was expressed to be subject to our standard terms and conditions.

> 2. There is a fundamental disagreement as to the respective works to be performed by the parties. The Claimants' case is that they were merely to commission the installations once they had been properly installed, cleaned and pre-commissioned by us. We do not accept that we were to have installed and checked the installations to a certain minimum standard prior to the Claimants commencing their works.

> 3. We don't wish to be too specific with regard to the various delays and defects alleged by the Claimants, as there may be some truth in some of them. However, we do not accept any responsibility for any increase in the contract time or the amount of additional works alleged to have been occasioned.

Once again, you are cordially invited to have a go yourself, and then to compare your analysis and draft with that below. The results will, it is hoped, convince you of your own superiority of style and accuracy — there's little so fulfilling as reassurance!

Obviously we do not need to do anything about paragraph 1. I trust it has not even entered your mind.

Paragraph 2 likewise appears to convey all necessary information, and we will leave it well alone.

Paragraph 3
This alleges that the oral agreement contained certain express or implied terms. Although these are, to a certain extent, a matter on which evidence may have to be given in due course, there is no escaping the fact that these must be tied up with what was said at the time that the Claimants say the oral agreement was made. However, it may be important for us to know which of the terms of the alleged agreement

are supposed to have been expressly agreed, and which are alleged to arise by implication. This will ensure that the Claimants are thereafter held to their case, and will be denied the luxury of flexibility. After all, certain of these terms are going to be fundamental to the outcome of this dispute, and the issues should be made completely clear.

The Request that we are about to make will require certain technical decisions as to layout. We will be asking much the same question of all the various sub-paragraphs, and yet must prevent our Request from being unwieldy or repetitious. In order to help us make this decision, we could map out the various possibilities.

First, we could simply deal with each and every sub-paragraph in turn. This would involve our setting out the individual sub-paragraphs, and then asking two or three questions of each. Thus, for example:

Under paragraph 3
Of: 'There were, amongst others, the following express or implied terms of the said agreement:

(a) That the said commissioning works would be carried out on a date to be agreed between the parties;'

Please state:

1. Whether the said term is alleged to be express or implied;

2. If express, the gist of all words spoken which it is alleged gave rise to the said term;

3. If implied, all grounds upon which the said allegation is made.

Of: '(b) That the systems to be commissioned would be fully and competently installed by the Defendants prior to the Claimants commencing the said commissioning works;'

Please state:

4. Whether the said term is alleged to be express or implied; etc.

However, this process is tedious and pedantic. You could, I suppose, 'roll-up' the questions into one, and repeat them for each paragraph, so:

> Of: 'There were, amongst others, the following express or implied terms of the said agreement:
>
> (a)   That the said commissioning works (etc.);'

1.   Please state whether it is alleged that the said term was express or implied; if express giving the gist of all words spoken which it is alleged gave rise to the same; if implied giving full particulars of the grounds upon which the said allegation is made.

> Of: (b) 'That the systems to be commissioned (etc.);'

2.   Please state whether it is alleged (etc.) ...

but I will have fallen asleep long before drafting the final question in that format.

The solution once again involves our being thoroughly conversant with the means by which we are trying to achieve our goal. The questions that we wish to ask are common to each of the sub-paragraphs. If we look carefully at paragraph 3 of the Particulars of Claim, we should notice that the sub-paragraphs follow an allegation which is also common to all of them, i.e., that they are all, amongst others, express or implied terms of the agreement. Thus, the thrust of our Request should be at those first two lines, rather than at the sub-paragraphs that follow. If we aim our Request accordingly, a little ingenuity should produce the following:

Under paragraph 3
Of: 'There were, amongst others, the following express or implied terms of the said agreement:'

Please state with the necessary changes in relation to each sub-paragraph thereafter set out:

1.   Whether the said term is alleged to be express or implied; if express giving particulars of the gist of all words spoken which it is alleged gave rise to the same; if implied, giving full particulars of the grounds upon which the said allegation is made.

In the above format, the whole series of questions has been rolled up into one, and the format is such that the Claimants should not be hindered in setting out their Further Information with clarity and precision. I have deliberately used the 'long sentence' style, but incorporated in the overall 'multi-question' style, to provide an example of when the two can happily meet in the same document. This has been done not for the mere purposes of illustration, but also because the Claimants can easily respond to the present style by use of sub-paragraphs:

> (a) (Answer to question 1 in relation to sub-paragraph (a); ...)
> (b) (Answer to question 1 in relation to sub-paragraph (b); ...)
> etc.

Moving on, we must, of course, beware of falling into the trap of asking unnecessary questions, merely because we have decided in the first place to embark upon a Request for Further Information. Although having taken this decision we may wish to ask about one or two matters which would not by themselves have justified the making of a full Request, we must not thereafter simply lash out in all directions. Each individual paragraph must be approached with the same care and precision. So, looking at **paragraph 4**, I hope you will agree that there is no point in requesting Further Information. Although we could possibly ask for the reasons whereby the implied term is alleged, it is best to leave well alone. The term has been set out with particularity, the Claimants have given their estimation of a 'reasonable time', and the rest can be thrashed out in Court if necessary. In short, there is nothing in that paragraph which should, in any way, hinder us in the preparation of our case.

Likewise, **paragraph 5** should be left alone. Our case is that the Claimants did not 'agree' to complete the works by 1st September, but that the same were 'envisaged' (see Defence filed in Chapter 4). However, there is nothing to be gained by trying to make any capital out of this in the Request for Further Information.

Paragraph 6

This raises a problem of a different nature from those previously experienced. On the face of it, the paragraph is perfectly clear and particularised. The issue between the parties is, however, that we deny that we were required to perform pre-commissioning checks, and that this was a

purported unilateral variation of the contract by the Claimants, unsupported
by any form of consideration. Is there any opportunity here of reinforcing
our case, or should we let the first sentence of the paragraph go by?

There are times when it may be counter-productive to press too much
in a Request for Further Information. By all means fire as many broad-
sides as you can when the claim is patently both a 'try-on' and badly
drafted. However, whatever the merits of our case, there is clearly a genuine
dispute between the parties in the instant case, and we would be foolish
were we to proceed otherwise. On reflection, I would leave this paragraph well alone, although I will not follow my own advice here, merely
for the purposes of demonstration.

If we did decide to make a Request under this paragraph, we would be
aiming not so much at facts which would assist us in preparing our case,
but at particulars of the nature of the Claimants' case. They are alleging
that there was an agreement, whereby they would commission the system
once it had been installed and pre-commissioned by us. To facilitate this,
they sent us their standard checklists. If we are correct in our assertion that
we did not have to perform any pre-commissioning checks, it might
appear strange that the Claimants would have sent us their checklists.
As it happens, there is no allegation by any party that the Claimants **would**
send these checklists, so we could at this stage enquire the Claimants' case
in this regard. As I have said, I think we should refrain from so doing, but
were I to be overruled, the Request might read:

Under paragraph 6
Of: 'In order to assist the Defendants to conduct the necessary pre-commissioning checks,'

1.   Please state:
    (a)   whether it is the Claimants' case that it was at any
time agreed between the parties that the said check sheets
would be supplied by them to the Defendants, and if so, give
full particulars of when and between whom it is alleged that
the same was so agreed, and the gist of all words spoken;
    (b)   whether it is alleged that the said check sheets were
at any time requested by the Defendants, and if so, giving
the like particulars with the necessary changes as requested
in Request 1(a).

Note that I have not asked **why** the Claimants sent the sheets to the
Defendants. This is, first, because a reason is given in the first line of

paragraph 6 itself and, secondly, because I would be tempting the Claimants to give an answer which would itself reinforce their case. I have thus preferred to ask two direct questions (or rather, series of questions). However, these will themselves provide the Claimants with a useful tactical means of response which will not redound to our advantage, but you will have to wait until the next chapter to discover what they should do (if they know what they are about). ...

I will not include this particular part of the Request in the final document. It is set out here merely as a warning not to attempt to go too far!

Paragraphs 7 and 8
These make allegations as to breaches of contract, and consequent loss and damage allegedly suffered by the Claimants. The allegations themselves are not set out with any great particularity, but both paragraphs do make reference (under the heading 'Particulars'), to detailed documentation which it is alleged has been supplied to the Defendants. Thus, the nature and extent of the Claimants' case appears to have been fully set out in this regard, and there seems nothing to be gained by making a Request for the whole matter to be regurgitated in the statement of case, where the format will possibly be less easy to understand than the documentation originally supplied. This documentation will, in any event, form part of the bundle of documents in the case, and schedules can, if necessary, be drawn up by one or either side to make their comprehension more easy to the Court.

Of course, were we to deny that we had received the documents, we could make a Request for Further Information of their identity, and could then allege accordingly in our Defence. For the present purposes, I have refrained from making any Request for Further Information of the remaining paragraphs of the Particulars of Claim, and now reproduce our finished document below. However, for the purposes of illustrating various points pertinent to answering the Request, I will reproduce the same document in the following chapter, but with certain additions.

IN THE HIGH COURT OF JUSTICE   2006 T No. 0000
QUEEN'S BENCH DIVISION

BETWEEN:

TURNONN LIMITED

Claimants

— and —

THUNDER ENGINEERING LIMITED

Defendants

REQUEST FOR FURTHER INFORMATION ABOUT
THE PARTICULARS OF CLAIM

Under paragraph 3

Of: 'There were, amongst others, the following express or implied terms of the said agreement:'

Please state with the necessary changes in relation to each sub-paragraph thereafter set out:

1.   Whether the said term is alleged to be express or implied; if express giving particulars of the gist of all words spoken which it is alleged gave rise to the same; if implied, giving full particulars of the grounds upon which the said allegation is made.

HERMANN COWPAT

At the end of the day, this Request did not turn out to be a very long document at all. However, it is better that it is short, relevant and incisive, than long-winded, nebulous and unnecessary. As with all draftings, one cannot provide examples which cover every eventuality, or which illustrate every possible style or approach. However, I shall now turn to the way that I consider we should approach a case where we wish for further information of a factual kind (akin to the old interrogatories) in order to assist us either to draft a statement of case in response, or (more likely) to seek to expose weaknesses in the other side's case, to assist an early settlement or, one hopes, capitulation!

Remember, as I have already said, that the ethos of the CPR will almost certainly mean that we must be more restrained in our approach than hitherto. Nevertheless, the art of requesting such information is to do so in such a manner a to put your opponent very much 'on the spot', so that the answers will tend either to support your case, or (much more fun) to damage his! Therefore, care must be taken to draft your request in a precise and unambiguous format, and in a calculated and logical manner. The fact that we must not be scandalous or oppressive, and that we must be proportionate to the amount in issue, does not mean that we should lean over backwards to be gentle to the other side!

Let us take a short example of a fairly straightforward case in which we wish to ask the Claimant some embarrassing questions:

EXAMPLE

We act for Theobald Snoot, a grocer, who is being sued for £10,000 by Hermunculus Cosh, a local wholesaler. Mr Cosh alleges that he supplied us with a quantity of groceries which he in turn had purchased from Makerprofit Ltd, a huge area warehouse supplier. The arrangement was that Mr Cosh would receive a 20% discount from Makerprofit Ltd, provided he paid in full within 7 days of purchase. He would then sell the goods to various local retailers, including Mr Snoot, for a price equivalent to 15% off the full Makerprofit Ltd price. Thus, Mr Cosh would effectively make 5% for being the middleman.

The Particulars of Claim allege that Mr Snoot had agreed to pay for the goods within 7 days of delivery to him, and that he had defaulted on this particular consignment. As a result, it is claimed, Mr Cosh had been unable to pay Makerprofit Ltd within the 7-day period of grace, and had lost his 20% discount. He therefore claimed the full Makerprofit Ltd price, together with his 5% commission.

In his Defence, Mr Snoot admitted that he had had cash-flow difficulties, and had not paid the full sum due to Mr Cosh. However, his agreement provided that payment should be made within 7 days, but contained no provision that he would pay any increased sum in default. Additionally, he had made a part payment of £1,500, for which he had not been given credit, and in any event did not admit that Mr Cosh had been forced to pay the full price to Makerprofit Ltd. In the event, Mr Snoot admits that he is liable for £8,500 (being the Makerprofit Ltd full price less 15%), less the £1,500 already paid, being a total liability of £7,000. He states that a cheque for that sum has been paid to the Claimant's solicitors, who have refused to accept the same in full and final satisfaction, save for costs.

We have in fact discovered that there is reason to believe that Makerprofit Ltd were paid by Mr Cosh within the 7 days, and that he is therefore attempting to make a profit from our default. Of course, the terms and conditions of the various agreements will ultimately be a matter for the Court to decide if the matter comes to trial, but we wish to try to delineate the issues, and see if we can put some legitimate pressure on Mr Cosh to accept our payment, by making him realise the difficulty of his position if he persists in the litigation.

IN THE AVARICIOUS COUNTY COURT   Case No. AV990000

BETWEEN:

Mr HERMUNCULUS COSH
Claimant

— and —

Mr THEOBALD SNOOT
Defendant

REQUEST FOR FURTHER INFORMATION ABOUT THE CLAIMANT'S CASE

Note at this stage that the heading is quite straightforward, and as we are not in fact seeking further information of a statement of case, I have entitled the document 'Request for Further Information about the Claimant's Case' to avoid confusion. Unlike the old interrogatories, where the questions were directed for the answer of a specific person, it does not seem necessary to do so here, and therefore the questions will be set out in the impersonal form. Of course, it may well be that only Mr Cosh will be able to answer them, but that need not be specifically stated in the Request. Remember that there is now no difference between the old Request for F&BP and Interrogatories, and indeed, the Request for Further Information can contain a mixture of the two formats.

Now let us commence the question:

1.   Is it not the case:
      (a)   that Hermunculus Cosh received a cheque from the Defendant dated 10th May 2003 in the sum of £1,500?

Pray — Tell Me 181

(b)   that Hermunculus Cosh, or some person on his behalf, subsequently presented the cheque and that it was duly met and cleared through the Defendant's bank account on 20th May 2003?

(c)   that such sum falls therefore to be deducted from the Claimant's claim against the Defendant?

You will with your customary perspicacity doubtless have observed the use of sub-questions to deal with this particular subject. This is, of course, not strictly necessary, but I considered it to be appropriate for clarity and style. You could, I suppose, attempt to ask all three questions in 'rolled-up' form, i.e., in one question, but I still think that it is better to split them up. Note that I have been very pedantic, and have asked the Claimant to confirm not merely that the cheque was tendered to him but that it was in fact met, and met for the purposes of this particular contract. If I had not done so, it would have been open to him to say, 'Yes, you tendered a cheque,' but to leave open the question whether it was met and, if so, for what purpose. After all, the Claimant is not going to assist us by answering any more than he is asked! Furthermore, before asking the question, it would be as well for us to check with our client that the cheque had actually been met, otherwise we will have handed the Claimant a golden opportunity to make the obvious comment, to our considerable embarrassment!!

Now to the next part of the exercise:

2.   Has the Claimant at any time paid any sums to or for the benefit of Makerprofit Ltd for the goods supplied to the Defendant, in respect of which the present claim is made?

The object of this question is, of course, to endeavour to discover whether the Claimant has in fact at any time paid Makerprofit Ltd for these particular goods. Notice that I have deliberately used the words 'to or for the benefit of', because there is always the possibility that a payment was made, but to a third party. If the question had simply asked 'Has the Claimant at any time paid any sums to Makerprofit Ltd ... ?' the legitimate answer could be 'no', even though payment for the goods had actually been made by the Claimant. It is a matter for your own judgment and discretion whether and when you should use such careful language.

We are naturally not looking to a negative answer to the above question, but if we get one it will help us to advise our client, or (if we have reason to disbelieve the answer) to collate evidence to show that the Claimant is being economical with the truth! However, if, as we suspect, the reply is to the

effect that some payment has been made, we must narrow down the scope
of the answer, in order to assess its value to us:

>   3.   If the answer to question 2 above is 'yes':
>   (a)   On what date or dates were such sums paid?
>   (b)   How much was paid on each occasion?
>   (c)   Is any sum presently alleged by Makerprofit Ltd to
>   be outstanding to it in relation to the said goods, and if so
>   how much?

The first two sub-questions under this part are designed to take account of
the possibility that more than one payment was made against the invoice
from Makerprofit Ltd. The third is to ascertain whether full and final payment has been made. I do not, in the circumstances, think it necessary
further to subdivide the question. From the answers to these, we can see
whether the Claimant has been allowed his 20% discount but is nevertheless trying to make some money out of the present claim. It would, of
course, be possible for us to ask, as an alternative to the last sub-question:

>   (c)   Has the Claimant received any discount or other
>   bonus from Makerprofit Ltd in respect of the said goods?
>   If so, what was the value of the same?

but I think that the information will be more clearly obtained in the first
manner. So to recapitulate:

IN THE AVARICIOUS COUNTY COURT   Case No. AV990000

BETWEEN:

Mr HERMUNCULUS COSH

Claimant

— and —

Mr THEOBALD SNOOT

Defendant

REQUEST FOR FURTHER INFORMATION ABOUT
THE CLAIMANT'S CASE

8878878787878787878787878787878878878888878887878878887878878878788878878888788887887888778878878787888878788878788878888788878787878778878888887888888788788788878788788878887888787788887788788788788888887888878788787888788888788878787878878787888878888778787878787878

---

1. Is it not the case:

(a) that Hermunculus Cosh received a cheque from the Defendant dated 10th May 2003 in the sum of £1,500?

(b) that Hermunculus Cosh, or some person on his behalf, subsequently presented the cheque and that it was duly met and cleared through the Defendant's bank account on 20th May 2003?

(c) that such sum falls therefore to be deducted from the Claimant's claim against the Defendant?

2. Has the Claimant at any time paid any sums to or for the benefit of Makerprofit Ltd for the goods supplied to the Defendant, in respect of which the present claim is made?

3. If the answer to question 2 above is 'yes':

(a) On what date or dates were such sums paid?

(b) How much was paid on each occasion?

(c) Is any sum presently alleged by Makerprofit Ltd to be outstanding to it in relation to the said goods, and if so how much?

P. LAU-RICE

With a little confidence under our belts, let us now look at a somewhat more complex example in which we act on behalf of the Claimant. I do not propose to analyse it in any great detail, but I hope that an understanding of the facts and an awareness of the imperfections of the statements of case will prompt you to have a go at drafting your own Request, before examining the effort below. If not, see how the questions are designed to exact the maximum assistance from the Defendants, even though our case is by no means without its own difficulties. I shall start by setting out the Particulars of Claim and Defence:

IN THE BOGGLE COUNTY COURT   Case No. BL990000

BETWEEN:

Mrs TRUDY PELLET

Claimant

— and —

ROWEHORNE & Co. (A Firm)

Defendants

PARTICULARS OF CLAIM

---

1.   The Claimant was at all relevant times the wife of Tony Pellet. In about August 1989 the Claimant and her husband jointly purchased 3 Old Soak's Alley, Boggle, Kent (the property). The Claimant and her husband provided a deposit of £1,000 in equal shares. The property was subject to a mortgage in favour of the Boggle Building Society. At all relevant times, the Claimant and her husband occupied the property as the matrimonial home.

2.   The Defendants are and were at all relevant times a firm carrying on business as solicitors. In or about the early part of 2001, the Claimant's husband instructed the Defendants, in the course of their said business, to act on behalf of himself and the Claimant in the sale of the said property to a Mr and Mrs Roller-Blind.

3.   At all relevant times the Defendants knew, alternatively ought to have known, of the Claimant's interest in the said premises, and owed her a duty of care to act on her behalf using all due and proper professional care, skill and judgment.

4.   In breach of the said agreement, and/or negligently, the Defendants caused the said property to be transferred to Mr and Mrs Roller-Blind without due and proper consideration for the Claimant's interest in the same.

PARTICULARS OF NEGLIGENCE

The Defendants were negligent in that:

(1)   Notwithstanding that they owed the Claimant a duty of care to take proper instructions from her and her husband over the sale and transfer of the said property, they failed so to do.

(2)   They signed a contract and exchanged contracts to sell the property on the Claimant's behalf, without obtaining her authority to do so.

(3)   They paid the net proceeds of sale of £50,000 to the order of the Claimant's husband, without obtaining the Claimant's instructions and/or authority to do so.

(4)   They failed to account to the Claimant for the net proceeds of sale.

5.   By reason of the Defendants' said negligence, the Claimant has suffered loss and damage:

PARTICULARS

(1)   The Claimant lost all her legal interest in the net proceeds of sale.

(2)   The Claimant lost security of possession of a matrimonial home for herself and her two children.

(3)   Inconvenience and distress.

6.   The Claimant also claims interest on such damages as may be awarded to her, at such rate and for such period as the Court may deem fit pursuant to section 69 of the County Courts Act 1984.

7.   The value of this action exceeds £15,000.

AND the Claimant claims:

1.   Damages.
2.   Interest as aforesaid.

                                          MARCUS DOWN

Statement of Truth (etc.)

Those of you who have read, absorbed and inwardly digested the earlier chapters of this book may consider, at this stage, that the above is not exactly the finest example of a statement of case that you have ever seen. It is not. However, it is by no means untypical of the quality of drafting with which you may have to deal, and it would be unrealistic invariably to cite perfection. The Defence reads as follows:

IN THE BOGGLE COUNTY COURT   Case No. BL990000

BETWEEN:

                       Mrs TRUDY PELLET
                                                    Claimant

— and —

ROWEHORNE & Co. (A Firm)

<u>Defendants</u>

DEFENCE

---

1.   Save that it is admitted that the property was subject to the said mortgage, no admissions are made as to paragraph 1 of the Particulars of Claim. It is further averred that the property was subject to a second charge in favour of Longshot Bank plc, to secure an overdraft facility to Trudytone Ltd ('the Company') of which the Claimant was a director and company secretary.

2.   It is admitted that in about April 2001 the Defendants received instructions to act in the sale of the property to Mr and Mrs Roller-Blind. Save as aforesaid, no admissions are made as to paragraphs 2 and 3.

3.   It is denied that the Defendants were negligent as alleged by the Claimant in paragraph 4 or at all.

4.   It is denied that the Claimant has suffered the loss and damage alleged and the Claimant is put to strict proof thereof.

5.   Without prejudice to the matters set out above, it is averred that:

(1)   By reason of the first charge to the Boggle Building Society and the second charge to Longshot Bank plc, there was no remaining equity in the property as at the date of sale.

(2)   The Claimant accepted that it was necessary to sell the property in order to clear the debts of the Company and on 6th April 2001 in her capacity as company secretary and director, she resolved jointly with her husband and co-director that the property should be sold to clear the mortgage and to pay the remaining proceeds to Longshot Bank plc.

(3)   Following exchange of contracts on 6th May 2001, the Claimant signed the transfer document enabling the transfer to Mr and Mrs Roller-Blind to take place as of 18th May 2001.

6.   In the circumstances, it is denied that the Claimant is entitled to the relief claimed, or any relief, for the reasons alleged or at all.

HEALEY O'TROPE

Statement of Truth (etc.)

In so far as the facts are not clear from the statements of case, we have the following additional instructions:

> Mrs Pellet married her husband Tony in June 1989. They jointly purchased the matrimonial home.
>
> In 1997, the Pellets set up a company called Trudytone Ltd. The directors were registered as being Mr and Mrs Pellet, together with Mr Pellet's father Percy. Mrs Pellet was also the company secretary. In order to finance the business, the company obtained an overdraft facility of £50,000 from Longshot Bank plc, secured by way of a second charge over the Pellets' property. Mrs Pellet says that she signed the security, but in the general enthusiasm of the venture, she did not really apply her mind to what might happen if the company could not meet its liabilities.
>
> Unfortunately, however, the company (in which Mrs Pellet played no active part) got into difficulties, and by March 2001 the overdraft had been completely taken up, and the bank was calling for a substantial repayment. It had not, however, sought to exercise its security. Mrs Pellet says that she was aware that the company was in trouble, and that in March 2001 she, together with the other directors, attended a meeting with the company accountant, who advised that the company should be put into liquidation and that the house should be sold. Her husband was, however, adamant that he could still save the company, and in view of the fact that Mrs Pellet was most anxious that the property should not be sold, the accountant advised her that she should resign her positions with the company.
>
> Nothing happened for a few days, but Mrs Pellet states that after the meeting her husband said that he was going to draw up a minute of what had been said, so that he could take it to the proposed liquidators, to see if they would support him in his proposed scheme. On the morning of 6th April 2001,

he spoke to his wife at home, and asked her to sign a document, keeping his hands over the wording. Mrs Pellet was also in a hurry to go out, and she signed the document without reading it, understanding it to be her resignation as director and company secretary. Her husband then said he was going over to see the liquidators.

In fact, the document did contain her resignation, but also purported to be a minute of a directors' meeting held that day, which contained a resolution that the property would be sold, and that after clearing the mortgage, the remaining balance would be given to Longshot Bank plc to reduce the company's liability. Mrs Pellet is adamant that she never intended to sign such an agreement, and did not want the property to be sold.

About a week later, Mrs Pellet, by a long-standing appointment, went into hospital for a serious operation, where she remained until 5th May 2001. On 9th May, she was sitting downstairs in the house, when the doorbell rang. It was a Mrs Roller-Blind, who asked if she could have a quick look round, prior to her moving in on 18th May. Mrs Pellet was thunderstruck, and on questioning Mrs Roller-Blind, discovered that contracts had been exchanged the previous day, and completion was due on the 18th.

When Mr Pellet returned home that evening, he found that his dinner was not on the table!!! After a brief but tempestuous scene, he left the property, and the parties have since been divorced.

It transpired that Mr Pellet had put the property on the market without telling his wife, having made enquiries of an agent as far back as February 2001. He had instructed the Defendants to act on behalf of himself and his wife, and had at some later time provided them with the so-called 'minute', in which she had apparently consented to the sale. He then gave the solicitors his written authority on behalf of both of them, to sign the exchange of contracts with the Roller-Blinds and to transfer the balance of the proceeds of sale to Longshot Bank plc, telling them that his wife was seriously ill in hospital, had given written consent to the sale, and did not wish to be disturbed.

At no time until after exchange of contracts was there any contact between the Defendants and Mrs Pellet, who was, to put it mildly, somewhat aggrieved. When she contacted the Defendants she was informed that a binding contract existed, and that she would be best advised to sign the transfer of the property to the Roller-Blinds. In the light of her state of health, she felt she had no alternative but to do so.

Whatever the rights and wrongs of the situation between herself, the company, the bank and her husband, she contends that the solicitors had no business in purporting to act on her behalf without contacting her to ensure that her alleged instructions were correct.

We feel that, whatever the other problems faced by Mrs Pellet, there are grounds for requesting further information from the Defendants, in an attempt to point out to them the weakness of their position on liability.

IN THE BOGGLE COUNTY COURT   Case No. BL990000

BETWEEN:

Mrs TRUDY PELLET

Claimant

— and —

ROWEHORNE & Co. (A Firm)

Defendants

REQUEST FOR FURTHER INFORMATION ABOUT THE DEFENDANT'S CASE

---

1.   Did not the Defendants receive their original instructions to act in the sale of the property to Mr and Mrs Roller-Blind, from Mr Pellet?

2.   Thereafter, and until after exchange of contracts on the sale, did the Defendants not invariably take their instructions from Mr Pellet (whether or not he purported to be acting on behalf of both himself and the Claimant)?

3.   Did the Defendants at any time between receiving their original instructions and exchange of contracts, seek to obtain the personal instructions of the Claimant with regard to the sale of the property?

4.   If the answer to question 3 above is 'yes':
   (a)   Which member or members of the Defendants sought the said instructions?
   (b)   When were such instructions sought?
   (c)   Was the request or were the requests made orally or in writing?
   (d)   If they were in writing, identify the document or documents.
   (e)   If oral, what was the substance of the request or requests?

5.   Did the Defendants not fail at any time between receiving their instructions and exchange of contracts, to obtain personal confirmation from the Claimant that she consented to the sale of the property?

6.   If the answer to question 5 above is 'no':
   (a)   When was such confirmation received?
   (b)   Which member of the Defendants received the alleged confirmation?
   (c)   Was the confirmation made orally or in writing?
   (d)   If it was in writing, identify the document or documents.
   (e)   If it was received orally, what was the substance of the confirmation given?

7.   When did the Defendants first become aware that the property was subject to a second charge in favour of Longshot Bank plc, as set out in paragraph 2 of the Defence?

8.   Which member or members of the Defendants became aware of the second charge?

9.   By what means did the Defendants become aware of the second charge?

10.   When did the Defendants first become aware that the Claimant was a director and company secretary of Trudytone Ltd (the 'Company') as averred in paragraph 1 of the Defence?

11.   Which member or members of the Defendants became aware of the Claimant's position in the company?

12. By what means did the Defendants become aware of the Claimant's position in the company?

13. Did the Defendants not know that the Claimant had resigned her position as a director and company secretary of the company before they received their instructions to act in the sale of the property?

14. If the answer to question 13 above is 'yes':
  (a) When did they first know of the said resignation?
  (b) Which member or members of the Defendants became soaware?
  (c) By what means did they become aware of the said resignation?
  (d) Identify any document or documents which they saw concerning the said resignation.

15. Did the Defendants become aware that the Claimant had allegedly resolved jointly with her husband and co-director that the property should be sold, as averred in paragraph 5(2) of the Defence, before contracts were exchanged for the sale of the same to Mr and Mrs Roller-Blind?

16. If the answer to question 15 above is 'yes':
  (a) When did the Defendants first have knowledge of the alleged resolution?
  (b) Which member or members of the Defendants became soaware?
  (c) By what means did they become so aware?
  (d) Identify any document or documents which were seen by the Defendants concerning the alleged resolution.

17. Is it the Defendants' case that the alleged resolution bound the Claimant in her personal capacity to consent to the sale of the property?

18. Were the Defendants aware at any time prior to the exchange of contracts with Mr and Mrs Roller-Blind, of any requirement by the Boggle Building Society that the property should be sold in order to discharge the first charge set out in paragraph 5(1) of the Defence?

19. If the answer to question 18 above is 'yes':
  (a) When did the Defendants first have knowledge of the alleged requirement?
  (b) Which member or members of the Defendants had the said knowledge?

(c)   By what means did they become so aware?

(d)   Identify any document or documents which were seen by the Defendants concerning the alleged requirement.

20.   Were the Defendants aware at any time prior to the exchange of contracts with Mr and Mrs Roller-Blind, of any requirement by Longshot Bank plc that the property should be sold in order to discharge the second charge set out in paragraph 5(1) of the Defence?

21.   If the answer to question 20 above is 'yes':

(a)   When did the Defendants first have knowledge of the alleged requirement?

(b)   Which member or member of the Defendants had the said knowledge?

(c)   By what means did they become so aware?

(d)   Identify any document or documents which were seen by the Defendants concerning the alleged requirement.

22.   Was not the contract to sell the property signed by a member of the Defendants and not by the Claimant or Mr Pellet?

23.   If the answer to question 22 above is 'yes':

(a)   Was the instruction to sign the contract on behalf of the Claimant and Mr Pellet not received solely from Mr Pellet?

(b)   Which member of the Defendants signed the contract?

24.   What is the exact title and number of the account into which the net proceeds of sale of the property were paid by the Defendants?

25.   Was not the instruction to pay the net proceeds of sale in the manner set out in the answer to question 24 above given by Mr Pellet?

26.   If the answer to question 25 above is 'yes':

(a)   to which member of the Defendants was the instruction to pay the net proceeds of sale given?

(b)   When was the instruction given?

(c)   Was the same made orally or in writing?

(d)   If orally, what was the substance of the instruction given?

(e)   If in writing, identify the document or documents.

SALLY FORTH

If some of the above seems to you rather like 'cross-examination on paper', well, you may not be so far out. See how, for example, the questions have been divided into groups, and that the format of some of the groups is repeated. First, we deal with the fact that it appears that the Defendants did not consult us at all, during the course of ostensibly acting on our behalf. In the knowledge of what the answers to the first 6 questions are likely to be, we can feel reasonably safe in goading the Defendants into admitting that they did not take initial instructions from us, and then compounded the situation. It is most unlikely, according to our instructions, that the third question will be answered in the affirmative, but if it is, it will assist us to know whether the Defendants are calling us a bare-faced liar, or whether they claim to have attempted to make some contact but were unable to do so. In the latter event, of course, we will be interested to know in due course why the Defendants considered it necessary to try to obtain instructions, and then gave up.

The next 3 questions pertain to the Defendants' knowledge of the second charge. Is this something that they knew from the inception, or are they just using this as a form of excuse, notwithstanding their own default? Likewise, questions 10–12 concern their knowledge of our position in the company. If all their information was obtained from our husband, that may be ammunition which we will use later to support our case that the Defendants should have realised the necessity to ensure that he was genuinely acting with our consent.

Questions 13–14 are directed to the Defendants' knowledge of the internal affairs of the company. Taken with questions 15 and 16, it will be interesting and pertinent to discover when, and to what extent, the Defendants became aware of the company's difficulties, and thus the need to sell the property. Bearing in mind that the Claimant allegedly signed the minute in her capacity as a company director, question 17 hints at the fact that perhaps the Defendants should have made enquiry as to whether the document actually amounted to her personal consent as co-owner of the property to the sale.

Questions 18–21 add fuel to the flames, bearing in mind our case that there was no formal call by either the first or second mortgagees for sale of the property. Questions 22 and 23 require admissions from the Defendants that they allowed Mr Pellet alone to give them authority to sign the contract themselves, and the final 3 questions, as a parting shot, ask for explanation of the fact that they allowed the proceeds of sale to be paid out, again on the sole instructions of Mr Pellet. All very embarrassing … we hope!!

As I have said, this case is far from being one-sided, and it may well be that if and when the case ever got to trial, Mrs Pellet would have a deal of trouble explaining her signature on the minutes, and her apparent ignorance of the fact that the property was up for sale. Thus, even if she was successful against the solicitors, it may be shown that no loss has been suffered as a result. However, fortunately, we are not involved in that side of affairs at the moment, and our task has been to maximise our position, and obtain the greatest amount of legitimate information at the cost of the greatest amount of discomfort for our opponent. Just what the job's all about!

You may also have noticed that the form of some of the above questions is not entirely dissimilar to the format of a question requesting further information about a statement of case. Although there is no reason why such questions cannot be intermingled with 'interrogatories', you may find that, in a case where you wish to ask both types of question, it would be wiser to commence with requests dealing with identifiable passages in the statement of case, and then move on to more specific questions. It is, of course, a matter of style, and therefore entirely up to you.

Chapter Seven

'Just to Let You Know ...' (The Answer to a Request for Further Information)

'I'm afraid I can't put it more clearly',
Alice replied, very politely, 'for I can't
understand it myself, to begin with.'

Once you receive a Request for Further Information, you must of course give consideration to answering it. I use my words advisedly, as it does not necessarily follow that you are obliged to respond merely because you have been served with a Request. If the Request is for matters to which the other side is not entitled, or is disproportionate to the case, it is usually advisable not to provide the particulars.

However, should you decide that the Request, or any part of it, is not a proper one, it is nevertheless not considered polite merely to sit back and do nothing. Now it is true that the other side may, in the absence of any response, make an application to the Court for an order that you give the information, with all sorts of horrible sanctions in default. You can always defend this application on the basis that the Request is improper, and that you should not be obliged to give an answer thereto. On the other hand, there seems no reason why the alleged impropriety of the Request could not have been communicated to the other side in any event, merely by a formal refusal to give an answer to that part, or all, of the Request that you find offensive. Should they then wish to take the matter further, you have made your position clear at all times, and would not be subject to criticism for having failed to make any response. Put another way, your credibility is enhanced by coming clean about your position, and there seems no advantage in doing otherwise.

Sometimes being on the receiving end of a proper Request for Further Information may be an indication that we have not done our job properly in the first place. In other cases it may well have been that full information was not available for some reason at the time of drafting the statement of case, and that there was some compelling reason for going ahead with it in any event. This, I suggest, is unlikely under the CPR. Whatever the reason, it is a natural (and not improper) response to be as parsimonious with the Further Information as is compatible with our professional duty and the rules of drafting. As in all theory, there is room for the honourable exception, but the basic premise still holds good.

The answer itself need not be in the full and formal sentences necessary in a statement of case. If the Request can be answered in one word, so be it. Although (or possibly because) the answer becomes part of the statement of case, it is necessary to ensure only that a proper answer is given to a proper Request. For example, in response to a typical Request:

> Under paragraph 1
> Of: 'By an agreement made on 2nd April 2005 ...'

> Please state whether it is alleged that the said agreement was made orally or in writing; if orally, state where the same was allegedly made, the parties to the agreement, and the gist of all words spoken; if in writing, give the same particulars with the necessary changes, identifying any document or documents which it is alleged formed or evidenced the agreement, and attach a copy of such documents to the answer.

We could respond:

> Orally, at the Defendant's house, between Mr Surtees for the Claimants and the Defendant in person. The Defendant asked how much the Claimants would charge for rebuilding his wall, and Mr Surtees replied £1,000. The parties then came to the agreement set out in paragraph 1 of the Particulars of Claim.

It is not therefore necessary to make any specific averment as to the written documents, as by implication they do not exist. Were the Request to have been written as follows:

> Please state:
>
> 1.   Whether the said agreement was made orally or in writing.
>
> 2.   If orally, giving particulars:
>   (a)   of the place where made;
>   (b)   the parties thereto;
>   (c)   the gist of all words spoken.
>
> 3.   If in writing, give particulars:
>   (a)   as in question 2 above;
>   (b)   and identify the document(s) which it is alleged formed or evidenced the agreement, and attach a copy of such documents to the answer.

We could reply:

> 1. Orally.
>
> 2. (a)   At the Defendant's home;
>
> 2. (b)   Mr Surtees for the Claimants, and the Defendant in person;
>
> 2. (c)   The Defendant asked Mr Surtees to quote the Claimants' price for rebuilding his wall. Mr Surtees quoted £1,000, whereupon the parties came to the agreement set out in paragraph 1 of the Particulars of Claim.
>
> 3. Not applicable.

In the latter example, a specific response was given to question 3, simply because there was no other way in which it could be covered without doing so. There is nothing wrong with this.

Although the format and content of Further Information may not be the most intellectually demanding of disciplines, there are some tactical advantages that can be gained from skilful use of this medium.

Obviously there are 'points to be scored' from a tactful (or sometimes not too tactful!) pointing out that your opponent is not entitled to the information requested, or that he has got the wrong end of the stick, or that the matter has been sufficiently set out, or that, were he to look at paragraph 14, he would find the answer to his problems. There are several ways in which you can indicate that your opponent should merrily go about his way without further interference from your good self. The golden rule is to make sure that he is **not** entitled to his Request, or you'll end up looking a lot less cocky in front of the District Judge — with costs!

'… your opponent should merrily go about his way…'

One way in which a withering retort can rock you to the marrow is the exploitation of a defect in your Request when you have tried to be too clever by half! This happened to me several years ago, as I shall now illustrate. I cannot remember the facts of the case (I have tried ever so hard to forget!) but my jumped-up Request, written under the old rules, went along the following lines:

Under paragraph 3
Of: (whatever it was)…

State whether it is the Plaintiff's case that the said agreement was made at the Defendant's premises; if so, further state whether the same was made orally or in writing; if orally, give the date and time thereof, the parties thereto, and the gist of all words spoken; if in writing, give the like particulars *mutatis mutandis*, together with full particulars of each and every document relied upon in support.

A grand piece of legal flatulence! The answer, when it arrived, went as follows:

No.

I felt devastated! However, my opponent had done no more than respond accurately to a perfectly proper Request. It was not the Plaintiff's case that the agreement took place on the Defendant's premises, and as a result the remainder of the paragraph was utterly irrelevant. A large point scored against my own self-importance (and flabby drafting), and a big lesson learned.

The layout of your Further Information is provided for in the Rules, and you should not deviate from this. Look at CPR Part 18 (it should take you all of 10 seconds!) and its associated Practice Direction (which will take slightly longer), and it is all there set out for you.

I do not think it necessary to burden you with a large number of examples, but it may be useful to trace through the Request for Further Information in the case of *Turnonn Ltd* v *Thunder Engineering*, from the last chapter, although I will add one or two 'extras' for the purposes of illustrating certain types of answer and showing how it is possible to 'mix' questions of both types in the same Request. This time, we are again, of course, acting on behalf of the Claimants, in answering the Request for Further Information about the Particulars of Claim:

IN THE HIGH COURT OF JUSTICE   2006 T No. 0000
QUEEN'S BENCH DIVISION

BETWEEN:

TURNONN LIMITED

Claimants

— and —

THUNDER ENGINEERING LIMITED

Defendants

REQUEST FOR FURTHER INFORMATION ABOUT
THE PARTICULARS OF CLAIM

Under paragraph 3
Of: 'There were, amongst others, the following express or implied terms
of the said agreement:'

Please state with the necessary changes in relation to each sub-paragraph
thereafter set out:

1.   Whether the said term is alleged to be express or implied; if express
giving particulars of the gist of all words spoken which it is alleged gave
rise to the same; if implied, giving full particulars of the grounds upon
which the said allegation is made.

Under paragraph 6
Of: 'In order to assist the Defendants to conduct the necessary pre-
commissioning checks ...'

2.   Please state:

    (a)   Whether it is the Claimants' case that it was at any time agreed
between the parties that the said check sheets would be supplied by them to
the Defendants, and if so, give full particulars of when and between whom
it is alleged that the same was so agreed, and the gist of all words spoken;

    (b)   Whether it is alleged that the said check sheets were at any time
requested by the Defendants, and if so, give the same particulars with the
necessary changes as requested in Request 2(a).

Under paragraph 7
Of: '(a) caused the Claimants to suffer excessive and unreasonable delay in
commencing, and thereafter carrying out the said works of commissioning;'

3.   Please specify the delay in each case allegedly suffered by the
Claimants.

Of: '(b) failed on repeated occasions to ensure that the said systems were
completely installed ...'

4.   Please identify each occasion upon which the Defendants allegedly failed to ensure that the systems were completely installed, and in respect of each system, state the failures complained of.

Of: '(c) failed adequately or at all on numerous occasions properly to conduct the necessary pre-commissioning checks ...'

5.   Please state:

(a)   each such occasion alleged;
(b)   the necessary pre-commissioning check required on each occasion.

Of: '(d) failed on repeated occasions to ensure that the said systems were in a proper state for works of commissioning to be carried out.'

6.   Please state in respect of each occasion when that system was not in a proper state for works of commissioning to be carried out.

Under paragraph 8
Of: '(2) The failure of the Defendants adequately or at all to ensure that the said systems were totally free of all foreign matter prior to commissioning.'

7.   Please state:

(a)   each occasion and each system which was not free from foreign matter;
(b)   the foreign matter relied upon on each occasion.

SALLY FORTH

The first thing we must do in respect of each question, is to decide whether or not it requests information to which the other side is entitled. Even if we are not convinced that the question is a proper one, it is occasionally possible that we may wish to answer it in any event, if we can score a suitably telling point.

Once we have decided to give an answer, we must then decide the manner in which it should be expressed. For example, do we wish to be monosyllabic or expansive. This may to a certain extent depend on our ability to answer the question. There are occasions where we may simply not have the information, possibly due to weaknesses in our case, or deficiencies in recollection, and we must then look upon our answer as being an exercise in damage limitation. This in fact may well have to be our approach to the first question, as we simply do not know the answer. Let us recall our instructions from previous chapters:

> The oral agreement in September 2004 was preceded by negotiations in which the Claimants originally quoted just over £102,000 to perform the full commissioning works. The ultimate quote of £78,450.00 was given on the basis that the Defendants would perform all necessary installation and pre-commissioning, and that the Claimants would not supervise or give advice as they would in normal circumstances.
>
> The negotiations were concluded between Mr Tapp of the Claimants and Mr Thunder of the Defendants. The date, place and gist of the conversation in which the agreement was concluded were, as required by the Rules, set out in the Particulars of Claim.

Now let us look at the various requests for Further Information, and see how we should approach them.

Paragraph 3
This provides a useful example of how to answer a question which is 'rolled up', as it requests the same information in respect of a number of sub-paragraphs. The paragraph in question alleges four express or implied terms of the agreement, and it will clearly be preferable if we can set out our answer in a form which refers easily and directly to each allegation.

The questions require information as to the gist of all words spoken in the event of an alleged express term, or the grounds upon which implied terms are alleged. These are of course, matters of law, and although the Rules do permit us to expand on any points of law that we may wish to raise at the hearing, I consider that it is not necessary in the present circumstances to do any more than state the general principle that will be relied on — after all, we are hardly going to be breaking any new legal territory, or stun the Court (or the other side) with the genius of our legal inventiveness!

Before answering the individual questions, however, we may wish to be alive to the possibility of refusing certain information as to words spoken if we consider that the nature and extent of our allegation have been sufficiently set out. For example, since the effect of our allegation has been that a telephone conversation took place between Mr Tapp and Mr Thunder in the course of which an agreement took place, and that one of the terms expressly agreed was that the works would be carried out on a date to be agreed, one wonders what possible additional further information can be given of the conversation without descending to matters which are purely evidence. We shall bear this in mind.

In so far as the layout of this answer is concerned, I suggest we should do as follows:

> ANSWER
> Under paragraph 3(a)
>
> [Answer]
> Under paragraph 3(b)
>
> [Answer]
> etc.

This ensures that the Judge will be able immediately to refer the answer to the sub-paragraph in question, even though this has not been made clear in the Request itself. Now let us deal with the questions themselves.

3.   (a)   That the commissioning works would be carried out on a date to be agreed between the parties
It is clear that this was an express agreement between the parties. It is also clear that the works could only have been carried out once the installation (at the very least) had been completed, and this date would almost certainly not have been known at the date of the agreement. We are asked to set out the gist of all words spoken giving rise to the alleged term. Of course, we have not so far expressly set out the fact that the Defendants had agreed to accept a limited service from the Claimants in view of their reduced price for carrying out the commissioning works, and now it seems appropriate to set this out, in order that our case is clear.

The above will, of course, be enough to enable us to draft our answer. However, the question does enable us to take another 'swipe' at the other side. Our case is that not merely was there an express agreement to start the works at a later date, **but that such was a matter of common sense in the light of the circumstances**. Put another way, it would be normal practice to incorporate a term of this nature in view of the usual difficulties in estimating a precise date upon which the works would have been completed. There seems to me to be no reason whatsoever why our answer cannot be reinforced by the inclusion of this last matter. It is by no means essential, but it is perfectly proper to do so, and it colours the picture in our favour.

3.   (b)   That the systems would be fully and competently installed by the Defendants prior to the Claimants commencing the works
The fact that they should be fully installed was, of course, part of the express agreement. The question of their being competently installed was not mentioned, but must, we say, be by necessary implication or implied in the interests of business efficacy.

3.   (c)   That the Defendants would ensure that all water systems were totally free from all foreign matter prior to the start of commissioning works
This is in the nature of pre-commissioning and therefore express, and implied by necessity or business efficacy.

3.   (d)   That the Defendants would conduct all necessary pre-commissioning checks
On our case, this was expressly agreed, in consideration of our accepting a reduced price for the contract.

Have a go yourself at drafting the answer. It is not really very difficult; as ever, my version is set out below:

ANSWER

Under paragraph 3(a)
In the course of the said telephone conversation, it was agreed that the Claimants would perform the said commissioning for the sum of £78,450 rather than their original quotation of £102,000, the reason for this being that the Defendants indicated that they were seeking only a limited service from the Claimants, and would carry out all works of installation and pre-commissioning themselves, and would further not seek the Claimants' advice and assistance in relation thereto. The said term was expressly agreed in the course of the said conversation, and was necessary in view of the difficulty in estimating the progress to be made on site prior to the said works of commissioning being necessary.

Under paragraph 3(b)
It was expressly agreed that the Defendants would carry out
the installation of the said systems. The Claimants repeat
the information set out in the answer to 3(a) above. It was
implied that the Defendants would carry out the same in
a competent manner, the same being by necessary implication and/or in order to give business efficacy to the said
agreement.

Under paragraph 3(c)
The works alleged therein are comprised in pre-commissioning
checks and were expressly agreed between the parties. The
Claimants repeat the information set out in the answer to
3(a) above.

Under paragraph 3(d)
The Claimants repeat the information set out in the answer
to 3(c) above.

I have deliberately incorporated a variety of different techniques in the
above answers in order to illustrate the way in which one can avoid
unnecessary and prolix repetition of the case, by reference to previous
answers.

It is only in paragraph 3(a) that I have made any specific reference to
the contents of the telephone conversation. The remaining answers are
accomplished by reference to that information. In 3(d), it is clear that the
answer is going to be identical (or almost identical) to the previous
answer, and there is thus little point in repeating it.

Although this is not particularly so in the present case, there are times
when it is tactically advantageous continually to refer the other side back
either to previous answers or to the original statement of case. This can carry
the implication that the Request for Further Information is unnecessary or
repetitious, or even that the other side may not fully understand the
weaknesses of its own case.

Paragraph 6

You may recall that in the previous chapter I considered this request
to be unnecessary. However, I have included it in this chapter for the
purposes of demonstrating ways in which it can be answered. Remember,
of course, that in the previous chapter we were considering matters from
the **Defendants'** point of view. Here we are doing the opposite.

Our case is that there was no agreement to send our standard check sheets to the Defendants, but that we did so in order to facilitate their carrying out the necessary pre-commissioning checks which we say they agreed to do. The requests for Further Information are clearly aimed at embarrassing us into revealing that there was no agreement to send the check sheets, with the implication that there was thus no agreement that the Defendants would perform any works of pre-commissioning. It is, of course, important for us, wherever possible, to understand the other side's reasons for making any particular request, in order that we can prepare our answer to our best advantage.

Here, we have to weigh up a number of possibilities. We could be 'smart' and answer the questions in monosyllables, along the lines that so embarrassed me all those years ago! However, the drawback to that in the present case is that a mere denial would give rise to the question why we **did** supply the check sheets. The Defendants' objectives would thus have been achieved. We must therefore seek to angle our answer in a positive manner, and so as to avoid falling into the above trap. I propose to do this by means of a restatement of our case, even if this has not specifically been asked. However, I will not pass up the opportunity to have a bash at the first question:

> (a)   Whether it is the Claimants' case that it was at any time agreed between the parties that the said check sheets would be supplied by them to the Defendants, and if so, give full particulars of when and between whom it is alleged that the same was so agreed, and the gist of all words spoken;

> ANSWER
> No.

Of course, you could (and possibly should) be more polite and put:

> It is not the Claimants' case that it was agreed that they should supply the said check sheets to the Defendants;

although it would stick in my craw to do so!

> (b)   Whether it is alleged that the said check sheets were at any time requested by the Defendants, and if so, giving the like particulars with the necessary changes as requested in Request 2(a).

ANSWER
The same is not so alleged. The Claimants repeat that it was
the Defendants' responsibility to carry out the said checks,
and that the Claimants merely sent the said check sheets by
way of courtesy, and in order to assist them in so doing.

In this way, we have gently but firmly restated our position, and have not
lost any 'face' by virtue of our denials.

Paragraph 7
Essentially this Request wishes particulars of:

All delays allegedly suffered by the Claimants;
All alleged acts of failure by the Defendants to ensure that the systems
were properly installed;
All alleged acts of failure by the Defendants to conduct the necessary
pre-commissioning checks;
All occasions on which it is alleged that the system was not in a proper
state for commissioning works to be carried out.

Now there is no doubt that these are important matters, of which the
Defendants are entitled to particulars. Clearly, to set them out here will
involve a very detailed and involved schedule. If this has to be done, so
be it. We cannot evade our responsibilities merely because it may
involve a lot of work.
   On the other hand, not merely have we already set out certain information in paragraph 7 of the Particulars of Claim, but in sub-paragraph 3
we have alleged that the information now being requested was contained
in various site reports, which were supplied to the Defendants on site.
That having been the case, there is no reason whatsoever to repeat those
matters again by way of Further Information. We have not so far received
any indication of any denial by the Defendants that they received the site
reports, and could, of course, supply further copies were we to be
requested. However, the point of a statement of case is to ensure that the
Defendants are aware of the particulars of the case against them, and
these have already been supplied.

We shall tell them to get lost!

We can do this in a number of ways. The first is by a simple:

   Not entitled.

Alternatively we can put:

> Sufficiently set out.

These phrases have a certain elegant simplicity and may be employed if we wish to be particularly dismissive of a badly drafted Request. Should we wish to be more polite, we can of course put:

> The matter has been sufficiently set out in the Particulars of
> Claim;

or some other fancy words to the same effect. However, in the present case, we should perhaps make our point a little more firmly. I would again do this by reference to matters already set out, and a formal restatement of our case:

> The above matters have been sufficiently set out in paragraph 7
> of the Particulars of Claim. The Claimants repeat the infor-
> mation therein, and in particular sub-paragraph 3 thereof.

The use of this style of response should be appropriately dismissive in the circumstances.

Paragraph 8
This is another irrelevant request, and I have included it only in order to illustrate again the way in which one can deal with an irrelevance by reference to a previous answer. There is also a rare opportunity to indulge in a bit of fun at the other side's expense, although this should be done only sparingly!
    The first part of the question is easy. The answer is identical to the previous question:

> Please see the previous answer.

That is all you need to do.
    The next question is positively mind-boggling. Is an answer seriously expected? In the light of instructions we can put:

> Dirt and dust of a nature normally associated with such
> installation, and which the Claimants have not (and do not
> intend to have) analysed.

I include the above merely as an illustration of the flexibility with which it is possible to approach answers to a Request for Further Information, and not as any encouragement to be flippant. Always be careful, it may be the other side's case that the systems were clogged by one of our workmen's gloves being dropped in a duct!

Here, therefore, is the final layout:

IN THE HIGH COURT OF JUSTICE   2006 T No. 0000
QUEEN'S BENCH DIVISION

BETWEEN:

TURNONN LIMITED

Claimants

— and —

THUNDER ENGINEERING LIMITED

Defendants

FURTHER INFORMATION ABOUT THE PARTICULARS
OF CLAIM SERVED PURSUANT TO A REQUEST DATED [date]

Under paragraph 3
Of: 'There were, amongst others, the following express or implied terms of the said agreement:'

Please state with the necessary changes in relation to each sub-paragraph thereafter set out:

1.   Whether the said term is alleged to be express or implied; if express giving particulars of the gist of all words spoken which it is alleged gave rise to the same; if implied, giving full particulars of the grounds upon which the said allegation is made.

ANSWER
1.
Under paragraph 3(a)
In the course of the said telephone conversation, it was agreed that the Claimants would perform the said commissioning for the sum of £78,450 rather than their original quotation of £102,000, the reason for

this being that the Defendants indicated that they were seeking only a limited service from the Claimants, and would carry out all works of installation and pre-commissioning themselves, and would further not seek the Claimants' advice and assistance in relation thereto. The said term was expressly agreed in the course of the said conversation, and was necessary in view of the difficulty in estimating the progress to be made on site prior to the said works of commissioning being necessary.

Under paragraph 3(b)
It was expressly agreed that the Defendants would carry out the installation of the said systems. The Claimants repeat the information set out in the answer to 3(a) above. It was implied that the Defendants would carry out the same in a competent manner, the same being by necessary implication and/or in order to give business efficacy to the said agreement.

Under paragraph 3(c)
The works alleged therein are comprised in pre-commissioning checks and were expressly agreed between the parties. The Claimants repeat the information set out in the answer to 3(a) above.

Under paragraph 3(d)
The Claimants repeat the information set out in the answer to 3(c) above.

Under paragraph 6
Of: 'In order to assist the Defendants to conduct the necessary pre-commissioning checks.

2.   Please state:
   (a)   Whether it is the Claimants' case that it was at any time agreed between the parties that the said check sheets would be supplied by them to the Defendants, and if so, give full particulars of when and between whom it is alleged that the same was so agreed, and the gist of all words spoken;
   (b)   Whether it is alleged that the said check sheets were at any time requested by the Defendants, and if so, giving the like particulars with the necessary changes as requested in Request 2(a).

ANSWER
2. (a)   No.
2. (b)   The same is not so alleged. The Claimants repeat that it was the Defendants' responsibility to carry out the said checks, and that the

Claimants merely sent the said check sheets by way of courtesy, and in order to assist them in so doing.

Under paragraph 7
Of: '(a) caused the Claimants to suffer excessive and unreasonable delay in commencing, and thereafter carrying out the said works of commissioning;'

3. Please specify the delay in each case allegedly suffered by the Claimants.

Of: '(b) failed on repeated occasions to ensure that the said systems were completely installed ...'

4. Please identify each occasion upon which the Defendants allegedly failed to ensure that the systems were completely installed, and in respect of each system, state the failures complained of.

Of: '(c) failed adequately or at all on numerous occasions properly to conduct the necessary pre-commissioning checks ...'

5. Please state:
    (a)   each such occasion alleged;
    (b)   the necessary pre-commissioning check required on each occasion.

Of: '(d) failed on repeated occasions to ensure that the said systems were in a proper state for works of commissioning to be carried out.'

6. Please state in respect of each occasion when that system was not in a proper state for works of commissioning to be carried out.

ANSWER Questions 3, 4, 5 and 6
The above matters have been sufficiently set out in paragraph 7 of the Particulars of Claim. The Claimants repeat the information therein, and in particular sub-paragraph 3 thereof.

Under paragraph 8
Of: '(2) The failure of the Defendants adequately or at all to ensure that the said systems were totally free of all foreign matter prior to commissioning.'

7.   Please state:

(a)   each occasion and each system which was not free from foreign matter;

(b)   the foreign matter relied upon on each occasion.

ANSWER

7. (a)   Please see the previous answer.

7. (b)   Dirt and dust of a nature normally associated with such installation, and which the Claimants have not (and do not intend to have) analysed.

                                                                          P. NUTBUTTER

Statement of Truth (etc.)

(Remember, the information supplied forms part of a statement of case, and therefore your answer (but not the Request for Further Information itself) must contain a Statement of Truth.)

As I indicated earlier, this has not perhaps been the most intellectually demanding of chapters. On the other hand, it is important to appreciate that the techniques of replying to a Request for Further Information are somewhat different from those employed in other statements of case, and some illustration of these techniques has been shown above.

We have now been through most of the basic statements of case and documents which you will find in an ordinary action. The rest of this book will be concerned with other disciplines which you will come across from time to time. There is also a chapter each on affidavits and witness statements, drafting Orders, the skeleton argument, and a short chapter on writing opinions. By and large, I do not propose to treat the following matters in quite the same degree of depth, as the basic techniques of drafting still hold good for all of them. Each document or statement of case does, however, have its own characteristics and peculiarities, and it is these on which I will mainly concentrate.

Chapter Eight

Come and Join In
(Additional Claims Against
Third Parties)

'See how eagerly the lobsters and the
turtles all advance!
They are waiting on the shingle — will
you come and join the dance?'

The Additional Claim (formerly known as the 'Part 20 claim' is, amongst other things, a procedural device, whereby a Defendant to a claim can bring an action against someone else in respect of the subject matter of the claim, without having to go to the trouble and expense of instituting fresh proceedings. As this is a book on drafting, I shall not concentrate on the procedural aspects of the Additional Claim, but you should be aware of the basic situations in which one may arise.

Most commonly, your client may be served with proceedings to which he may or may not have a defence, but in any event claims that someone else is wholly or partially to blame for the matters complained of. In other words, even if your client is held liable to the Claimant, he claims to be entitled to slough off all or part of that liability onto someone who got him into the mess in the first place. A common situation is when your client claims to have incurred liability (if he has) as a result of something said or done by the Third Party, on which he has relied.

In such circumstances it is normally (but not invariably) desirable that all issues between all parties should be thrashed out in the same proceedings. The Claimant will pursue his remedy against the Defendant; and in the event of liability being established, the Defendant will pursue his claim for an indemnity or a contribution from the Third Party, depending on the circumstances.

A less common but still valid use of the procedure is when your client may wish to claim some remedy or relief against a third person connected with the subject matter of the claim, even though his claim does not depend for its success on the Claimant being able to prove liability against him. Sometimes there are questions or issues which need to be determined, rather than remedies or relief. The principle is nevertheless broadly the same.

The Additional Claim is commenced on Form N211. I shall assume, for the purposes of this work, that the Particulars of Claim will be drafted as a separate document and not endorsed on the Form. The Rules also provide that a copy of all other statements of case in the action should be served with the Additional Claim.

Form N211 contains detailed guidance notes, including 'notes for defendant', which include a warning of the dreadful tortures and other nasties which will be inflicted upon him in the event of his failing, within 14 days, to reply to the claim (essentially he will be deemed to have admitted that claim against him)! I shall therefore concentrate on the most common type of Additional Claim, in which we will claim for an indemnity or a contribution.

A few words about style. In all our previous attempts at drafting a statement of case, we have kept to the tradition of setting out our claim in the third person, i.e.: 'On 17th June 2005 the Claimant was walking along Buttercup Road, London SW44 when he was bitten by a Yorkshire Terrier dog owned by the Defendant', etc. Normally, that presents no problems. However, the situation becomes more complicated where there is a multiplicity of parties, each of whom may have more than one status in the action. This is recognised in the CPR by the provision (in the accompanying Practice Direction) that where there are fourth or subsequent parties, additional parties should be referred to in the text of statements of case or other similar documents by name, suitably abbreviated if appropriate. Since April 2006 the rules as to the naming and status of parties have (thank heavens!) been considerably simplified.

When the CPR were originally brought out, all 'third party' claims were to be known as 'Part 20 claims', with the Defendant bringing the action being called the 'Part 20 claimant' and the Third Party being called the 'Part 20 Defendant'. To make matters worse, all parties had to have their full status reflected (at least for the first time) in their title, so that, to take a perfectly horrible example, it was (technically) possible to have:

IN THE PIED WAGTAIL COUNTY COURT   Case No. 02445566

BETWEEN:

BORIS OLAF PABLO-ESTERHAZY-ARCHIBALD-PLOTNIK
Claimant and Part 20 Defendant (2nd Claim)

— and —

THE PERPETUAL MOTION EXPLORATION COMPANY LIMITED
Defendant and Part 20 Claimant (1st Claim)

— and —

HAZEL WITHERSPOON
(Trading as Witherspoon and Co., (a firm))
Part 20 Defendant (1st Claim) and Part 20 Claimant (2nd Claim)

— and —

HUBERT KARAOKE
Part 20 Defendant (2nd Claim)

Since April 2006, however, the basic rule is that when there are Additional Claims which add parties, the title to the proceedings should comprise a list of all parties, describing each by giving them a single identification, which should be used throughout. Claimants and Defendants in the original claim should always be referred to as such in the title, even if they subsequently acquire an additional procedural status. Additional parties should be referred to in the title in accordance with the order in which they are joined to the proceedings, e.g. 'Third Party' or 'Fourth Party', whatever their actual procedural status. If proceedings are brought against additional parties jointly, they should be named 'First Named Third Party' etc., accordingly. In the case of group litigation, the Court should give directions as to the designation of parties.

It should be clear that this ought to lead to a great deal less confusion.
The title to the above action would now read:

IN THE PIED WAGTAIL COUNTY COURT   Case No. 02445566

BETWEEN:

Mr BORIS OLAF PABLO-ESTERHAZY-ARCHIBALD-PLOTNIK
Claimant

— and —

THE PERPETUAL MOTION EXPLORATION COMPANY LIMITED
Defendant

— and —

Mrs HAZEL WITHERSPOON
(Trading as Witherspoon and Co., (a firm))
Third Party

— and —

Mr HUBERT KARAOKE
Fourth Party

and the matter can proceed from there, with the precise roles of the
parties being reflected in the text of the statement of case.

Now, let us assume that we have the privilege and pleasure of acting
for Mrs Witherspoon, and that we are about to draft her Fourth Party
claim against the hapless Mr Karaoke. Even here it can be seen that the
continued description of the parties by their status in a statement of case
could lead to confusion, and that using some common sense, and a judicious application of the rules, it would be possible to commence our
masterpiece thus:

1. For the purposes of clarity, the following abbreviations
will be used in this Additional Claim:

The Claimant will be referred to as 'BOPEAP';
The Defendant will be referred to as 'Perpetual';

The Third Party will be referred to as 'Mrs Witherspoon' or 'Witherspoon and Co.,' as the context requires;
The Fourth Party will be referred to as 'Mr Karaoke'.

2. At all relevant times, Mrs Witherspoon carried on business as a supplier of musical instruments, trading under the name of 'Witherspoon and Co.'.

3. By a written agreement dated 2nd February 2005 (a copy of which is attached to this claim), and made between Mrs Witherspoon and Mr Karaoke, Mrs Witherspoon agreed to supply Mr Karaoke with an 'Orpheus' pipe chamber organ, at a price of £24,750.

This will, in the majority of cases, solve the problem and lead to a clear exposition of what is intended. However, in a case where there is a relatively straightforward claim for an indemnity or contribution against a third party, I would suggest that it would be appropriate to use the format favoured before the CPR, in which the use of names and titles can be avoided by addressing the claim in the personal rather than impersonal mode, thus:

IN THE MARTLE COUNTY COURT   Case No. 02 23232

BETWEEN:

Mr ALAN SHARPE

Claimant

— and —

Mr CYRIL CUTTS

Defendant

— and —

Mr IVOR POUND

Third Party

DEFENDANT'S ADDITIONAL CLAIM AGAINST THE
THIRD PARTY

---

1. At all relevant times, you carried on business as an investment adviser.

2. In the course of a telephone conversation between Mr Cutts and yourself, on 3rd May 2005, you agreed, in the course of your business, and in consideration of a fee of £750, to investigate the potential of an business investment opportunity being proposed by the Claimant to Mr Cutts, and to advise Mr Cutts as to the viability of the proposed enterprise, and as to the amount (if any) of money that he should invest therein.

etc.

I have straightaway to confess that there is no express provision in the Practice Direction for the use of this format. However, at the end of the day, the aim is to be clear and succinct, and I consider that these worthy objectives are achieved in the above example. The emphasis of the CPR is on the substance rather than the form, and I am pretty confident that you would not be the subject of judicial criticism for drafting your case in this way.

Once you have settled on your approach, there is nothing in this form of drafting that is any different from a standard Particulars of Claim. I propose therefore to depart from my normal practice of analysing every paragraph of the following example, but will merely postulate a set of facts, and demonstrate the way in which these could be incorporated into an Additional Claim.

EXAMPLE

We act for Fallow Fruiterers Ltd who have been carrying on business for a fairly short time as wholesale suppliers of fruit trees. The Company was in the process of building up a good business supplying trees to smallholders.

In April 2004, Mr Fallow was approached by a Mrs Pippin, who was intending to plant a considerable number of pear trees in order to sell the produce to local market traders. She required 5,000 late-flowering pear trees, and asked Mr Fallow to recommend a variety. She stated that she was starting her own business and, provided that the first order was successful, hoped to have a long and profitable relationship with Fallow Fruiterers Ltd.

Mr Fallow therefore telephoned Mr Comice of Pearadventure Orchards Ltd with whom he had done a little business, having opened an account some months earlier. He explained the situation and asked for a recommendation. He also let it be known that the trees were for a very important customer, who had a lot of future business, and that it would be in everyone's interests for the best possible service to be given. Mr Comice said that he had no hesitation in recommending a variety known as Passe Crassane as being 'very sweet, late-flowering', and as a result Mr Fallow recommended the variety to Mrs Pippin who ordered 5,000 at a total cost of £64,750.

The trees were duly supplied by Pearadventure Orchards Ltd to Fallow Fruiterers Ltd at a price of £40,500, and then to Mrs Pippin, who paid the purchase price, and planted the trees.

In August 2005, Mrs Pippin came in to see Mr Fallow and informed him that Passe Crassane were an early-flowering variety of pear, and that she had therefore planted the trees at the wrong time and given them the wrong treatment, as a result of which they had all died.

Furthermore, she had entered into a contract with the local market trading organisation which she had been unable to keep, and had thus lost profit on her outlay. At the end of August, Fallow Fruiterers were served with proceedings claiming damages totalling £62,000.

At this point I suspect that all those of you who know far more about fruit trees than do I, may be saying that it would be impossible for the trees to have died merely because they were planted at the wrong time. That may well be the case! I have made this example up, and I shall tell you here and now that Fallow Fruiterers Ltd intend to contest at least that part of the action as claims damages in this regard, on the basis that the trees died as a result of the Claimant's own lack of care and/or expertise. That need not concern us here (or tax my imagination any further). If you fancy drafting Particulars of Claim and/or a Defence thereto, please do not let me stop you!

Although Fallow Fruiterers Ltd intend to contest part of the action on the basis that the Claimant herself was to blame for the loss of the fruit trees, the company wishes to bring an action against Pearadventure Orchards Ltd on the basis that they had relied on Pearadventure's skill and judgment in purchasing the trees, and that Pearadventure knew the purposes for which they were to be supplied and the likely loss that would

be incurred in the event of any breach of contract and/or
duty of care by them.

Exercising your own skill and judgment for a moment, it may come as
no surprise to discover that this part of the action will be commenced by
way of an Additional Claim.

IN THE HIGH COURT OF JUSTICE   Case No. 0000
QUEEN'S BENCH DIVISION—

BETWEEN:

Mrs PAULA PIPPIN

Claimant

— and —

FALLOW FRUITERERS LIMITED

Defendants

— and —

PEARADVENTURE ORCHARDS LIMITED

Third Party

DEFENDANTS' ADDITIONAL PARTICULARS OF CLAIM
AGAINST THE THIRD PARTY

---

1.   In her claim against the Defendants, the Claimant claims
damages together with interest, for alleged breach of contract
and/or misrepresentation. A copy of the Claim Form and
Particulars of Claim, and the Defendants' Defence thereto,
are attached to this Particulars of Claim against yourselves.

I have not wasted time and space by including the Particulars of Claim
and our Defence with this example (they are basically irrelevant for our
purposes), but remember that **every** statement of case which has already
been served in the proceedings must accompany the Additional Claim
form when it is served. As the full case and defence should (one hopes)

be obvious from the Particulars of Claim and the Defence, I have therefore not considered it necessary here to set out more than a basic summary of what is being alleged against the Defendants.

> 2. If, contrary to their Defence, the Defendants are held
> liable to the Claimant, they claim against you to be indem-
> nified in respect of the Claimant's claim, or a contribution in
> respect thereof, and in any event damages against you
> together with interest, on the grounds set out below.

The front part of Form N211 contains a space for a brief summary of
the Additional Claim (which must of course be completed), but this will
ordinarily be no more than a very concise encapsulation of the claim
(similar to the old 'general endorsement' on a writ), and in any event,
I am firmly of the view that the Particulars of the Additional Claim
which we are drafting should stand on its own as a complete recital of
the reasons for which we are bringing our claim against the Third Party,
as well as the claim itself.

By way of an alternative approach, it is, as I have already explained,
possible to draft paragraph 2 as follows:

> 2. If, contrary to their Defence, the Defendants are held
> liable to the Claimant, they claim that they are entitled to be
> indemnified by the Third Party in respect of the Claimant's
> claim, or a contribution in respect thereof, and in any event
> damages against the Third Party together with interest, on
> the grounds set out below.

or even:

> 2. If, contrary to their Defence, Fallow are held liable to
> Pippin, they claim that they are entitled to be indemnified by
> Pearadventure in respect of Pippin's claim, or a contribution
> in respect thereof, and in any event damages against Pear-
> adventure together with interest, on the grounds set out below.

although I think such a paragraph would need to be prefaced with a paragraph defining the names by which it is proposed to refer to the parties.

I remain convinced that the first specimen is far preferable — it is
clearer and easier to read. If you do not agree, please feel free to adopt
one of the alternatives.

We are now about to set out what is essentially a Particulars of Claim against the Third Party for the relief outlined above. You may have observed that we are going to claim an indemnity or a contribution, and damages in any event. This is because we wish to be indemnified against the Claimant's claim, due to the fact that we allege we were acting entirely as a result of advice given to us by Pearadventure, who know the purposes for which the advice was required. If we are unsuccessful in our submissions that we are entitled to a full indemnity, the next best thing, of course, is a contribution. That takes care of the Claimant's claim! However, additionally we claim to have suffered loss and damage to our business as a result of the bad reputation that we now have, and from the loss of promised future orders from Mrs Pippin.

3.   At all relevant times you carried on business as suppliers of fruit trees, including the giving of advice in connection therewith.

4.   By an oral agreement made in the course of a telephone conversation between your Mr Comice and Mr Fallow of the Defendants on 27th April 2004, you agreed to supply the Defendants with 5,000 Passe Crassane pear trees for a total price of £40,500 inclusive of VAT.

5.   In the course of the said telephone conversation, Mr Comice was told by Mr Fallow, and you consequently knew that:
    (1)   The Defendants carried on business as wholesale suppliers of fruit trees;
    (2)   The Defendants required the said trees on behalf of one of their customers who wished to purchase late-flowering pear trees, for use in her business as a grower of fruit for onward sale;
    (3)   The Defendants were relying on your skill and judgment in purchasing the said pear trees from you, in that they requested you, in the course of your said business, to advise them as to a suitable late-flowering pear tree to sell to their said customer, and that you advised the purchase of the said Passe Crassane pear trees.
    (4)   The Defendants' said customer was minded to place further business with the Defendants in the event of the satisfactory supply to her of late-flowering pear trees.

6. Further, as a result of the said telephone conversation, you know or ought to have known that the Defendants and/or their said customer would suffer loss of business in the event of the said trees not being of the nature and quality required by them and agreed to be supplied by you.

7. In the circumstances it was an express term of the said contract that you would supply the Defendants with late flowering pear trees.

8. Further or alternatively, it was an express and/or implied term of the said contract that the said pear trees should be reasonably fit for their required purpose, namely as late-flowering pear trees for onward supply to a customer requiring the same.

9. Further or alternatively, at or before the time of the said agreement, and in order to induce the Defendants to enter into the same, you orally represented to the Defendants during the telephone conversation:

(1) That Passe Crassane pear trees were a late-flowering variety; and/or

(2) That Passe Crassane pear trees were suitable for the supply by the Defendants to their customer who required late-flowering pear trees.

10. The Defendants entered into the said contract with you as a result of your said representations.

11. The said representations and each of them were false in that Passe Crassane pear trees are of an early-flowering variety and were thus not suitable for supply by the Defendants to their said customer.

12. Further or alternatively, you were in breach of your said agreement with the Defendants in that you supplied pear trees which were not of a late-flowering variety, and/or were not fit for the purpose for which they were required.

13. By reason of your said misrepresentation and/or breach of contract, the Defendants have suffered loss and damage.

PARTICULARS

(1)   Liability on the Claimant's claim, to the extent that the same may be successful;

(2)   Loss of reputation and/or future business.

14.   The Defendants further claim to be entitled to interest on such sums as may be recovered from you under their claim herein, at such rate and for such period as the Court shall deem fit, pursuant to section 35A, Supreme Court Act 1981.

15.   The value of this claim exceeds £15,000.

AND the Defendants claim against you:

1.   An indemnity in respect of the Claimant's claim, to such extent as the same may be successful, alternatively a contribution in respect thereof.

2.   Damages.

3.   Interest as aforesaid.

PADDY FIELD

Statement of Truth (etc.)

Essentially, that's it! I could go through the claim point by point, but hope that by now that should not be necessary. Part of the claim is a bit of a 'try on', but then so is probably much of the Particulars of Claim itself. I am not so concerned with the claim itself, but more as to the way in which one sets it out by way of the Additional Claim. The above example is, I hope, useful, in that it deals not merely with the effects of the Claimant's claim upon the Defendant, and then the Third Party, but also with an additional head of claim by the Defendant against the Third Party which does not inevitably depend for its success or failure upon the view that the Court takes on the Particulars of Claim.

So far in this book, we have dealt only with actions that begin by way of a 'standard' Part 7 claim form. Although the CPR have simplified the manner in which an action is commenced, there are still, technically, at least 11 ways in which a claim can be started. Fear not, the vast majority will be by Part 7 claim form, and most of the rest will use the 'Part 8 procedure' provided for (yes, you've guessed it) in CPR Part 8. This is intended for cases where the nature of the relief or remedy sought, or the lack of factual dispute, would make the standard procedure unnecessarily cumbersome. It will doubtless be used in many instances where formerly the old 'originating summons' procedure would have been the appropriate way of starting an action, although the Part 8 procedure will not be limited to these. As a common law practitioner, my experience was not unnaturally more extensive in the fields that have already been covered. Nevertheless, the aim of this work is to demonstrate that there are techniques that are common to all types of drafting, and that these can gainfully be employed in all cases, subject of course to the individual prerequisites of the case in hand at any given time. So we will now brave the world of the Part 8 procedure.

Chapter Nine

Pieces of Eight
(The Part 8 Procedure)

> *'What do you know about this*
> *business?', the King said to Alice.*
> *'Nothing', said Alice.*
> *'Nothing whatever?', persisted the*
> *King. 'Nothing whatever', said Alice.*
> *'That's very important', the King said.*

The Part 8 procedure is a strange beastie, and has to be approached in a somewhat different manner from the so-called 'contentious' statements of case, such as a Particulars of Claim or a Defence, etc. It is used in circumstances where the nature of the relief or remedy sought, or the lack of factual dispute, would make the standard procedure unnecessarily cumbersome. This will usually (but not invariably) be when a party seeks the Court's decision on a question which is unlikely to involve a substantial dispute of fact, or where a Rule or Practice Direction permits use of the procedure. Examples of such instances are set out in the Practice Direction to CPR Part 8. The purposes of the Part 8 claim form is thus to set out the question you wish the Court to decide, or the remedies you are seeking, and the legal basis for making the claim, specifying (should this be the case) the Part of the CPR or the Practice Direction on which your case is based.

The format of the claim will thus be different from a claim under CPR Part 7. For a start, although an action is started by issuing a Part 8 Claim in Form N208, there is no provision in the Form for incorporating a Particulars of Claim. Instead, the Claimant may rely on the matters set out in the claim form as evidence if (as is required by the Rules) it is verified by a statement of truth. Additionally, the Claimant must, when filing the claim form, file any written evidence on which he or she intends to rely, and must serve such evidence, with the claim form, on the Defendant. Although it is possible for such evidence to be contained in the claim form itself, it will normally be in the form of a witness statement or an affidavit, which must be verified by a statement of truth.

The aims and intentions of the Part 8 procedure are very different from those of a claim under Part 7, and it would thus be inappropriate to approach such a document using the same drafting techniques. In order to illustrate and (I hope) explain the discipline, I will concentrate on the manner in which the claim itself should be drafted (whether on the form itself, or attached thereto). It would, dare I suggest, be very helpful were you to read CPR Part 8 and its accompanying Practice Direction, and even (whilst you are in the mood) Form N208 itself!

Having divested myself of all the above, there are nevertheless basic principles of drafting which are obviously common to both types of claim. All drafting should be approached with the aim and intention of producing a result which is logical, clear, concise and comprehensible. The necessity for having a clear understanding of what it is you are trying to achieve is every bit as important in the drafting of a Part 8 Claim as it is in a Particulars of Claim. Indeed, there are strong grounds for arguing that it is even more important (were it possible), in that one main purpose of the Part 8 procedure is to define a series of questions and alternatives with which the Court will be invited to deal. Precise, clear and logical thought is therefore vital.

On the other hand, we must not draft a Part 8 Claim with the same tactical considerations in mind as would be the case were we drafting a Particulars of Claim. The reason for this is that whereas a Part 7 action is essentially adversarial in the way in which it is drafted, the same is not so when the Part 8 procedure is used. The latter is almost invariably used in circumstances where there is no substantial dispute as to the facts but the Court is asked to deal with questions of construction. As a result, the Part 8 procedure is frequently used in the field of trusts, or wills, or actions concerned with the construction or interpretation of documents.

In many ways, the problems with which you may be confronted in the course of a Part 8 Claim lie outside the scope of this work. The claim itself will almost invariably require legal argument as to the construction of the circumstances giving rise to the proceedings, and the particular questions that require to be answered. Furthermore, one of the most difficult decisions you may have to make is whether or not to commence the proceedings by way of the Part 7 or Part 8 procedure. If you decide on the latter, you will then have to decide the parties to the action, using considerations very different to the former. All these matters require legal and procedural considerations, which are (thankfully) outside the ambit of a book about drafting! There are several learned and profound works on the subject, and I would respectfully commend you to them.

I shall therefore assume that you have taken the decision to proceed by way of Part 8, and will discuss some of the basic principles which I hope will assist you in formulating your draft. I will then follow this by a short example of a fairly conventional nature to illustrate the points I have made. I will not attempt anything too complicated, if only because it would necessarily involve legal issues which would confuse, rather than clarify, the required techniques of drafting.

As I have said, the first matter that we must understand, is the purpose for which the Part 8 Claim is being drafted. It is essentially to formulate the questions that the Court is being asked to decide. It is better at this stage **not** to expound on the background facts or to tell the story of the action, or to colour the issues in any way in favour of your case. The Part 8 claim form will almost invariably be accompanied by an affidavit or a witness statement, and it is there that the above matters will be contained. By fortuitous coincidence, I will be discussing these in the next chapter!

Thus, as there should be no 'party political' objectives to be achieved in drafting the Part 8 Claim, we have to concentrate entirely on ensuring that the issues to be decided are presented accurately, concisely, and with clarity. With all thoughts of tactical advantages out of our heads, we should concentrate on setting out the case with objectivity. Some common lawyers may find this difficult!

It may be of assistance if I now outline the way in which I consider a Part 8 Claim should be perceived in concept. I say straightaway that we should be totally flexible in our approach, and should not hesitate to modify what comes below to suit the case with which we are dealing:

1.   We should, of course, commence with the title to the action. There is, naturally, room for this on the Part 8 claim form. If a party is claiming

(or being sued) in a representative capacity, this should also be clearly set out in the title.

2. Curiously, there is no requirement (or provision) in the Form to identify any document or enactment on which the action is premised. Under the old originating summons procedure, it would be normal to add to the title of the action something such as:

> In the matter of the Strip Poker and Underwater Knitting Act 1991,
> AND
> In the matter of the Will of Silas Juniper (deceased)

and I see no reason whatsoever why we should not continue to do this if it makes the purpose of our action more clear and, most importantly of all, assists the comprehension of the issues to be decided.

3. We should seek to identify the capacity or interest which has caused each Defendant to become a party to the action, if this adds anything further to his formal identification in the title to the claim.

4. Having done that, it may be necessary to introduce the Claimant(s) in the same manner, together with any document or enactment that requires construction, and mentioning any schedule of, e.g. property, attached to the claim form, to which reference will be made in the course of the claim.

5. The next paragraph(s) should then set out the questions (if any) which the Court is asked to determine, followed by the relief claimed.

Let us now look at each of these in turn.

THE TITLE

The first matter which we must consider is the title of the action. Although superficially similar to a Part 7 Claim, the heading requires different considerations. For example, where the action concerns the construction of a document, the Defendants may well comprise all those parties who it is felt may have some interest that would be affected by any decision made by the Court, and/or who it is felt may have a claim of some sort in the action or a right to be heard. Being made a Defendant does not necessarily indicate that the Claimant is of the view that that party has done something wrong!

At this stage, I shall introduce a set of facts, which will be used to illustrate the layout of a typical Part 8 Claim:

EXAMPLE

By his will dated 12th May 1988, Brian Portcullis appointed his sister Eva Portcullis together with Henry Slow, a local publican, to be his executors and trustees. By clause 3 of his will, he left a house at 2 Moat Road, Durham to Eva '… to be held jointly by her with such person with whom, at the date of my death, she may intend at that time permanently to live'.

The reason for that somewhat strange clause was that Eva was an elderly spinster who had lost her fiancé during the war, and had consequently taken a vow never to marry. However, a recent fall had left her permanently disabled, and Brian hoped that the prospect of a share in the property would encourage a companion to look after her in her time of need. He did not consider that he needed the services of a solicitor to draft his will, and did the job himself.

Brian Portcullis, although not a wealthy man, had originally purchased the house in Moat Road as an investment, his own residence being in another part of the city. The house was divided into a number of flats, and in 1986 he had allowed his sister to live there free of charge.

At the time of his death in July 1991, Eva had for 2 years been living with an 'unclaimed treasure' called Daisy Banks, who did not pay any rent but who looked after Eva full time. Miss Banks had no other home, and had often expressed her intention of looking after Eva for the rest of her days, even though she did not know of the terms of Brian's will.

Eva, however, was unfortunately not over-endowed with intelligence, and it did not occur to her that Miss Banks might be counted as a beneficiary under the terms of the will, even though she was hoping that she would continue to stay and care for her. Henry Slow did not even realise that Eva was sharing with Daisy Banks, and thought that the will was referring to a potential husband for Eva. As a result, the property was ultimately transferred to Eva absolutely, and registered in her sole name. Henry Slow died in 2002.

Life continued as normal, with Eva now collecting and
keeping the rents from the property. Daisy Banks continued
to reside rent free in the house and to look after Eva.
However, in early 2004, Daisy was cleaning out some cup-
boards when she came across a copy of the will, and appreciated that she might be entitled to a share in the property.
She raised it with Eva that evening, and a most unfortunate
argument ensued, in the course of which Daisy was given her
'marching orders'. Eva maintained that she never intended
that Daisy should live permanently at the property, and that
Daisy was not entitled to any interest.

Daisy then left the house, and has never returned.
Although Eva has now engaged a paid housekeeper, Daisy
is of the view that she will shortly need to go into a residential home. In any event, Daisy now needs money in order to
find rented accommodation for herself, as her funds are very
limited. She wishes to apply for an order declaratory of her
interest in the house, and for an order for sale of the property, which is valued at £400,000. The sorry mess lands up
on your desk.

The first thing that you have to do when faced with this unlikely tale, is
to decide on the form of action that is to be taken. We shall assume that
the appropriate thing to do is to bring an action for a declaration of
Daisy's interest in the house, and for an order for sale under s. 14 of the
Trusts of Land and Appointment of Trustees Act 1996. Conveniently for
us, this will involve the use of the Part 8 procedure.

The basic title of the case should be quite straightforward. It will
be in the Chancery Division of the High Court. The Claimant will be
Daisy Banks, the sole Defendant Eva Portcullis, in view of the death of
Henry Slow. However, before putting pen to paper, we must consider
whether and to what extent it is necessary to refer to any representative
capacity of any of the parties in the title itself, rather than in the body of
the claim.

The capacities of Eva Portcullis must be considered with care. She is,
of course, an executor and trustee of the will. As this is the capacity in
which she is being sued, it should be mentioned in the title to the action.
Because of this, there seems little point in additionally identifying the
will in the title. (I said we should adopt a flexible approach.) Further,
however, it must be remembered that Eva is also a **beneficiary** under
the terms of the will, and has an interest to protect in that regard. This is

not a capacity in which she is being sued, and we should therefore mention this in the body of the claim. The Claimant, Daisy Banks, although claiming to have a beneficial entitlement, is not suing in any form of representative capacity, but in her own name and for her own benefit. We shall therefore leave any description of her status until a little later.

The title should therefore read as follows:

IN THE HIGH COURT OF JUSTICE   Ch 2005 No. 0000
CHANCERY DIVISION

BETWEEN:

Miss DAISY MAY BANKS

Claimant

— and —

Miss EVA PORTCULLIS
(Sued in her capacity as executor and trustee of the Will of
Brian Portcullis (deceased))

Defendant

So far so good! Now we must turn to the body of the claim itself. Using what I trust is sound common sense, I think that we should begin by defining the interests and capacities of both parties. There are any number of ways in which this can be done, and I shall choose what I hope is the most logical and straightforward. In so far as Eva Portcullis is concerned, I have already observed that she is not merely an executor and trustee, but also a beneficiary under the terms of the will, and thus has an interest to protect in that regard. It may also be worthwhile setting out the fact that she is the sole surviving such executor and trustee. So we commence:

1.   The Defendant is the sole surviving executor and trustee of the Will dated 12th May 1988 of Brian Portcullis deceased; a beneficiary thereof under the terms of the same, and a Trustee of the property at 2 Moat Road, Durham, at which she presently resides.

There may be room for slight variations in the manner of setting out the above, but I do not warrant them sufficiently important to set them out here. The identity and address of the Defendant has been set out, and we can see precisely why she may have an interest in the subject matter and nature of the application to be made.

INTRODUCING THE CLAIMANT AND THE NATURE OF THE RELIEF SOUGHT

The purpose of the next paragraph is to introduce the Claimant and her capacity or interest in the proceedings, in exactly the same way as has been done with the Defendant. When this has been done, we will lead in to the questions on which the Court will be asked to rule, and the nature of the relief claimed by the Claimant.

A common mistake is to claim that the Claimant is entitled to a one-half (or some other) interest in the property itself. That is of course incorrect. The Claimant is entitled to an interest in the **proceeds of sale** of the property, which, if her claim is made out, will be held by the trustees on a Statutory Trust for Sale with power to postpone on the usual considerations. Furthermore, of course, it is only correct here to say that the Claimant **claims** to have an interest in the proceeds of sale. The position is thus different from a Particulars of Claim, in which I would have had no hesitation in setting out that claim in more forthright terms.

Another matter that we must consider at this stage is the manner in which we will set out our application. As I have intimated before, this can take two basic forms: the application to the Court to determine questions, and the seeking of relief. In the present case we are not merely applying for an order for sale, as there may be some dispute as to our entitlement to an interest in the proceeds of such a sale. If we have no such interest, the question of the Court making an order for sale would, of course, not arise. Technically, therefore, we should ask the Court to determine the question of whether or not we are entitled to the claimed interest. As I propose to demonstrate, this can be done by analysing the possible effects of the deceased's Will as at the date of his death, and by postulating precise questions in respect of each option. On the other hand, the present circumstances are such that an application can be framed which will incorporate this particular area of uncertainty, and this can be achieved by asking the Court for relief by way of a **declaration** that the Claimant is entitled to an interest in the proceeds of sale. This will probably end up as being a more concise and equally proper and satisfactory method of application, but I will set out both approaches, simply by way of illustration. However, if we are to ask for the determination of questions, it might be helpful were we to state this in the final sentence of the ensuing paragraph. This would therefore read as follows:

> 2. The Claimant, Daisy May Banks, of 33 Grasslea, Durham, claims to be beneficially interested in the proceeds of sale of the property described in the Schedule hereto, and seeks the determination of the following questions and the following relief namely:

Notice that I have taken the opportunity to demonstrate the manner in which a Schedule may be employed in the course of the Part 8 Claim. Strictly speaking, this is not necessary in that the property has already been described in the course of stating the Defendant's address and capacity. On the other hand, there has not so far been any precise description of the property, e.g. whether it is held by way of freehold or leasehold interest, and whether or not the title is registered at Land Registry. This can conveniently be inserted in the Schedule, and I propose so to do.

QUESTIONS AND RELIEF

The following paragraphs will require the most careful drafting, and will to a great extent depend on what is being requested of the Court, and the particular circumstances of the case. As I have said, I will demonstrate a manner of doing this both by way of determination of a question, followed by a claim for relief, and then another way dealing only with the latter.

If we wish to formulate a question or series of questions, the usual and most logical approach is to refer to the document that requires construction, and then to ask a series of alternatives. From the answers to those questions may flow an alternative series of questions or applications for relief, and so on. I hope that this will become more clear if I do it by way of a skeleton:

1. The Claimant seeks the determination of the following questions and the following relief.

2. There is then a reference to the document in question, for example:

> Whether on a true construction of the said Will and in the events which have happened ...

3.   Then the question by way of alternatives, for example:

> 3.   The gift to Wilfrid Scroggins of the house at 3 The
> Meades, Kenton, Middlesex is:
> (a)   valid, or
> (b)   void for uncertainty or otherwise.

Or:

> 4.   The gift of £10,000 to the Cypress Tree Home for Aged
> Eunuchs comprises a valid and effectual gift to the Third
> Defendants (the Oak Tree Home for Aged Eunuchs).

4.   Then follows the next series of questions or applications for relief,
based on the answers to the former questions. These are conventionally
formulated after the manner:

> If the answer to question 3 is in sense (b):
> 4.   (next question).

Or to take the latter of the above examples:

> 5.   If paragraph 4 is answered in the negative, whether the
> property comprised in the said gift:
> (a)   is held on charitable purposes and is applicable
> cy-près, or
> (b)   is undisposed of by the said Will.
>
> 6.   If paragraph 5 is answered in sense (a), such directions
> with regard to a scheme for the application of the property
> comprised in the said gift as may be necessary. (etc.)

You can see that the whole layout is carefully and logically formulated
rather in the manner of a flowchart.

Is the answer (a), (b) or (c)?
If the answer is in sense (b), whether (x), (y) or (z)?
If the answer is in sense (c), such directions for [whatever it is] as may
be necessary.

It may well be that if the answer is in sense (a), no further applications
for relief will be necessary.

Taking our main example, were we to formulate our Part 8 Claim by way of the determination of a question, we may wish to ask:

> 1.   Whether on a true construction of the said Will, and in the events which have happened, the property at 2 Moat Road, Durham devolved upon:
>
> (a)   the Defendant absolutely; or
>
> (b)   the executors and trustees of the said Will on trust for sale for the Claimant and the Defendant in equal shares; or
>
> (c)   the executors and trustees of the said Will on trust for sale for the Claimant and the Defendant in some other, and if so what proportion.

The first thing to point out is the convenient phrase:

> Whether, on a true construction of the said [Will] and in the events which have happened ...

These words form part of hallowed tradition and, unlike some hoary old phrases, serve a useful purpose. I do not advocate trying your own alternatives when the above sets out precisely what it is you would be trying to say and, what is more, does so with economy and style.

Next, observe the way in which the questions have been formulated. It is not appropriate to phrase one general question along the lines of: 'Please tell us the result of what happened' as it is your responsibility to set out precisely what it is that you are asking the Court to determine. Having said that, there is still a 'catch-all' type question that you are permitted to ask at the conclusion of your catechism, and it is expressed above as:

> ... some other, and if so what proportion.

The questions themselves are, it is hoped, quite straightforward. First we have asked whether or not the disposition took effect as a direct gift to Eva Portcullis. Naturally, we are hoping that the answer to this will be 'no'. If it is not, that is the end of the matter as far as we are concerned.

If Eva did not receive the house as a direct gift, the only other realistic possibilities are that she shared the house with another person, and that person would almost certainly be Daisy Banks. In such a circumstance, the property would be held by the trustees of the estate on a statutory trust for sale for Eva Portcullis and Daisy Banks, in such proportions as they were entitled. Now it is almost certain that, in the event of the property

being held on such a trust, both parties would have an equal interest in
the proceeds of sale. However, just in case there is any possibility that
there may be unequal shares, the Court is asked in question (c) to determine this as an alternative to question (b). It is to be hoped that this too
will not be necessary.

Thereafter, we will continue by seeking the same relief as if we had
simply made an application for a declaration that the Claimant was entitled
to an interest in the proceeds of sale of the property, save that we must
commence:

> If paragraph 1 is answered in sense (a) or (b) ...

and then proceed accordingly.

Before setting out the manner in which I consider we should formulate our claims for relief, it is important that we take stock of **precisely**
what we wish to seek. Let us start by looking at our problems:

1.   We have not been recognised as a joint tenant of the property under
a statutory trust for sale.
2.   Because of the death of Henry Slow, there is now only one trustee
of the property (should the trust be held to exist), and that is insufficient
for the purposes of selling the same and administering the proceeds in
accordance with the terms of the trust.
3.   Eva Portcullis will not consent to the sale — at least not on the terms
of a statutory trust for sale, the power to postpone which has now been
terminated.
4.   If Daisy Banks is entitled to a share in the proceeds of sale, she will
also have been entitled to a share of the 'rents and profits' obtained in
the interim. Eva Portcullis has been pocketing the rents, and we claim to
be entitled to half.

The above should have given us some clue as to the type of relief that
we should seek. I shall now assume that you have decided what you
want by way of relief, and that coincidentally your view concurs with
mine. What we must now do is to set out the various applications for
relief, in the appropriate manner:

> 1.   A declaration that the said property is held by the
> Defendant on trust for sale to hold the net proceeds of sale
> and the net rents and profits until sale, upon trust for the
> Claimant and the Defendant in equal shares or alternatively
> in such shares as the Court shall determine.

This is framed in order to take account of the fact that the Defendant is presently the sole trustee of the trust for sale. It also mentions the net rents and profits, although I shall consider it appropriate to refer to these in more detail in a moment.

Next, we have to deal with the appointment of another trustee. Obviously we would prefer it to be Daisy Banks herself, although we must make provision for other eventualities:

> 2.   An order that the Claimant or some other fit and proper person be appointed as a Trustee of the trust for sale of the said property jointly with the Defendant, and that the property thereafter be vested jointly in the Claimant and the Defendant for the purposes of carrying out the orders of the Court, on the determination of this claim.

Now I confess that this is a little 'wrapped up', and that it is possible to be rather more blunt, namely to request:

> 2.   That the Claimant or some other fit and proper person be appointed as trustee of the said property jointly with the Defendant.

> 3.   That the said property be vested in the Claimant and the Defendant.

There is nothing whatsoever wrong with the above, although I prefer the first draft, as it is technically more accurate. Not only does it deal with matters in one paragraph rather than two, it also makes it clear that the purpose of vesting the property in the names of both Claimant and Defendant is so that effect can be given to the orders of the Court which are about to be requested. Once again, I leave the ultimate decision to you. The next paragraph gets to the heart of the whole matter:

> 3.   That the Defendant be ordered to sell the said property, together with the Claimant, notwithstanding that she refuses to consent to such a sale.

Again, I am not using 'statutory' language, i.e. you may use whatever form of words you consider most appropriate to your request.

> 4.   Alternatively, that the said property be sold by order of the Court.

This is a necessary legal alternative request. Now, we shall deal with the specific question of the rents:

> 5.   An inquiry as to all profits made by the Defendant (whether as a result of letting the said property or otherwise) during the course of the said trust.

And just in case I may have forgotten to ask for something that should have been requested, or anything important turns up in the course of making the specific inquiry requested:

> 6.   All other necessary accounts, directions and inquiries.

Now we deal with various technical matters to which we should have regard:

> 7.   That all necessary orders and directions may be given as to the execution of the said trust for sale, consequent upon the result of such accounts and inquiries as are taken.

> 8.   If necessary, that the said trust for sale may be carried into execution by the Court.

> 9.   That provision may be made for the costs of this application.

> 10.   Further or other relief.

NOAH SARK

This last is the great catch-all, and thank heavens for it too, bearing in mind the complexities of the average Chancery action. Put another way:

> 'If I've forgotten to ask for anything, or if there's something else that you would like to give me, please feel free ... !'

SECTIONS OF RELEVANT ACTS, AND
SCHEDULES OF PROPERTY

In the present case it is sufficient simply to state:

> This application is made under Section 14 of the Trusts of Land and Appointment of Trustees Act 1996

NOAH SARK

Statement of Truth

As I stated earlier, I would not normally consider it necessary to insert a Schedule of property into a comparatively straightforward case such as the present, but I do so here by way of illustration:

SCHEDULE

The freehold property situate at and known as 2 Moat Road, Durham, title to which is registered at HM Land Registry under Title Number ABC 2345678

Let us now regard the finished product:

IN THE HIGH COURT OF JUSTICE   Ch 2005 No. 0000
CHANCERY DIVISION

BETWEEN:

Miss DAISY MAY BANKS

Claimant

— and —

Miss EVA PORTCULLIS
(Sued in her capacity as executor and trustee of the Will of
Brian Portcullis (deceased))

Defendant

1.   The Defendant is the sole surviving executor and trustee of the Will dated 12th May 1988 of Brian Portcullis deceased; a beneficiary thereof under the terms of the same, and a Trustee of the property at 2 Moat Road, Durham, at which she presently resides.

2.   The Claimant, Daisy May Banks of 33 Grasslea, Durham, claims to be beneficially interested in the proceeds of sale of the property described in the Schedule hereto, and seeks the determination of the following questions and the following relief namely:

(1)   A declaration that the said property is held by the Defendant upon trust for sale to hold the net proceeds of sale and the net rents and

profits until sale, upon trust for the Claimant and the Defendant in equal shares or alternatively in such shares as the Court shall determine.

(2)   An order that the Claimant or some other fit and proper person be appointed as Trustee of the trust for sale of the said property jointly with the Defendant, and that the property thereafter be vested jointly in the Claimant and the Defendant for the purposes of carrying out the orders of the Court, on the determination of this claim.

(3)   That the Defendant be ordered to sell the said property, together with the Claimant, notwithstanding that she refuses to consent to such a sale.

(4)   Alternatively, that the said property be sold by order of the Court.

(5)   An inquiry as to all profits made by the Defendant (whether as a result of letting the said property or otherwise) during the course of the said trust.

(6)   All other necessary accounts directions and inquiries.

(7)   That all necessary orders and directions may be given as to the execution of the said trust for sale, consequent upon the result of such accounts and inquiries as are taken.

(8)   If necessary, that the said trust for sale may be carried into execution by the Court.

(9)   That provision may be made for the costs of this application.

(10)   Further or other relief.

NOAH SARK

This application is made under section 14 of the Trusts of Land and Appointment of Trustees Act 1996.

<u>Statement of Truth</u> (etc.)

SCHEDULE

The freehold property situate at and known as 2 Moat Road, Durham, title to which is registered at HM Land Registry under Title Number ABC 2345678.

Dated the 28th day of April 2005.

What I have attempted to do is to give an indication of the different techniques which have to be used when drafting a Part 8 Claim, when compared with those outlined in the earlier chapters on 'common law' statements of case. What I have not attempted to do is to analyse and explain each and every paragraph in the example in the same manner as I have done, say, in the Particulars of Claim. The Part 8 Claim requires different considerations, and the example that I have given above cannot be directly employed in all cases. Nevertheless the basic technique of drafting outlined in this chapter still holds good, and should, I trust, enable you to enter this field with greater confidence and understanding than hitherto.

Part 8 Claims are, of course, usually accompanied by witness statements or affidavits. These appear in many shapes and forms throughout the whole gamut of legal proceedings, and I will examine some of the relevant drafting techniques in the next chapter.

Chapter Ten

'To Tell You the Truth...' (Affidavits and Witness Statements)

> *'Give your evidence', said the King; 'and don't be nervous, or I'll have you executed on the spot.'*
>
> *The White Rabbit put on his spectacles. 'Where shall I begin, please your Majesty?' he asked.*
>
> *'Begin at the beginning', the King said gravely, 'And go on till you come to the end: then stop.'*

The previous chapters have been full of admonitions not to set out evidence unless and save in so far as is necessary to found the allegation that you are making.

Affidavits and witness statements are different! Here we are required to set out evidence by virtue of the very nature of the document which we are drafting. This is because they comprise the written evidence of a witness, and are either used in circumstances when it is not considered necessary or expedient for 'live' evidence to be called, or are, at the very least, used as the evidence-in-chief of the witness.

The formal requirements for both are contained in CPR Part 32, and more particularly in Practice Direction 32, and you would be well advised to consult those to ensure that you have complied with the Rules, and that your work is in the necessary format. Even before the CPR, many people considered that there was little practical difference between a witness statement and an affidavit, and to a great extent they were right, and are even more so today! I suspect that in a fairly short time the difference between the two will disappear altogether; and in any event, from the point of drafting technique, there is little or nothing between them. Therefore, in a radical departure from previous editions (and with a consequent saving in paper), I shall deal with both in the same chapter.

The body of both documents should be written in the first person, in a clear, straightforward narrative form using the witness's/deponent's own words. In the days of the RSC, the requirement was that the language should be the witness's '*ipsissimma verba*', a phrase which you may think was totally inappropriate to the concept it was supposed to describe! Thankfully that has now gone. Both documents must contain a statement that the contents are true to the best of the **witness's** knowledge and belief (affidavits are sworn, witness statements must contain a statement of truth), both must contain the author's name, address, occupation and status in the action, be written in consecutive numbered paragraphs, and should properly contain only matters on which the witness would be competent to give evidence at trial (i.e., the evidence must be relevant, admissible, and be of fact and not opinion).

Affidavits are, of course, used in a large variety of different situations, and in a number of different configurations. Sometimes they may be required as formalities in order to support certain applications. In many such cases they may be both short and highly stylised, effectively constituting no more than a signed (and sworn) affirmation of a number of preconditions to the validity of an application.

A variation from the above is where the affidavit is not in standard form but is nevertheless required to contain certain specific information. These are also pretty straightforward and need no special drafting expertise. That leaves, of course, merely a few hundred thousand instances in which an affidavit may be required to be drafted. There is no 'official' format, save that certain preliminaries are required, and the whole document must conform to rules of relevance and admissibility. Thus, the scope for individual expression in an affidavit is very much greater than in drafting a statement of case, and I cannot possibly cover all possible permutations.

Now, you may have thought that none of the above would tax the intellectual or drafting abilities of the most humble of lawyers (or even witnesses). However, true stories abound of tens of thousands of pounds being expended in some heavy cases on drafting, and the 'massaging' of witness statements, and much court time used to be taken up with attacking witnesses on real or imagined inconsistencies between their statements and their oral evidence, to the extent that the real objectives of the case were often forgotten. Today this happens considerably less frequently, particularly as the giving of oral evidence in chief is now rare — the witness statement standing in its place. However, such was the paranoia of the profession that specialist courses were (and as far as I know may still be) set up to educate us all on the required techniques, and I was approached some years ago by a number of souls who suggested that the subject should be allotted a hallowed place in this humble work. Being unable to resist such earnest entreaties, I duly succumbed, but consider that the following hints should be as relevant today as they were hitherto.

The first thing that I have to say is that the spirit of the CPR means that the Court should come down pretty hard on anyone who spends too much (or even a little) time drawing attention to inconsistencies between oral and written evidence, when it detracts from a trial on the real issues. Don't try to do so in my home Court! The hoary old submission, 'well your Honour, it goes towards establishing credibility' will meet with a fairly pithy riposte! So our drafting techniques should be focused on ensuring that as full, logical and clear an account as possible is given, rather than on seeking any tactical advantage in the manner of our drafting. Of course, persuasive effect is another matter altogether!

In any event, I have to confess that, in so far as drafting these documents is concerned, I do not understand what the fuss is all about. After all, the principle is quite simple, and nothing additional seems to be required over normal preparation and logical analysis about which I have expounded much earlier in this work. There nevertheless seems to be a feeling in the profession that any change in procedure or alteration in established techniques necessarily involves the learning of new disciplines, although all that may really be required is a return to fundamental values and concepts. Before the practice of exchanging witness statements came into effect, proofs of evidence were (or should have been) invariably taken, and the only real change was that such proofs had to be refined and put into a format which confines itself to a clear and unadorned exposition of relevant facts. What is so difficult about that?

Before the onset of the CPR, I felt that there were occasions when tactical considerations may have been justified when deciding what to include in a witness statement. These flowed from the rule that a party serving a witness statement may not lead evidence from his witness, the substance of which is not included in the statement served, save with the consent of the other parties or leave of the Court (neither of which was likely to be forthcoming). The distinction between 'new evidence' and what is merely the amplification of matters, the substance of which is already included in the statement, is thus of some importance. Although this is not a work on advocacy, you will I hope readily appreciate that there are disadvantages to the following scenario:

You:	'Your Honour, I call my next witness, Mr Ytosis'
Judge:	'Very well'
You:	'Is your name Hal Ytosis?'
Witness:	'Yes'
You:	'Is this your witness statement in this case?'
Witness:	'Yes'
You:	'Are the contents of this statement true to the best of your knowledge and belief?'
Witness:	'Yes'
You:	'Thank you. Please wait there' ...

at which stage, your witness, who (unless he is an expert and/or mad) is extremely nervous at being in Court, is left to the tender mercies of your opponent, who will do his best to kick seven bells out of him before he has even had time to get used to the sound of his own voice in the court-room!

It is therefore both natural and desirable that you will want to be able to ask a few questions of your witness to settle him down, and also to give the Judge the opportunity of assessing him on 'home ground' before he is subjected to cross-examination, where he will inevitably be on the defensive. A witness statement which contains each and every word that the witness could reasonably be expected to say on the subject, will leave you with no scope whatsoever for such examination-in-chief, unless you start to take him through his statement, which will (or should) subject you to instant judicial disapproval!

Now, it was usually possible to get away with that in the past. It is very difficult indeed to do so now! The fact that, for example, a fast track case has to be heard within 5 hours, coupled with the Judge's con-siderable powers to abridge the degree and extent to which a party can examine or cross-examine a witness on certain issues, has meant that the ability to ask 'supplemental' questions of a witness, as a matter of course, is very considerably curtailed. This means that most witnesses will be called into the witness-box and almost immediately be subjected to cross-examination. Thus it may well be taking too much of a risk to leave room in a witness statement for 'filling out' matters, in order to get the witness comfortable and prepared for what is to come.

Let us therefore look at some of the principles that we should bear in mind when drafting our statement. The examples that I use are for illustrative purposes only — it may be that under the CPR you would wish to use a statement rather than an affidavit, or even to rely on the statement of case — but the following examples simply illustrate drafting principles assuming that you have decided the appropriate medium to use.

First, of course, a statement is to be used to impart information, and thus should do so in a manner which is comprehensible. Remember as well that the person reading the statement will be required to assimilate a great deal of information within a very short time — he or she will not have had the advantage of the leisurely opportunity to consider the case that will, of course, have been afforded to you! Thus, the object of the exercise must be to communicate that which is desired, in the most digestible fashion, and in a manner which will be the most persuasive to our case.

Secondly, as in all drafting, it is necessary to remind ourselves of the reason for which the particular statement is being drafted. Although on occasions it will be necessary to set out the whole history of the case, in many instances we will be using a statement or affidavit to support an application where we may only be required to deal with specific issues. It is thus a complete and oppressive waste of time to impose a huge document on the other side (and on the Court), and thus unreasonably to add to the costs of the case. Remember as well, that in the majority of applications, the statement of case (having been endorsed with a statement of truth) will itself be evidence of the facts contained therein, which will not have to be repeated. Thus, the **objectives** of the exercise must always be borne in mind.

Thirdly, we must ensure that the statement is set out according to the Rules, i.e. that it bears the proper heading and indorsement at the top, and that it contains the necessary averments as to truth, that the exhibits are properly laid out and labelled, and, of course, that the thing has either been sworn or endorsed with a statement of truth, or that arrangements are in hand for this to be done.

Lastly (for the moment), we must check that the statement contains any necessary 'required elements', i.e. matters which have to be included in the particular circumstances of the case. A comprehensive and beautifully laid out statement will get us nowhere if it does not contain matters required by the relevant Rules pertaining to our case.

Let us commence by looking at the heading. You must now remember that a witness statement is required to bear the same formal endorsement in the top right-hand corner as was previously required (and frequently ignored) in the case of affidavits. All affidavits and/or witness statements must bear the title of the case, and as such should cause no problems. However, we are required also to indorse the document, at the top right-hand side, with information as to:

(a) the party on whose behalf the witness statement or affidavit is made;

(b) the initials and surname of the witness/deponent;

(c) the number of the statement/affidavit in relation to that witness/deponent;

(d) the identifying initials and number of each exhibit referred to; and

(e) the date made or sworn.

These requirements are mandatory. Unfortunately, they still seem to be honoured more in the breach than in the observance, and some Judges are getting more than a little stroppy about this. Make it a habit always to ensure that the statement is appropriately indorsed in all cases, and you will not be bawled out or, worse, be deprived of your costs! The method of this indorsement used to vary from the frankly cryptic, to the rather more clearly labelled. I have seen thus:

JS Barnes/P1/1st/26/1/01/JSB1, 2 & 3

(which is hardly 'clearly marked' and which I do not advocate) and the rather more comprehensible:

Deponent [Statement of]: JS Barnes
1st affidavit [statement]
For: Claimant
Sworn [dated] 26th January 2001
Exhibits JSB 1, 2 & 3

(which I do)!

After the main title should come the centre heading, in which you have the option (which you should seize) to state precisely what the document is to comprise. You could of course simply put 'Affidavit', as a main centre heading, but I think it is more helpful (and hardly onerous) to put:

AFFIDAVIT [STATEMENT] OF NICHOLAS MINK

or

AFFIDAVIT [STATEMENT] IN SUPPORT OF APPLICATION TO SET ASIDE JUDGMENT

or even

AFFIDAVIT [STATEMENT] OF NICHOLAS MINK IN SUPPORT OF APPLICATION TO SET ASIDE JUDGMENT

An exception may be made in cases when the affidavit is extremely short and formal — as ever, use common sense in order to aid clarity and assimilation.

The first paragraph of the body of the statement will be the full name of the witness, together with a declaration of oath by the deponent if it is an affidavit, followed by:

(a)   his residential address (unless the evidence is being given in a professional, business or other occupational capacity, in which event the job title and business address should be given);

(b)   his occupation or description;

(c)   his status in the action, or whether he is employed by any party in the case (should either be relevant).

The appropriate declaration on oath for an affidavit (which has now changed since the CPR) is:

I, Nicholas Mink, of 42 Sun Street, Fishbourne, Hertfordshire, state on oath:

The first substantive paragraph will normally provide further introduction of the author and, if necessary, a brief statement of the reasons for which the affidavit is made. This may not always be necessary in the case of a witness statement. Both affidavits and witness statements should indicate which of the statements made in it are made from personal knowledge, and which are matters of information and belief, and the source of any such information or belief. This is so as to declare the possibility of hearsay evidence being used, and thereafter to identify such hearsay if and when it occurs:

> 1.   I am a self-employed tripe boiler carrying on business from the above premises, and the Claimant in the present action. I make this affidavit in support of my application to set aside the order of Master Grouch dated 10th April 2006, by which I was debarred from calling expert evidence in support of my claim, due to my failure to serve a copy of an expert's report on the Defendant within the stipulated period. The facts set out in this affidavit are true to the best of my knowledge and belief, and are within my own knowledge unless stated to the contrary.

There are, as ever, other forms of words that can be used, but the above example is fairly typical, and is as concise a statement of the necessary declarations as possible.

The rest of the affidavit will contain the information that you wish to use in support of, or against, the application that is being made, or whatever the purpose of the affidavit may be. It is here that a curious but necessary make-believe takes place. The affidavit is, naturally, in the name of the deponent, and as such contains evidence for which he is entirely responsible. It is thus strange how even the most illiterate and philistine of deponents usually manages to create an affidavit which, if not exactly matching the peerless style of the present work, nevertheless communicates its message with staggering literacy and facility. Is this due to a sudden onset of scholarship due to respect for the law and a sense of occasion? Not a bit of it! Of course, **you** wrote it. You know, your opponent knows, your client knows, and the Court knows. Nevertheless we persist in this pretence that it is the unencumbered work of the deponent.

There is a simple explanation for this, which is almost convincing. You have put your instructions into a form which is best calculated to provide the appropriate evidence in the most suitably persuasive manner. However, the responsibility for the accuracy of the contents is that of the deponent.

This explanation would perhaps carry greater authority were it to be carried out into the field of oral evidence as well. Rather than have Ignatius Sproat stammering out his evidence in halting tones, scared out of his wits, why should **you** not give the evidence based on instructions that you have been given, with your client taking responsibility for the contents? Ah well, you may say, that deprives the Judge of the opportunity of assessing the veracity of the witness by observing his demeanour in the witness-box. However, does a cleverly worded affidavit drafted by a lawyer provide any greater assistance? Perhaps it may be that the client would fare better under cross-examination than would you acting as his substitute. Anyway, I digress.

'... the most illiterate and philistine of deponents ...'

What does matter, however, is that you take even greater pains than usual not to 'gild the lily' and misrepresent your instructions in order to give your case some added authenticity. It is surprising how easy it is to do this even unconsciously, in genuine enthusiasm to make a silk purse out of a sow's ear. Avoid doing this at all costs. Remember that your client will almost invariably swear on the dotted line as to the truth of the affidavit or statement, on the basis that you presumably know what you are doing and therefore the document must be OK, even if you do remind him that the responsibility of swearing (or signing a statement of truth) is his alone. You cannot, in conscience, hide behind your client's responsibility for the affidavit, in order to absolve yourself from professional impropriety. Warning the client of his responsibility for the contents is simply not good enough. After all, he hasn't hired a dog in order to do his own barking!

It is still arguable that an affidavit should perhaps be somewhat more persuasive in the manner in which it is drafted than a witness statement and I will illustrate this later on in this chapter. However, this does not mean that a witness statement should not be drafted in terms which put the evidence in the most persuasive light. Although, as I have already said, I consider this subject requires little in the way of new techniques, it may be helpful if I append an example of a rather detailed witness statement, where dates, times and places are clearly of great relevance. In this case, we act for the Defendants in an action in which they are being sued by the purchasers of their house for additional sums that they had to pay in order to obtain a clear title. We in turn are suing our previous solicitors, for allowing exchange of contracts to take place before obtaining the consent of the building society to the release of their charge on the property (which was in substantial negative equity). If this sounds confusing, I hope the witness statement will make it all clear:

> On behalf of the Defendants
> A. Chance
> First Witness Statement
> No exhibits
> Dated:

IN THE HIGH COURT OF JUSTICE   2006 P No. 1234
QUEEN'S BENCH DIVISION

BETWEEN:

(1)   Mr ERNEST BARRY POLLOCK
(2)   Mrs ELSIE POLLOCK

Claimants

— and —

(1)   Mr ARTHUR CHANCE
(2)   Mrs MARGARET CHANCE

Defendants

— and —

AUSTIN and FOXHOLE (A Firm)

Third party

WITNESS STATEMENT OF ARTHUR CHANCE

Background

1. I am Arthur Chance, of Highho, Village Lane, Milton, Yorkshire, and the First-named Defendant in these proceedings. My wife is the Second-named Defendant. This litigation concerns the sale of our former property known as 17 Old Street, Barrington, North Yorkshire, which was bought by us jointly in 1997 for £220,000, with the assistance of a mortgage to Convent County Building Society of £210,000.

2. At about the same time, I entered into negotiations with Riley Motor Company Ltd, to take over a dealership, which I did at the beginning of 1997. This involved my introducing £50,000 capital into the new business. Unfortunately it proved to be a disaster, and I was dismissed in January 2000. By 2000 I was in a parlous financial position. I owed money to Convent County, Furness Bank plc and Northeast Bank plc, and my property was fully charged. Although I attempted to set up new businesses, these were not successful, largely due to poor trading conditions. In November 2001, Convent County obtained a possession order on the property, suspended to May 2002, dependent upon my reducing the mortgage arrears, and putting the house on the market.

Voluntary arrangement

3. In view of my financial position, I sought advice from an insolvency practitioner called Tony Hunt, of Hunt & Co., in the Autumn of 2001. I was advised to apply for a voluntary arrangement in order to attempt to clear all family liabilities, both secured and unsecured. Unfortunately, however, my wife owed substantial sums of money to HM Revenue & Customs, and she was unable to avoid being adjudicated bankrupt in summer 2002. In so far as I was concerned, however, an arrangement was eventually concluded on 29th November 2002.

Marketing of 17 Old Street

4. In view of the suspended possession order, it was inevitable that we would have to dispose of the property, and it was put on the market at the beginning of 2002, through the joint agency of Grover Greene & Co. and Peter Potts & Co. The property was initially marketed at £425,000. Various advertisements were placed in the *Yorkshire Post* etc., but there was very little interest. I recollect that eight couples saw the property. As the property was not moving, we indicated that we would be prepared to accept lower offers.

Mr Thaw

5.   In March or April 2002, I received a telephone call from a Mr Thaw. He introduced himself as a neighbour, although I had never spoken to nor seen him before. He suggested that we met at the York Doone Hotel, to discuss something which he said would be to our mutual advantage. We did meet, and he said that his wife had always wanted to live in our house, and that he had a substantial amount of cash with which to purchase the property. I had already explained to Mr Thaw that the property was charged to the hilt, and that all the proceeds of sale would go to the mortgagees. He indicated that he would be prepared to pay £350,000 for the house, but that he would formally offer £320,000, and deposit £30,000 in a Jersey Bank account for me. This was to be outside the sale. I understood from this that I would receive a 'present' which, in view of the way it was offered, would be something which I would be able to keep from my creditors and the voluntary arrangement. I was not interested in a deal of this nature, which seemed to me to be totally dishonest, and I politely told him that I was not interested.

6.   Because of the unusual nature of the approach by Mr Thaw, I immediately reported the discussion to Mr Hunt, Charles Coote of Messrs Austin and Foxhole, and Arthur Hill, an accountant, who advised me from time to time. As a result of advice I was given by them, I did not pursue the matter with Mr Thaw. However, two or three weeks after this meeting, I had a visit from various neighbours who lived behind Mr Thaw's house. As a result of what they told me, I formed the view that not only was Mr Thaw's approach improper, but that he had not been full and frank about his motives for wishing to purchase the property. I therefore telephoned Mr Thaw on 3rd May 2002, and arranged to meet him on 6th May at the Palace of India Curry House in York. At the meeting I made it clear that I was not impressed by his lack of candour at our first meeting, and told him that if he wished to make an offer, he should do so through the agents, Grover Greene. The reason I met Mr Thaw again was that although he had not been straightforward with me, I would clearly have been prepared to consider a genuine offer made by him in the conventional way, if he wished so to do.

Negotiations with Mr and Mrs Pollock

7.   My wife and I have known the Claimants socially, for about 15 years. I knew that they were potentially interested in buying the house, but not for the initial asking price. In about August or September 2002, I received

a telephone call from Mr Wolfe, the manager at Convent County. As a result of this conversation, I was left with the firm impression that if we did not dispose of the property quickly, Convent County would apply to reinstate the possession order. This would, of course, have caused us considerable problems, which we wished to avoid if at all possible.

8.   I therefore spoke to Mr and Mrs Pollock, who confirmed that they were interested in buying the property. They made an offer via Grover Greene of £310,000. This was attractive in so far as they did not require vacant possession until January 2003. At this stage, the only other person interested was a Mrs Maggot, who was also prepared to pay £310,000, but who said that if we were prepared to wait for her exchange of contracts, she might be able to increase the offer to £350,000. I was not particularly attracted to this, however, as there was no binding commitment on her to increase the offer, and she could well merely have repeated her original offer. Additionally, there was clearly a risk that Convent County would not wait until such time (if at all) as she exchanged contracts on her existing property.

9.   I was conscious of the fact that Mr Thaw might approach Mr and Mrs Pollock to acquire part of the garden. This led to negotiations between the Pollocks and us, concerning the land at the rear of the garden, described as 'the back land'. It was eventually agreed in September 2002 that the Pollocks would proceed at £310,000, but in the event that they ever sold the back land (whether to Mr Thaw or otherwise) the profit would be shared equally between us. Mr Hunt was made aware of the situation, and the benefit of this agreement would have formed part of my assets in the voluntary arrangement.

Austin and Foxhole's retainer
10.   I retained Messrs Austin and Foxhole to act on my behalf in September 2002. The firm had acted for me on a number of matters for about 5 years. I explained the nature of the transaction including arrangements concerning the back land, and left them to deal with all matters. My principal contact was Charles Coote, although the work was carried out by Mrs Dingle, under the supervision of S. A. Tombs, a partner in the firm. On 27th September 2002 my wife and I signed a letter of disclosure to Austin and Foxhole to obtain the necessary information regarding the sale from the mortgagees. Further, as we were due to go away on holiday on 4th October 2002, I signed an Authority for

Mrs Dingle to sign the contract of sale, on our behalf. I did this, of course, on the assumption that this would not be done until they had obtained the necessary consents from the various mortgagees.

Mr Thaw's intervention

11.   My wife returned from Portugal on 14th October, and I returned the following day. During the course of our holiday, we had received a telephone message from someone from Austin and Foxhole (I do not remember who), to tell us that contracts had been exchanged.

12.   However, on our return, Mr Coote told me that there had been problems concerning the sale. He said to me that one of his staff had been guilty of an act of negligence, in exchanging contracts with only a verbal consent from the mortgagees. Apparently Furness Bank were now refusing to release their charge.

13.   When I opened the post on returning from holiday, I discovered a letter from Peter Potts dated 14th October 2002, confirming a message which had apparently been left on my telephone answering machine on Friday 11th October. The letter enclosed an offer from Mr Thaw, to purchase the property at £365,000. As far as I was aware, this was the first time that Mr Thaw had made a formal offer to purchase the property. Of course, I did not receive the telephone call, as I was away, and contracts had been exchanged by the time I had sight of the letter.

14.   I believe that Mr Coote endeavoured to resolve matters with Furness Bank, but without success. I had various meetings with him, during the course of which he confirmed that the property would have to be sold to the Pollocks, and he informed me that his firm's insurers would be responsible for any shortfall due to Furness Bank. On 22nd November 2002 we had a further meeting, in the course of which he told me that his practice could no longer continue acting for us, and recommended that we sought independent advice elsewhere. I therefore contacted Mr Steven Sheep of Messrs Rottweiler and Dogg, who agreed to act.

Re-negotiations

15.   I understand that there were then protracted negotiations between Rottweiler and Dogg, solicitors for the Claimants, solicitors for the mortgagees, and the Official Receiver. On 29th November 2002 I attended a meeting at the offices of Hunt & Co. Mr Thaw attended the meeting, and

alleged that he was representing a former employee of mine (a gardener), who was asserting a claim. After the meeting, Mr Thaw waited outside and approached me to see if we could still come to terms. I immediately reported the conversation to Tony Hunt.

16.   Subsequently the contract was re-negotiated by Steven Sheep. The revised deal was that the Claimants would pay £350,000, which was paid to Furness Bank plc. An agreement was entered into between the Pollocks, my wife and I, her Trustee in bankruptcy, and Mr Hunt, which provided that the Trustee in bankruptcy and Mr Hunt would each have a charge over the back land. This would entitle them to a quarter each of any profit derived on a sale. Thus neither my wife nor I would receive any personal benefit. In so far as the Pollocks were concerned, they had to pay £40,000 more for the property.

17.   On 30th September 2003, Rottweiler and Dogg sent me accounts in respect of the work carried out over and above standard conveyancing work, which amounted to a total of £7,406.91 inclusive of VAT.

Signed ...

Statement of Truth (etc.)

...

This is, of course, a complex set of facts in a fairly substantial case. You can see that I have divided the statement using sub-headings, in the same manner as may from time to time be appropriate in an affidavit, applying, once again, the cardinal rule: 'If it helps to make the case more clear, it is the right thing to do.' Other than that, I hope that the example explains itself and embodies the principles that I have advocated throughout this work. Even though it may be argued that we should employ different techniques here than we should use in an affidavit, I think that a clear and logical exposition of our case has its own persuasive force. Of course, I do not put the example forward as being the ultimate that can be achieved, and if you feel that you can do better, please do not let me for one moment stop you. Above all, do not be induced into believing that the drafting of witness statements requires any fresh or radical techniques of drafting, and be wary of those who would have you think otherwise.

Let me deal now with a situation where it may be thought permissible to inject a little more persuasive effect into a statement. As I have indicated above, this should not normally be done in the case of a witness state-ment, subject to the best possible presentation of the evidence. However, where an affidavit is being sworn in support of some relief claimed where the Court has a discretion which you want to have exercised in your favour, slightly different drafting considerations may apply. In accordance with hallowed tradition, here is an example. I have chosen an instance which may equally be in affidavit or sworn statement format, it matters not. I will draft it as an affidavit. It will be an application in a family matter, for a non-molestation order and for a residence order, requiring the other party to leave the home in which the parties have been cohabiting. The bald facts, which we shall assume are developed to a greater extent in our instructions from the Applicant, are:

> The parties began a relationship in 1996. In 1997 they decided to live together in the Applicant's council property, which was (and still is) held by her under a tenancy in her sole name.
>
> There are two children of the relationship. In June 2005 the Applicant discovered that the Respondent was having an affair. This affair has continued, and he has never sought to hide it, often using it to cause distress to the Applicant. However the Respondent continued to live in the property. This may be because his girlfriend is also married.
>
> Although the Applicant 'hung on' for a long time, in the hope that she could save the relationship, she became fed up with the girlfriend constantly telephoning the house. Relations with the Respondent had not unnaturally become very strained, and from about June 2005 he began to drink a lot. From time to time he has used violence to the Applicant, mainly the occasional slap or kick. He often abuses her ver-bally, and has tried to make her life a misery by stopping her watching television, and telling her that all the contents of the home belong to him and that she should not touch any of them without his permission.
>
> In May 2006 the girlfriend again telephoned the home, and the Applicant asked her not to do so. She then decided that she had had enough, and told the Respondent that he should either get rid of the girlfriend or get out. In the course of the ensuing argument, he slapped her across the face a few times, and kicked her several times on the shins. The Applicant had to go to the chemist to get some medication.

After this, the Respondent left the house, and didn't come back until the early hours of the following Friday, 7 days later. He started screaming abuse at the Applicant, who was asleep in the bedroom and who had locked the door. He then banged on the door, upsetting one of the children. When the Applicant went downstairs to placate him, he punched and kicked her, called her a 'slag', and then left the house, threatening to return.

Let us review the situation, and our objectives, before putting pen to paper.

First, there should be little if any difference between an affidavit in support of an application without notice, and one made in the course of proceedings on notice. In both you are under a duty to inform the Court of any matters detrimental to your case, or which may prompt the Court not to make an order in your favour. We are, of course, always under a duty not to mislead the Court, and every affidavit is supposed to be a full and frank exposition of our case.

Secondly, we must, as usual, be certain as to the principles of law upon which the Court will act in deciding whether or not to grant the relief claimed. The affidavit should ideally be angled towards demonstrating that the facts deposed to are such that the Court would feel compelled to grant what we seek.

Next, we must be alive to the relevant matters which are required to be stated in the course of our affidavit. Even if we have a rock-solid case, we must comply with the Rules. Failure to do so may have severe results in human terms, in that an unacceptable situation may have to continue due to non-compliance with essential Rules of Court. The rationale is that these Rules are there to protect the other side from injustice. Whether or not you agree, it is better not to have to argue the point in the first place!

Having apprised ourselves of all the above, we must now turn to the facts of the case in hand. Let us assume that we have already correctly decided that the case is appropriate for an application of the nature that we have made, and are about to support by means of the affidavit. We must now consider the most appropriate form in which to present the affidavit itself. Although such an affidavit can be endorsed on a standard form, the facts here require some exposition; and in any event, this is an illustration of drafting techniques, so just bear with me please!

I suggest that we must adopt the same form of tactics as we would in 'normal' advocacy. Remember that our objectives must be:

To impart all necessary factual and other information in as concise a manner as is consistent with it being easily digested by someone who has not had contact with the case before;

and then

To do so in a manner as supportive as possible to the application or proceedings in which the affidavit is being drafted;

subject to the overriding duty to do so in a manner consistent with professional integrity and ethics.

Having said all that, there is nonetheless a basic blueprint which may be applicable in most circumstances. Very broadly speaking, I would suggest that you should:

(a) state your objectives;

(b) deal with the facts in chronological order;

(c) submit what you say are the necessary inferences and conclusions that can be drawn from these facts;

(d) if necessary, express your (client's) fears as to the consequences if the relief asked for is not granted (that concentrates minds somewhat — let's not call it emotional blackmail!);

(e) sum up shortly, asking the Court to grant your application in all the circumstances.

However, for the purposes of comparison, let me start by drafting what would be a perfectly serviceable, if somewhat inadequate affidavit, on the Applicant's behalf.

Sworn on behalf of the Applicant
Deponent: P Hooligan
1st affidavit
Exhibit PH1
Sworn: 26th May 2006

IN THE EDGWARE COUNTY COURT   Case No. EG020000

BETWEEN:

Mrs PHILLIPA HOOLIGAN

Applicant

— and —

Mr TIMOTHY BUSTUP

<u>Respondent</u>

AFFIDAVIT OF PHILLIPA HOOLIGAN

I, PHILLIPA HOOLIGAN of 238 Canons Drive, Edgware, Middlesex, STATE ON OATH as follows:

1. I am a housewife, and am the Applicant in the present action, and I make this affidavit in support of my application for a non-molestation order against the Respondent, and for an order excluding him from occupation of 238 Canons Drive, Edgware, pursuant to section 8 of the Children Act 1989. The matters set out in this affidavit are within my personal knowledge and are true to the best of my knowledge and belief.

2. The Respondent and I commenced a relationship in late 1996. We have two children, namely Alex Hooligan, born on 12th September 1997, and Vanessa Hooligan, born on 13th March 2003. Prior to our relationship I was living at the above address as a council tenant. The Respondent and I lived there together since 1997. The tenancy is in my sole name.

3. In June 2005, I discovered that the Respondent had been having an affair with Winifred Rabbit-Feather, which had commenced in 1999. We have however, both continued to reside in the home, although our relationship has become extremely strained.

4. Since June 2005 the Respondent has commenced drinking to excess. He has also become extremely abusive to me, and is sometimes violent. He will not allow me to watch the television, and says that everything in the house belongs to him. He will therefore not allow me to touch anything in the house whilst he is at home.

5. Mrs Rabbit-Feather constantly telephones the Respondent at the house. I have answered the telephone on a number of

occasions, and find this quite upsetting. I have asked her not
to telephone at the house, but have been told by her that her
relationship with the Respondent is none of my business,
and that she will telephone if she wishes to do so.

6.   On 17th May 2006 Mrs Rabbit-Feather telephoned the
house once again. I answered the telephone, and again asked
her not to 'phone the house any more. The Respondent was
in earshot of my conversation and he became annoyed with
me, and told me that I had no right to speak to her in that
manner. There was then an altercation between the
Respondent and myself, in the course of which I told him
that he should either stop the relationship with Mrs Rabbit-
Feather, or get out of my house. At this he slapped me across
the face about 4 or 5 times, causing my nose to bleed. He
then kicked me several times on the shins. As a result of the
slaps, I had to go to the local chemist in order to get some
medication.

7.   Immediately after this assault, the Respondent left the
house and did not return until about 7am on Friday, 26th
May 2006. On his arrival, the Respondent commenced
shouting and screaming abuse at me, whilst coming up the
stairs towards the bedroom in which I was sleeping. I locked
the bedroom door, and the Respondent then started banging
on the door, and shouting threats and abuse at me. Vanessa
was sleeping with me in the bed and started to cry when she
heard the noise being made by the Respondent.

8.   After a few minutes the Respondent went downstairs,
and I went after him to try and placate him. As soon as
I entered the kitchen, the Respondent punched me in the face,
tripped me up and knocked me to the ground, and started
kicking me. He then left the house shouting 'I'll be back,
you slag!'

PH1 9.   As a result of this beating, I went to see my doctor, and
his report is now shown to me marked PH1.

10.   I am afraid that, unless prevented by this Court from so
doing, the Respondent will return to the home and beat me

again, possibly causing me even more serious bodily harm than has so far been the case. Additionally, I am concerned for the safety of the children, who are clearly very distressed by what has been going on. I therefore respectfully ask this Court to grant me the orders set out in my present application.

Sworn etc.

Now although this is quite adequate, it can be presented in a form far more attractive to our purposes than is presently the case. Let us therefore apply the principles outlined above in order to do so, albeit without over-gilding the lily or descending into melodrama. I will deal with each paragraph in turn.

> I, PHILLIPA HOOLIGAN of 238 Canons Drive, Edgware, Middlesex, STATE ON OATH as follows:
>
> 1. I am a housewife, and am the Applicant in the present action, and I make this affidavit in support of my application for a non-molestation order against the Respondent, and for an order excluding him from occupation of 238 Canons Drive, Edgware, pursuant to section 8 of the Children Act 1989. The matters set out in this affidavit are within my personal knowledge and are true to the best of my knowledge and belief.

There seems no reason to make any alterations to this paragraph. So far we have introduced the Deponent, and stated why this affidavit is being made. Logically, we should now draw in some background details that may be relevant to the application, and which will hopefully assist the Court in understanding the facts that we are about to set out:

> 2. The Respondent and I commenced a relationship in late 1996. We have two children, namely Alex Hooligan, born on 12th September 1997, and Vanessa Hooligan, born on 13th March 2003. Prior to our relationship I was living at the above address as a council tenant. The Respondent and I lived there together since 1997. The tenancy is in my sole name.

I can see no reason to play about with this paragraph either. It is factual and uncontroversial.

Now let us paint some more background detail, which is particularly pertinent to the present application. Here, I consider that we should differ from the original version, which reads:

> 3.   In June 2005, I discovered that the Respondent had been having an affair with Winifred Rabbit-Feather, which had commenced in 1999. We have however, both continued to reside in the home, although our relationship has become extremely strained.

This paragraph is very much in the mould of the previous one, in that it contains a bald statement of facts, which are presumably going to be admitted. On the other hand, this is the first allegation of wrongful behaviour by the Respondent, and is possibly worthy of a bit more in the way of explanation:

> 3.   Sometime during the course of 1999, the Respondent started a relationship with Winifred Rabbit-Feather, and I believe that they have continued their relationship to this day. This affair was admitted by the Respondent in about June 2005 after I became suspicious of his frequent absences from home, and he has never flinched from admitting the continuing affair. Indeed, on many occasions, particularly in recent months, he has flaunted the relationship whenever he feels that it will cause me particular distress.

Now, although some of the above is not strictly necessary for the purposes of our application, it nevertheless serves to show up the Respondent for the thoroughly unpleasant fellow we say he is, and certainly cannot be said to be gratuitous mud-slinging. At this stage, we should perhaps develop this in order to set out the background to our present application. We will insert another paragraph, continuing with an exposition of our client's long-suffering, nay, saintly, nature:

> 4.   Notwithstanding the Respondent's affair, I was hopeful that we could still keep our relationship together, particularly as he showed no signs of wishing to move out of the home. However, it became clear that he wanted the best of both worlds, and had no intention of giving up the relationship

with Mrs Rabbit-Feather, who seems to have no qualms about regularly telephoning our home, much to my distress.

What we have done here is to continue the relevant narrative, but in a style consistent with the picture we are attempting to paint of the Applicant. We have also introduced the distress caused by the telephoning, which, on our instructions, was ultimately the cause of the violence towards us of which we are presently complaining. Notice also that, whereas the previous draft referred to 'the house', the present example speaks of 'the home', which carries important psychological connotations.

Now let us continue the narrative, moving ever closer to the present day, and dealing only with matters relevant to our present application. The paragraph in the previous example went as follows:

> Since June 2006 the Respondent has commenced drinking to excess. He has also become extremely abusive to me, and is sometimes violent. He will not allow me to watch the television, and says that everything in the house belongs to him. He will therefore not allow me to touch anything in the house whilst he is at home.

The difficulty with this paragraph is that it is 'flat'. It recites facts, yet is not persuasive. It does not specifically relate to the present application. Thus, in deciding how to 'ginger it up', we must seek to make it more relevant:

> 5.   Since I discovered the affair, the Respondent's behaviour has changed considerably for the worse. He began to drink to excess, and has often yelled abuse at me. From time to time he has been violent, mainly by [describing the nature of one or two incidents, such as throwing plates about the kitchen, and occasionally slapping me across the face]. He has also (incorrectly) maintained that the entire contents of our home belong to him, and will not allow me to touch anything whilst he is there. He also prevents me from watching the television.

What we have done is to describe his behaviour in the context of the relationship between the parties. Whether or not the drinking was prompted by the discovery of the affair we cannot say, but it is nevertheless true that it started at much the same time. The Court may wish to draw its own conclusions in the absence of any explanation by the Respondent. Additionally, as we are making an application for an order as a result of allegations of violence, it is incumbent on us to be specific about the violence that has been offered. However, although it will be necessary to describe the latest or 'active' event in detail, we can deal with previous matters in more general terms, although I consider the original example to be too general. Again the words 'our home' have been substituted for 'the house' in order to give a more personal touch to the paragraph.

At this stage, we should link in Mrs Rabbit-Feather with the cause of the present problem. Instead of:

> Mrs Rabbit-Feather constantly telephones the Respondent at the house. I have answered the telephone on a number of occasions, and find this quite upsetting. I have asked her not to telephone at the house, and have been told by her that her relationship with the Respondent is none of my business, and that she will telephone if she wishes to do so.

let us put:

> 6. As I have said, Mrs Rabbit-Feather does not seem to have any conscience about telephoning the Respondent at our home. I have answered the telephone on a number of occasions, and have found this quite upsetting. I have asked her not to telephone at the house, but have been told by her that her relationship with the Respondent is none of my business, and that she will telephone if she wishes to do so. It is this that has led to the recent incident in which I was assaulted by the Respondent.

All this has done is to link the conduct of Mrs Rabbit-Feather (who is clearly painted as a co-conspirator with the Respondent in this case) with the matters which are to form the basis of the present application. The next paragraph of the original draft can be inserted almost in its entirety, save that we may wish to be a little more specific about the pain caused by the assault, so we adapt the original:

> On 17th May 2006 Mrs Rabbit-Feather telephoned the house once again. I answered the telephone, and again asked her

not to 'phone the house any more. The Respondent was in earshot of my conversation and he became annoyed with me, and told me that I had no right to speak to her in that manner. There was then an altercation between the Respondent and myself, in the course of which I told him that he should either stop the relationship with Mrs Rabbit-Feather, or get out of my house. At this he slapped me across the face about 4 or 5 times, causing my nose to bleed. He then kicked me several times on the shins. As a result of the slaps, I had to go to the local chemist in order to get some medication.

to read:

7.   On 17th May 2006 Mrs Rabbit-Feather telephoned the house once again. I answered the telephone, and again asked her not to 'phone the house any more. The Respondent obviously overheard the conversation and became annoyed with me, telling me that I had no right to speak to her in that manner. There was then an altercation between the Respondent and myself, in the course of which I told him that he should either stop the relationship with Mrs Rabbit-Feather, or get out of my house. When I said this, he slapped me across the face about 4 or 5 times, causing my nose to bleed. He then kicked me several times on the shins. As a result of the slaps, I was in considerable pain, and my nose was so badly hurt that I had to go to the local chemist in order to get some medication to relieve the pain and stop the bleeding.

The minor changes in construction are designed to make the paragraph flow in a convincing manner, and in accordance with the mood that we are trying to paint.

The next two paragraphs describe the incident which has given rise to the present applications, and need not, in my view, undergo any modification:

8.   Immediately after this assault, the Respondent left the house and did not return until about 7am on Friday, 26th May 2006. On his arrival, the Respondent commenced shouting and screaming abuse at me, whilst coming up the stairs towards the bedroom in which I was sleeping. I locked the bedroom door, and the Respondent then started banging

on the door, and shouting threats and abuse at me. Vanessa
was sleeping with me in the bed and started to cry when she
heard the noise being made by the Respondent.

9.   After a few minutes the Respondent went downstairs,
and I went after him to try and placate him. As soon as
I entered the kitchen, the Respondent punched me in the
face, tripped me up and knocked me to the ground, and
started kicking me. He then left the house shouting 'I'll be
back, you slag!'

So far, so bad! We have now completed the narrative section of the
affidavit. What now remains is to describe the nature of the injuries
inflicted, and the effect of the Respondent's present and threatened
future behaviour on the Applicant (and the children), in order to provide
the basis for the relief which we are seeking. The bald statement in paragraph 9 of the original draft:

As a result of this beating, I went to see my doctor, and his
report is now shown to me marked PH1.

can be redrafted to better effect. How about:

PH1   10.   As a result of this beating I suffered [give particulars
of injuries, e.g., bruising to the ribs, etc.] and was forced to
see my doctor, whose report describing my injuries is now
shown to me marked PH1.

The difference between this and the original draft is not great, but once
again sets the facts in the context appropriate for the applications that we
are making, and without being melodramatic or (much worse) making
things up. Note incidentally the new format for identifying exhibits —
far more straightforward than before the CPR. However, we are now
required to identify any documents referred to in the text, by an indication in the margin, and I have done so here. Those of you who find, like
me, that your word-processors decide to re-format the whole text when
performing this exercise, should please contact the Lord Chief Justice —
I didn't make the rule!

Now we must continue with the essential paragraph describing the
Applicant's fears for the future. This is the sole justification for granting

the orders that the Court is being asked to make. All the previous paragraphs are to show that there is a real, and not an imagined, risk of future violence, thus making it appropriate to grant the Draconian orders applied for. The final paragraph of the original draft is again adequate for these purposes, although it may not be thought to communicate sufficiently the fears that the Applicant has for the safety of herself and her children:

> I am afraid that, unless restrained by this Court from so doing, the Respondent will return to the home and beat me again, possibly causing me even more serious bodily harm than has so far been the case. Additionally, I am concerned for the safety of the children, who are clearly very distressed by what has been going on. I therefore respectfully ask this Court to grant me the relief asked for in my present application.

There seems no reason why we should not fully express the Applicant's real fears:

> 11. I am now very afraid of the Respondent, particularly when he is in drink. I believe that in his present state of mind he is quite capable of returning to the home and causing damage and injury to myself and possibly the children. Both of the children are young and need looking after, and I cannot leave the home, having nowhere else to go with them. On the other hand, the Respondent managed to stay away from the home for 7 days, and clearly has some form of accommodation elsewhere.

and then finish in the manner expressed in the original draft:

> 12. I believe that, unless prevented by this Court from so doing, the Respondent will return to the home and beat me again, possibly causing me even more serious bodily harm than has so far been the case. Additionally, I am concerned for the safety of the children, who are clearly very distressed by what has been going on. I therefore respectfully ask this Court to grant me the relief set out in my present application.

Sworn etc.

Again, I have made minor changes to the last paragraph for reasons of style and emphasis. The finished product thus reads as follows:

> Sworn on behalf of the Applicant
> Deponent: P Hooligan
> 1st affidavit
> Exhibit PH1
> Sworn: 26th May 2006

IN THE EDGWARE COUNTY COURT   Case No. EG020000

BETWEEN:

Mrs PHILLIPA HOOLIGAN

Applicant

— and —

Mr TIMOTHY BUSTUP

Respondent

AFFIDAVIT OF PHILLIPA HOOLIGAN

I, PHILLIPA HOOLIGAN of 238 Canons Drive, Edgware, Middlesex, STATE ON OATH as follows:

1.   I am a housewife, and am the Applicant in the present action, and I make this affidavit in support of my application for a non-molestation order against the Respondent, and for an order excluding him from occupation of 238 Canons Drive, Edgware, Middlesex, pursuant to section 8 of the Children Act 1989. The matters set out in this affidavit are within my personal knowledge and are true to the best of my knowledge and belief.

2.   The Respondent and I commenced a relationship in late 1996. We have two children, namely Alex Hooligan, born on 12th September 1997, and Vanessa Hooligan, born on 13th March 2003. Prior to our relationship I was living at the above address as a council tenant. The Respondent and I lived there together since 1997. The tenancy is in my sole name.

3.   Sometime during the course of 1999, the Respondent started a relationship with Winifred Rabbit-Feather, and I believe that they have continued their relationship to this day. This affair was admitted by the Respondent in about June 2005 after I became suspicious of his frequent absences from home, and he has never flinched from admitting the continuing affair. Indeed, on many occasions, particularly in recent months, he has flaunted the relationship whenever he feels that it will cause me particular distress.

4.   Notwithstanding the Respondent's affair, I was hopeful that we could still keep our relationship together, particularly as he showed no signs of wishing to move out of the home. However, it became clear that he wanted the best of both worlds, and had no intention of giving up the relationship with Mrs Rabbit-Feather, who seems to have no qualms about regularly telephoning our home, much to my distress.

5.   Since I discovered the affair, the Respondent's behaviour has changed considerably for the worse. He began to drink to excess and has often yelled abuse at me. From time to time he has been violent, mainly by [describing the nature of one or two incidents, such as throwing plates about the kitchen, and occasionally slapping me across the face]. He has also (incorrectly) maintained that the entire contents of our home belong to him, and will not allow me to touch anything whilst he is there. He also prevents me from watching the television.

6.   As I have said, Mrs Rabbit-Feather does not seem to have any conscience about telephoning the Respondent at our home. I have answered the telephone on a number of occasions, and have found this quite upsetting. I have asked her not to telephone at the house, but have been told by her that her relationship with the Respondent is none of my business, and that she will telephone if she wishes to do so. It is this that has led to the recent incident in which I was assaulted by the Respondent.

7.   On 17th May 2006 Mrs Rabbit-Feather telephoned the house once again. I answered the telephone, and again asked her not to 'phone the house any more. The Respondent obviously overheard the conversation and became annoyed with me, telling me that I had no right to speak to her in that manner. There was then an altercation between the Respondent and myself, in the course of which I told him that he should either stop the relationship with Mrs Rabbit-Feather, or get out of my house.

When I said this, he slapped me across the face about 4 or 5 times, causing my nose to bleed. He then kicked me several times on the shins. As a
result of the slaps, I was in considerable pain, and my nose was so badly
hurt that I had to go to the local chemist in order to get some medication
to relieve the pain and stop the bleeding.

8.   Immediately after this assault, the Respondent left the house
and did not return until about 7am on Friday, 26th May 2006. On his
arrival, the Respondent commenced shouting and screaming abuse at
me, whilst coming up the stairs towards the bedroom in which I was
sleeping. I locked the bedroom door, and the Respondent then started
banging on the door, and shouting threats and abuse at me. Vanessa was
sleeping with me in the bed and started to cry when she heard the noise
being made by the Respondent.

9.   After a few minutes the Respondent went downstairs, and
I went after him to try and placate him. As soon as I entered the kitchen,
the Respondent punched me in the face, tripped me up and knocked me
to the ground, and started kicking me. He then left the house shouting
'I'll be back, you slag!'

PH1 10.   As a result of this beating I suffered [give particulars of
          injuries, e.g., bruising to the ribs, etc.] and was forced to see my
          doctor, whose report describing my injuries is now shown to me
          marked PH1.

11.   I am now very afraid of the Respondent, particularly when he is
in drink. I believe that in his present state of mind he is quite capable of
returning to the home and causing damage and injury to myself and possibly the children. Both of the children are young and need looking after,
and I cannot leave the home, having nowhere else to go with them. On
the other hand, the Respondent managed to stay away from the home for
7 days, and clearly has some form of accommodation elsewhere.

12.   I believe that, unless prevented by this Court from so doing, the
Respondent will return to the home and beat me again, possibly causing me
even more serious bodily harm than has so far been the case. Additionally,
I am concerned for the safety of the children, who are clearly very distressed
by what has been going on. I therefore respectfully ask this Court to grant
me the relief set out in my present application.

Sworn etc.

I hope that you will agree that this version is far more persuasive than the original draft, even though they are both accurately based on the same facts.

Lastly, let me give an example of an affidavit which is of a less emotive nature, in order to illustrate a fairly typical interim application. The Rules require merely that the application be supported by 'evidence', which in this case can mean either a witness statement or an affidavit, as it is unlikely that the subject of our action (security for costs) is going to be dealt with in any of the statements of case. I will use the affidavit form, as the facts that are going to be relied on have largely been obtained by or on the advice of a solicitor in the course of his instructions. I suppose he could make a witness statement, but I think that it would be more appropriate in the circumstances to use the more 'traditional' affidavit form:

> You, Zachariah Honk, are a partner in a firm of solicitors rejoicing in the name of Whinge and Co. You are privileged to act for Mr Rudolph Hiccup, who is the Defendant in an action brought against him by Jerribuild Ltd who claim £120,000 for building works carried out to his property.

You have reason to doubt the financial probity of the Claimant Company, and have advised your client to make an application that the Claimants therefore give security for costs.

I shall depart from my usual practice of setting a complete scene, as the facts are clearly subservient to the concept being discussed. Instead, I shall deal with the paragraphs in order, commenting on points of especial and gripping interest. For the present purposes, let us assume that Mr Honk has already filed an affidavit and exhibits in this case on, say, an application to strike out the Claimant's claim as disclosing no cause of action. Let us commence with the appropriate heading. First, the indorsement:

Sworn on behalf of the Defendant
Deponent Z. Honk
2nd affidavit
Sworn: 25th May 2006
Exhibits ZH1–ZH3

Then the heading of the action:

IN THE HIGH COURT OF JUSTICE   2006 J No. 0000
QUEEN'S BENCH DIVISION

BETWEEN:

JERRIBUILD LIMITED
                                                        Claimant
— and —

Mr RUDOLPH HICCUP
                                                        Defendant

---

AFFIDAVIT IN SUPPORT OF DEFENDANT'S APPLICATION
FOR SECURITY FOR COSTS

Next, we commence our identification of the Deponent etc. Note that
this paragraph is not given a number.

> I, Zachariah Honk, of Messrs Whinge and Co., 87 Whinding
> Road, Little Groaning, STATE ON OATH as follows:

It is quite possible in the above instance, to include his profession in this
paragraph, so as to read:

> I, Zachariah Honk, of Messrs Whinge and Co., 87 Whinding
> Road, Little Groaning, Solicitor and Partner in the above
> firm, STATE ON OATH as follows:

Were we to do that, we would, of course, omit the statement of his profession in the first substantive paragraph. Otherwise we would have to
describe him in addition to the other matters that must be contained
therein. These other matters will be:

(a)   the capacity in which he makes the affidavit;
(b)   the reasons for which the affidavit is made;
(c)   the truth of the affidavit and sources of his knowledge;
(d)   any references to previous affidavits sworn by him.

I will draft the appropriate paragraph, and then comment further:

> 1.   I am a solicitor of the Supreme Court, and a partner in the above firm. I have the conduct of this Action on behalf of the Defendant and am duly authorised to make this affidavit on his behalf. The matters to which I shall depose are true to the best of my knowledge and belief, and are either within my personal knowledge, or have been supplied to me in the course of my instructions. I refer to my previous affidavit in this Action sworn on 3rd March 2006 together with the exhibits thereto. I make this affidavit in support of the Defendant's application that the Claimant Company do give security for the costs of their claim,

When a solicitor is making an affidavit on behalf of his or her client, it is nevertheless a sworn statement of evidence which is believed to be true. Thus it is imperative for the Deponent to make it clear not only that he or she believes the matters to be true, but also the capacity in which the affidavit is made, and the circumstances in which the information contained therein has been acquired.

The reference to a previous affidavit may not always be necessary, but can be useful where the previous document contains a narrative history or other matter relevant to the present application, but which need not be repeated in the affidavit which you are about to draft. Do not forget to make reference to the exhibits to the previous affidavits, as these are also incorporated as evidence, and thus may equally be relevant to your present application. Remember also that the Practice Direction to CPR Part 32 requires (as I am sure you know) that exhibits should be numbered consecutively **from** the old affidavit, and should not start afresh.

Now we can turn to the 'meat' of the affidavit. We have already conveniently stated the purpose for which the document is being drafted, now we must state the basis of our application. I do not propose to discuss the facts in any great detail, but it is important to see how relevant documentation can neatly be incorporated into the body of the affidavit, by use of exhibits.

Exhibits themselves must be used in the most efficacious manner. Sometimes it will be better to discuss the basic outline of what you wish to say, and then 'tack on' the exhibit at the end of the paragraph, in order to provide proof of your contentions. Sometimes it is preferable to start with the exhibit, and then discuss relevant parts in the course of the paragraph.

We must also take care in the way in which the exhibits are set out and labelled. Each individual exhibit attracts a fee on swearing, and thus it is both cumbersome and uneconomical to set out each individual document as a separate exhibit. Thus, avoid:

> ABC 1   There is now shown to me marked ABC 1, a copy
>   of a letter from the Claimant to the Defendant
>   dated 3rd June 2004 in which ... etc. There is fur-
>   ther shown to me marked ABC 2
> ABC 2   a copy of the Defendant's letter in reply dated 10th
>   June 2004 in which ... etc.

The appropriate manner to deal with correspondence, and matters which can conveniently be dealt with together, is by doing just that — make a correspondence or other bundle as a single exhibit, number the pages and refer to the bundle as such:

> ABC 1   There is shown to me marked ABC 1, a bundle of
>   correspondence. Page 1 of the same consists of a
>   letter from the Claimant to the Defendant dated
>   3rd June 2004 in which he states ... etc. Page 2
>   comprises the Defendant's reply dated 10th June
>   2004 ... etc.

It is quite possible to do this with documents of a common nature, which may not require detailed analysis of every page, such as conveyancing documents etc., although you must use your own discretion as to whether it is better on occasions to deal with these by way of individual exhibits.

Continuing with our example, I will use the next three paragraphs to develop our case, using exhibits, facts and submissions in various ways, to demonstrate their most persuasive effect:

> ZH 1   2.   There is shown to me marked ZH 1 a copy of
>   a search made on the Claimant Company, which
>   shows that it was incorporated in December 1986,
>   and has failed to submit its last annual return on time.
>   Additionally, and importantly, it has never submitted
>   any accounts. The Claimant is a private limited com-
>   pany with a nominal share capital of 1,000 ordinary
>   shares of £1 each, of which only 10 have been
>   issued. The three Company officers all reside at the

same address, which is also the Registered Office of the Company. All Company correspondence has been signed by John Fastbuck, who is the majority shareholder.

3.   I respectfully submit there are substantial grounds for believing that the Claimant Company is in a parlous financial state, and would be unable to meet the costs of this Action in the likely event that

ZH 2   it loses the same. There is shown to me marked ZH 2 a bundle of documents relating to the financial position of the Claimant Company. Page 1 of the bundle comprises a letter from the Claimant to the Credit Controller of Trustybrick Ltd dated 23rd June 2003, in which it apologises for being unable to pay for work carried out at an address in London E15, and asks for time, on the basis that it had not apparently been paid itself.

4.   Page 2 of the bundle is a copy of an application by the Claimant for a reduction in an instalment order made in the Putney County Court, under a judgment against them in Case Number PT960000. The application, which was to be heard on 28th September 2004 was made on the basis that 'the Company is in great difficulty at the moment, and there is nothing to take, therefore we will make an offer of £50 per month until the debt is completed'. I add in passing that this implies that the Company does not own the premises which comprise its trading and registered office. I am informed and I believe that the amount of the judgment debt was £3,000, and the Claimant's inability to meet that comparatively minor sum is, in my respectful submission extremely significant.

In these paragraphs we have laid our ground for showing that the situation comes within the rules whereby the Court can make an order that the Claimant Company provide security for costs. It has incorporated both argument and evidence, and has (I hope) done so in a way such as to exploit the potential of the evidence for supporting our submissions.

Now we must continue with the equation, by showing that there is a real
likelihood that the Claimant's claim will fall, and that this is not simply
a delaying tactic made by the Defendant, to take advantage of the
Claimant's possible financial difficulties.

> 5.   I believe that the Defendant has an extremely
> strong defence to the present action, and in support
> ZH 3 of his case there is shown to me marked ZH 3 the
> report of his consulting engineers Ignaz Scaffold
> Associates, dated 15th February 2005, a copy of
> which has already been disclosed to the Claimant.

I pause at this stage to observe that where the contents of a report are
self-explanatory, there seems little point in paraphrasing it in the course
of an affidavit, unless this can be done so succinctly, and to such great
effect, as will add relevantly to the force of your affidavit. Otherwise,
there seems little point in merely repeating matters which will have to be
read in any event.

> 6.   As a result of what I respectfully submit are very
> real and well-grounded fears, I wrote to the Claimant's
> solicitors on 29th March 2005 requesting security for
> the costs of the claim. This letter appears at pages 3
> ZH 2 and 4 of the bundle ZH 2 and evinced the negative
> response dated 5th April 2005 at page 5 of the bundle.
> I have caused a skeleton bill of costs to be drawn up
> which has been divided into two parts, namely between
> the inception of proceedings and after discovery, and
> thereafter from discovery to trial. These costs total
> £5,680, and substantially exceed the County Court
> judgment against the Claimant which it had so much
> difficulty in meeting. Should this matter eventually
> proceed to a full trial, the costs awarded in favour of
> the Defendant, should he be successful, will be very
> substantially greater than those incurred to date.

There's nothing better than having a good argument and being able to
put the boot in on your opponent! Here, every available opportunity has
been taken legitimately to weigh the scales, and leave the Court with the
overall impression that the other side are going to have to come up with

a jolly good argument to get around the otherwise likely result of your application. If we can, let us round the matter off by some positive points about our client, and then, for good measure, take another bash at the other side:

> 7. I am informed by the Defendant, and believe that he owns his own property, and is both solvent and gainfully employed. In the light of the Claimant's non-compliance with Company legislation, its admitted precarious financial position, and what I would respectfully submit is the weakness of its case, I would respectfully ask this Court to protect the Defendant's position by ordering the Claimant to give security for costs in the sum of £5,000, and that the Action be stayed in default.
>
> Sworn etc.

What has been done at the end, of course, is to summarise the effect of the submissions made, to provide a short and pithy exposition of the case in favour of the application. Notice how the Deponent 'is informed and believes' about the Defendant's job and financial security. It is normal for the source of the information to be stated, such as:

> 'I am informed by Hubert Vacuum-Cleaner, the Defendant's personal secretary, and believe ...'

and as in the present case it has already been stated that the information has come from the Defendant in the course of the Deponent's instructions, it is not strictly necessary to repeat this, unless the particular information has come from a different source, although I have chosen to do so. If the Defendant's financial position was personally known to Mr Honk, it will naturally be unnecessary for him to make a declaration that the evidence is hearsay. However, it is usually considered wise for a solicitor not to get too personally involved with his client's case, as it could cause professional embarrassment in the event of certain deposed matters not being accepted by the Court.

Lastly, a word about language. Uriah Heep would have loved affidavits. Rarely has a better opportunity been granted to those of 'umble disposition to doff their hats and bend the knee, in the course of a written document. You can 'respectfully submit' to your heart's content to 'this Honourable Court' (note the capital letters). You can even 'humbly request, with the greatest respect' that your application be granted. This was all fine and dandy in the ages when one was required to resort to this kind of etiquette in order to obtain the appropriate relief. Without in any way suggesting that the greatest of respect should not be given to the Court (and the system of justice that it represents), it is today considered unnecessary to indulge in this persiflage. One may certainly use the occasional 'respectful submission', as one would do in open Court. It is not necessary to use the phrase three times in the same paragraph! Likewise, it is in my view, perfectly and sufficiently polite to 'ask' or 'respectfully ask', rather than 'humbly request', and although no one will object were you to continue to refer to this 'Honourable Court', the word 'Honourable' is not an indispensable adjective if the word 'Court' alone were not actively to convey any disrespect. Be genuinely polite. Do not grovel and writhe!

So, as we have seen, the drafting of a witness statement or an affidavit is very much a matter of taste and style, to be adapted to the exigencies of the situation in hand. However, there are fundamental rules of logic, expression, tactics and clarity, that apply equally to all the documents which from time to time you may be called upon to draft. Having divested myself of all the above, I hope you can see the enormous and legitimate possibilities for presenting the client's arguments in the best possible light, whichever medium you use.

Chapter Eleven

Just a Minute
(Minutes and Agreed Orders)

Another Rule of Battle, that Alice had not noticed, seemed to be that they always fell on their heads; and the battle ended with their both falling off in this way, side by side. When they got up again, they shook hands, and then the Red Knight mounted and galloped off.

A significant but little discussed problem often occurs at the time when you least expect it. Either you have successfully negotiated a conclusion to whatever dispute may be currently occupying your attention, or perhaps you may be seeking injunctive relief, when suddenly you are faced with recording the final product.

In the case of an order to be approved by the Court, you should, of course, present a draft minute of order with your application and evidence. However, it is quite possible, if not probable, that the relief (if any) obtained will not be exactly in the form that you have anticipated. If the agreement is one negotiated at the door of the Court, you may be sent away to draw up the order and submit it for approval. Usually you will not have the luxury of being able to do this anywhere else than in the corridor or robing room, returning to Court to interpose the order whenever it, (or the Court) is ready.

Furthermore, any settlement negotiated either before the Court hearing, or at the door of the Court, will have to be put into writing, possibly at short notice, and certainly in a form which will properly reflect the manner in which the parties intend the agreement to have effect. Very often this will include some form of disposition of legal proceedings currently between the parties. There are many different ways of recording your agreement, and these should form part of the essential compass of your drafting skills.

'There are many different ways of recording your agreement ...'

In this chapter, I shall draw a distinction between the drafting of the minutes of an order that you may be asking the Court to make, and the recording of the outcome of negotiations between yourself and the other side, which may or may not have to be submitted for approval. As ever, there are basic principles that are common to both.

MINUTES OF ORDER

These essentially consist of three parts (rather like Gaul).

1.   The title to the action, together with a record of the circumstances in which the Court has made the order.

2. The undertakings given, or the conditions imposed in 'consideration' of the order being made.
3. The order itself.

I like it... I like it...

Julius Caesar's Minutes of Order

There is little of tactical interest in the drafting of these minutes. What is however essential is that all necessary required legal conditions and safeguards are contained therein, and that we have made appropriate and full provision for that which we require. The above form no part of the business of this work. However, the manner of their recording does, and you should find this a relatively straightforward matter once a basic mental blueprint has been adopted.

In an application made without notice, you will almost invariably have to attach to your application a draft of the order sought. This will of necessity contain certain undertakings on behalf of your client. Normally these are fairly straightforward, and in certain types of action, e.g. for freezing injunctions and search orders (formerly *Mareva* and *Anton Piller* orders), these will be set out on a standard form.

Applications to the Court are started by completing an Application Notice (well that's pretty logical), in Form N244. Applications for injunctive relief are still to be made on what was the old County Court prescribed Form N16A, but which is now common to both the High Court and County Courts. The nature and extent of the relief sought is set out in the application form, and any order of the Court will then be drawn up on a separate form (N16 or N16(1)).

In a noble attempt to make legal language more 'plain', these prescribed forms use terminology which, it is hoped, will be understood by the vast majority of litigants, without recourse to a lawyer (or a legal dictionary). How far these worthy ends have been met is, perhaps, a matter of individual opinion, but there is no doubt that the new forms use language more readily understood by the layman.

The first and primary undertaking is as to damages. I have no intention of allowing this work to degenerate into a mere recitation of precedents, but this undertaking is normally expressed using standard wording, and there is no reason whatsoever to try to be different, just for the hell of it. The words at the foot of Form N16 state:

> The Claimant gave an undertaking [through his counsel or solicitor] promising to pay any damages ordered by the court if it later decides that the Defendant/Respondent has suffered loss or damage as a result of this order for which the Claimant is liable to pay.

Although this wording is in modern English, it does not, in my opinion, tackle the point that technically the undertaking is otiose. Surely it is quite unnecessary for the client to undertake to abide by any subsequent Court order made? Such an order would in any event be binding, and any failure to comply with it will land the defaulter in hot water! The rationale behind this, is that the Court may otherwise have no power to order a Claimant to compensate a Defendant for complying with a Court Order. Whether an undertaking to comply with a Court Order to such effect actually solves the problem, must be debatable. After all, if the Order is made without power, it is irrelevant that the Claimant agrees to comply with it! I have always felt that it should be redrafted, so as to amount to an undertaking by the Claimant to pay damages if it is subsequently found that the application should not have been made.

In my view this would be a more accurate representation of the true situation. However, for present purposes, let us abide by convention, both new and old, particularly as this undertaking is a necessary precondition to the granting of much interim relief, and there is recent authority requiring the applicant to show that he is capable of meeting such an undertaking if called upon to do so.

Other undertakings are required according to the type of order which is being requested, and the degree and extent to which the action has already got off the ground. For example, it is possible, in appropriate cases, to obtain an injunction even before proceedings have been issued. In such circumstances, the injunction will be granted only upon a recited undertaking by the Claimant to issue a Claim Form forthwith, and (if this has not already been done) to ensure that the draft affidavit before the Court is sworn.

In applications made without notice, we will have to undertake to serve the proceedings, and the affidavit and any Order made, upon the Defendant in short course, and to inform him of his right to apply to the Court to have the Order set aside. There are also special paragraphs which are inserted (where appropriate) in freezing injunctions, and search orders. These are set out in the new form of words and can be adapted to meet the individual requirements of the case.

The body of the order will be set out on the appropriate form after the undertakings (if any) have been recorded. Often, it will be necessary only to put:

IT IS ORDERED AND DIRECTED:

after which the various parts of the Order will be tabulated.

Often, this will not present any difficulties from a drafting point of view. All we may have to put is:

1.   That unless the Defendant serves the Claimant by 4pm on [date] with a copy of the Defence, verified by a Statement of Truth, the Defence be struck out.

2.   The Defendant pay the Claimant's costs of this application, assessed at £[ ].

The matter does become a little more complicated, however, when applying for an injunction, or for a number of injunctions. Here, precision is vital, as the Defendant is entitled to know exactly what he is and is not permitted to do in the event of the application being granted.

It is thus essential that the terms of the draft order be carefully considered prior to making the application, both to ensure that we have applied
for everything that we think necessary, and to make certain that we have
not unfairly applied for too much, such that the Court will strike out half
our application, and force us to redraft the minute before making an
Order. This will take time, and may prejudice the client in cases of real
urgency.

When considering how to record our application for injunctive relief,
all we need do is to apply the same principles of logical analysis that we
would in deciding how to formulate our claim in the first place. Think:

(a)   What it is that we want.

(b)   What is the most that we can apply for (adding in a reasonable
measure on our side of the balance under the title 'what we think we can
get away with')!

(c)   What do we know will **not** be granted by the Court.

(d)   The best and most comprehensible way of listing our applications.

Let us, as ever, consider an example:

EXAMPLE

We are instructed by Miss Gertrude Housefly. She works at
Tootle and Scrape Ltd in Mouthwash, Sussex. On three occasions, she went out with a fellow employee called Johnny
Gnat, but then went off him. Last week, she told him she didn't
wish to go out with him any more. The night before last, he
came round to her house at 123 Gargle Avenue, Mouthwash,
at about 11.30 pm. He had obviously been drinking, and was
shouting and swearing. In order not to upset the neighbours,
Miss Housefly let him in. He said he wanted to spend the
night with her. She said 'no way' and asked him to leave.
He refused, and an argument ensued, in the course of which
he punched her in the stomach, tripped her up and kicked
her. He then left, shouting 'I'll come by whenever I want,
you cow!'

The following day a large poster appeared on the staff
notice board at Tootle and Scrape. It was crudely drawn, and
obscene. A letter stuck to it simply bore the words: 'Housefly
is a stuck up cow'.

Miss Housefly is very upset, and worried about further
harassment by Mr Gnat.

Having given the matter due consideration, we have decided to apply to the local County Court for an injunction. Due to the short time involved, we have not had time to issue our claim form endorsed with Particulars of Claim, but we have this ready. Likewise, the supporting affidavit is in the name of the Claimant, but has not yet been sworn. We will, however, have to complete the General Form of Application for Injunction (N16A) and, as Miss Housefly will be in Court to give the various undertakings herself, through you, we will also have to complete a General Form of Undertaking in Form N117. For your assistance, blank copies of both these forms are now set out, and for good measure I have thrown in a sample N244 Application Form. Don't say I don't pander to your every need!

Assuming that we have had the wit and presence of mind properly to insert the parties' names in the right places, let us turn to the nature of the proceedings.

We clearly want an injunction:

(a)   to restrain the Defendant from assaulting the Claimant;
(b)   to stop him coming to the house;
(c)   to prevent him from putting up any more posters or letters;

and we must carefully consider the degree and extent to which we require protection, and then make our application accordingly. We could, of course, simply ask for an order that the Defendant be restrained from:

1.   assaulting the Claimant;

2.   entering the Claimant's premises at 123 Gargle Avenue, Mouthwash, Sussex;

3.   putting up posters or letters referring to the Claimant on the notice board at the Claimant's place of work.

However, what if the Defendant chooses to obey the letter of the proposed order in the above terms, but not the spirit? An Order restraining him from assaulting the Claimant may prevent him personally from physically bashing her. However, what if he employs someone else to do the job? Although you would not catch me first in line begging for the opportunity to put the argument, it could be said that the Defendant would not technically be in breach of the terms of the injunction. Thus it will be necessary to extend the scope of the application somewhat.

Application for Injunction
(General Form)

Name of court	Claim No.
Claimant's Name and Ref.	
Defendant's Name and Ref.	

☐ By application in pending proceedings

☐ Under Statutory provision _____

☐ This application is made under Part 8 of the Civil Procedure Rules

Seal

This application raises issues under
the Human Rights Act 1998   ☐ Yes   ☐ No

Notes on completion

Tick which boxes apply and specify the legislation where appropriate

(1) Enter the full name of the person making the application

(2) Enter the full name of the person the injunction is to be directed to

(3) Set out here the proposed terms of the injunction order (if the defendant is a limited company delete the wording in brackets and insert "whether by its servants, agents, officers or otherwise")

(4) Set out here any proposed mandatory orders requiring acts to be done

(5) Set out here any further terms asked for including provision for costs

(6) Enter the names of all persons who have sworn affidavits or signed statements in support of this application

(7) Enter the names and addresses of all persons upon whom it is intended to serve this application

(8) Enter the full name and address for service and delete as required

The Claimant(1)

applies to the court for an injunction order in the following terms:

That the Defendant(2)

be forbidden (whether by himself or by instructing or encouraging any other person)(3)

And that the Defendant(4)

And that(5)

The grounds of this application are set out in the written evidence of(6)   sworn (signed) on

This written evidence is served with this application.
This application is to be served upon(7)

This application is filed by(8)

(the Solicitors for) the Claimant (Applicant/Petitioner)

whose address for service is

Signed   Dated

*
Name and address of the person application is directed to

This section to be completed by the court

To*
of

This application will be heard by the (District) Judge

at

on   **the**   **day of**   **[20   ]   at**

o'clock

If you do not attend at the time shown the court may make an injunction order in your absence

If you do not fully understand this application you should go to a Solicitor, Legal Advice Centre or a Citizens' Advice Bureau

The court office at

is open between 10am and 4pm Mon - Fri. When corresponding with the court, please address all forms and letters to the Court Manager and quote the claim number.

N16A General form of application for injunction (09.04)   *Designed by Publication Branch*

General Form of Undertaking

In the	
	County Court

Claimant	
Applicant	
Petitioner	

Between _____

Claim No.	
Claimant's Ref.	

Defendant	
Respondent	

and _____

This form is to be used only for an undertaking not for an injunction

(1) Name of the person giving undertaking

On the   day of   [19   ][20   ]

(1)

[appeared in person] [was represented by Solicitor / Counsel]
and gave an undertaking to the Court promising(2)

Seal

(2) Set out terms of undertaking

(3) Give the date and time or event when the undertaking will expire

(4) The judge may direct that the party who gives the undertaking shall personally sign the statement overleaf

And to be bound by these promises until(3)

The Court explained to(1)

the meaning of his undertaking and the consequences of failing to keep his promises,

And the Court accepted his undertaking(4) [and *if so ordered* directed that

(1)   should sign the statement overleaf].

And   (enter name of Judge) **ordered that**(5)

(5) Set out any other directions given by the court

(6) Address of the person giving undertaking

Dated

To(1)
of(6)

Important Notice

- You may be sent to prison for contempt of court if you break the promises that you have given to the Court.
- If you do not understand anything in this document you should go to a Solicitor, Legal Advice Centre or a Citizens' Advice Bureau

The Court Office at

is open from 10 am to 4 pm. When corresponding with the court, address all forms and letters to the Court Manager and quote the claim number.

N117 General form of undertaking (4.99)   *Printed on behalf of The Court Service*

The Court may direct that the party who gives the undertaking shall personally sign the statement below.

Statement

I understand the undertaking that I have given, and that if I break any of my promises to the Court I may be sent to prison for contempt of court.

Signed

To be completed by the Court

Delivered

☐ By posting on:

☐ By hand on:

☐ Through solicitor on:

Officer:

Application Notice

	In the	

You should provide this information for listing the application

1. How do you wish to have your application dealt with

  a) at a hearing? ☐ ⎫

  b) at a telephone conference? ☐ ⎬ *complete all questions below*

  c) without a hearing? ☐ *complete Qs 5 and 6 below*

2. Give a time estimate for the hearing/conference
_____ (hours) _____ (mins)

3. Is this agreed by all parties? ☐ Yes ☐ No

4. Give dates of any trial period or fixed trial date _____

5. Level of judge _____

6. Parties to be served _____

In the	
Claim no.	
Warrant no. (If applicable)	
Claimant (including ref.)	
Defendant(s) (including ref.)	
Date	

Note You must complete Parts A **and** B, **and** Part C if applicable. Send any relevant fee and the completed application to the court with any draft order, witness statement or other evidence; and sufficient copies for service on each respondent.

Part A

1. Enter your full name, or name of solicitor

I (We)[1]   (on behalf of)(the claimant)(the defendant)

2. State clearly what order you are seeking and if possible attach a draft

intend to apply for an order (a draft of which is attached) that[2]

3. Briefly set out why you are seeking the order. Include the material facts on which you rely, identifying any rule or statutory provision

because[3]

Part B

I (We) wish to rely on: *tick one box*

    the attached (witness statement)(affidavit) ☐   my statement of case ☐

4. If you are not already a party to the proceedings, you must provide an address for service of documents

evidence in Part C in support of my application ☐

Signed [_____]

(Applicant)('s Solicitor)('s litigation friend)

Position or office held [_____]

(if signing on behalf of firm or company)

Address to which documents about this claim should be sent (including reference if appropriate)[4]

		if applicable
	fax no.	
	DX no.	
	e-mail	
Tel. no. Postcode		

The court office at

is open from 10am to 4pm Monday to Friday. When corresponding with the court please address forms or letters to the Court Manager and quote the claim number.

N244 Application Notice (4.00)   *Printed on behalf of The Court Service*

Part C   Claim No. [   ]

I(We) wish to rely on the following evidence in support of this application:

Statement of Truth

(I believe) (The applicant believes) that the facts stated in Part C are true

delete as appropriate

Signed [   ]   **Position or office held** [   ]

(Applicant)('s Solicitor)('s litigation friend)   (If signing on behalf of firm or company)

Date [   ]

In the 'old days', a technical legal distinction was drawn between the different ways in which other people could act at your behest. If, for example, a Defendant paid, or ordered someone to perform a little 'service' for him, such as bashing up the Claimant, such person would be classed as a 'servant', and would be restrained accordingly.

Additionally, what if the Defendant did not employ someone to pay the Claimant a 'little visit', but tipped off an obliging friend who owed him a favour, and who then assaulted the Claimant whilst the Defendant was miles away in the pub? Such a person may not be a 'servant' but an 'agent', and thus the injunctive relief would have to be extended further to restrain the Defendant 'by himself, his servants or agents'.

This was not, however, the end of the matter. An interesting, if somewhat bizarre, problem arose if the Defendant did not assault the Claimant himself but set a ferocious dog on her. If there was no direct causal link between the Defendant and the act of assault, it was arguable that this would not be by the Defendant, nor by his servants, nor by his agents. A dog is a chattel, and by definition cannot be an agent, which connotes human propensities. That is the reason why the words 'or otherwise howsoever' were conventionally included in the standard wording of 'non-molestation' injunctions. Thus the wording would restrain the Defendant 'by himself, his servants or agents, or otherwise howsoever ...'. In cases which did not involve violence, the conventional restraint was 'the Defendant, by himself, his servants or agents', but today we use a more modern format:

> 'That the Defendant...' (and again, you must put in his name, so that there can be no doubt about whom you are talking — or in case he has forgotten!) 'be forbidden **whether by himself or by instructing or encouraging any other person ...**'

These new words replace 'servants or agents or otherwise howsoever', and are intended to cover all the situations outlined above. It is only if the Defendant is a limited company that the words 'whether by its servants, agents, officers, or otherwise', replace the new format. It remains to be seen whether the words 'instructing or encouraging', include a passive lack of interference with a third party deciding to 'do the Defendant a favour', but it is almost certain that the words will be interpreted to cover all situations covered by the previous rubric. 'What about the dogs?' you may ask. Well, the answer is that there should be no difference between a Defendant using a chattel such as a baseball bat to beat the Claimant, and a chattel such as a dog. 'Ah then, why did we have the previous wording?' Let's get on with the lesson!

Anyway, the new language achieves its purpose, in that it is made quite clear to any Defendant, in plain and simple language, that he cannot get around the terms of the order by getting someone else to do his dirty work. That therefore takes care of the parties. Now to the first part of the order we require.

Here again there have been changes. The word 'assault' has a precise legal definition, and there are other means of abusive and offensive behaviour that may still continue to trouble the Claimant, notwithstanding an injunction restraining the Defendant etc., from assaulting her. Therefore the words 'molest' and 'otherwise interfere with', were conventionally included in non-molestation applications, although there were many Judges who disapproved of the last of the three categories. Sometimes the word 'threaten' was added in appropriate cases. The conventional words were to restrain the Defendant etc. from 'assaulting, molesting or otherwise interfering with the Claimant'. In keeping with the 'plain language' approach, this legalistic form of restraint is now less used than hitherto, although it has by no means entirely disappeared, and the new form of wording is to restrain the Defendant etc. from:

1.   Using any violence against the Claimant,

2.   Threatening, harassing or pestering the Claimant,

At the risk of standing alone amid the general delirium and rejoicing at the use of such simple language, I look forward to the eventual House of Lords decision when it comes, as to the precise legal distinctions between 'harassing' and 'pestering'. Or perhaps I won't!

Now we must consider the scope of the restraint we wish to have put on the Defendant with regard to his coming into the Claimant's house. Of course, we are assuming, for the purposes of this example, that the Court will consider there to be sufficient grounds for making an order of this nature. Ideally of course, we would like to keep the Defendant outside a 100-mile radius from the house. Apart from the question of enforceability, it may be that the Court would consider this just a tiny bit excessive! Additionally, it used to be thought that there was no power in the Court to restrain a person from approaching within a certain distance of a property whilst not actually trespassing thereon. However, in *Burris* v *Azadani* [1995] 4 All ER 802 the Court of Appeal held that there was, in appropriate cases, jurisdiction to restrain a person from entering an 'exclusion zone' outside the Claimant's home, as there was no rule that the Court was restricted to restraining conduct which was itself tortious or otherwise unlawful. I suggest that you do not consider this to be an open invitation routinely to seek to impose a '6 mile limit' on any Defendant coming within your forensic ministrations, but in the present case, 200 yards might perhaps not be thought excessive. The next part of the proposed order should therefore read:

> 3.   Entering the premises at 123 Gargle Avenue, Mouthwash, Sussex, or coming within a 200-yard (or metre — if you were born after about 1970) radius thereof.

I should at this stage add that much work has been done by various bodies, including in particular the North Eastern Circuit, in formulating precise forms of restraint in domestic violence and occupation applications, and although these may have to be slightly modified on occasions, it may not be necessary to depart radically from these just to prove your independence! As it is intended that there should be various 'standard' orders in such cases, creative drafting is clearly not applicable.

The fourth part of the injunction is a little more tricky. What we do not want to happen is to draft our proposed order in such a way as to tempt the Defendant to do something that has not yet occurred to him, or to manoeuvre him into a position whereby he can 'cock a snook' at the Claimant and the Court. Thus, it will not be sufficient merely to seek to restrain him from pinning up posters or letters on the notice board at work. Were he then to put individual abusive notes into employees' pigeon holes for example, he would not be in breach of the terms of the injunction, he will consider that he has scored a point off the Claimant, and the authority of the Court will have been impugned.

Obviously we must devise a form of words which will prevent the act complained of **together with any acts of a similar nature**. As usual, we should adopt a logical approach to the problem, dealing with each potential source of trouble in turn.

The first hurdle is the manner in which the previous abuse has been carried out. Letters and rude posters have been pinned on the notice board. It is clearly of no use whatsoever attempting to prohibit the Defendant from 'pinning' any notice on to the board. He may then use adhesive tape! Doubtless the House of Lords would have a rare old time handing down a judgment four years later on the question of whether 'pinning', in law, includes the use of sticky tape. I do not think that our client will thank us for this — the object of coming to see us has been to prevent the Defendant from making a nuisance of himself, not in order to achieve legal immortality!

The way to approach this problem is to find a word which will cover all forms of pinning, sticking, tacking, etc. That word is 'affixing'. Unfortunately, this does not cover all our problems.

The trouble is that although the use of this word should effectively prevent any form of attachment, it does not cover any form of display which does not involve such attachment, e.g. leaning a board against a wall, or marching around the grounds with a banner. This is linked with the fact that, were we to limit our application to posters and letters, this would not cover other forms of communication, which the Defendant's cunning brain may devise. Therefore it appears that we shall have to use additional wording to cover this situation.

Another obstacle is that we will have to cover a display which may take place elsewhere than on the notice board originally complained of. Were we to direct our application for injunctive relief merely towards the use of the notice board, the Defendant may be tempted to do his damage at some other venue.

To deal with these problems, we must devise a form of wording sufficiently wide effectively to prohibit **any** form of this type of behaviour, at **any** place. One of the ways in which to achieve this end, is by use of **catch-all** words such as 'whatsoever', and 'howsoever'. There are also other **generic** words which can be useful to cover articles of a nature similar to those specifically complained of. Therefore, search for these generic words, and put them in your draft after dealing with the specific complaint.

In principle, we shall deal with the problems as follows:

1.   The specific word 'affixing', together with an additional catch-all phrase to preclude alternative methods not covered by the specific word;
2.   Specific words 'poster' or 'letter', together with a generic word to cover like things. This will be supplemented with a catch-all phrase for absolute security;
3.   A few words defining what it is about the posters etc. that we do not like, so as to ensure that the Defendant is absolutely certain what he is to be prevented from doing;
4.   The specific words 'Claimant's place of work', plus a further generic word and catch-all phrase, to ensure that the Defendant does not simply work his mischief elsewhere.

In practice this should work out as follows:

> 4.   Affixing, or in any manner howsoever displaying or exhibiting any poster, letter or other material whatsoever, purporting to relate to the Claimant, at the Claimant's place of work, or in any place whatsoever.

The word 'affixing' has been supplemented by use of the catch-all phrase 'or in any manner howsoever'. After that we have two generic words covering acts of affixing, attaching, etc., these being 'displaying or exhibiting', and this phrase will hopefully cover the basis of all the acts which have been complained of, or which could be repeated in different form.

When it comes to what should not be affixed, displayed or exhibited etc., we have the specific 'poster', and 'letter', and then the generic 'material', together with the catch-all 'whatsoever'.

To describe the material further (as it would be improper to restrain the Defendant from putting up **any** notices on the board, after all he may be the secretary of the company's snooker club), we use a general 'purporting to relate to the Claimant'.

Finally, dealing with the areas covered by the injunction, we use the specific 'at the Claimant's place of work' (which covers the whole area, and not just the notice board), and then for good measure the generic 'or in any other place', then catch-all 'whatsoever'.

I certainly do not advocate that you sub-divide your phraseology in the above manner every time you set out to draft an application or a minute of order. Rather, the principles should become an automatic frame of mind, so that the appropriate points would be covered comprehensively, yet succinctly, with as little time wasted as possible.

Two further matters. The principles of 'tight' phraseology apply equally to applications, or draft minutes of order, as they do to other forms of drafting. Unnecessary repetition of standard phrases betrays a mind that has not fully thought things through.

Secondly, note here that, strictly speaking, the Action has not formally commenced. Mr Gnat is no more than an 'intended' Defendant, and Miss Housefly is a 'proposed' Claimant. However, as the proceedings will almost certainly have been formally commenced by the time the injunction is served, it is common in both the County and High Court, to ignore the technicality.

For the sake of clarity, I now reproduce the completed paragraph, applying for the various orders against Mr Gnat:

> That the Defendant, John Gnat, be forbidden, whether by himself or by instructing or encouraging any other person, from:
>
> (1) Using any violence against the Claimant,
> (2) Threatening, harassing or pestering the Claimant,
> (3) Entering the premises at 123 Gargle Avenue, Mouthwash, Sussex or crossing within a 200-yard radius thereof;

(4)   Affixing, or in any manner howsoever displaying or exhibiting any poster, letter or other material whatsoever, purporting to relate to the Claimant, at the Claimant's place of work, or in any place whatsoever.

I will not proceed to deal with the remainder of Form N16A, as no mandatory order is required here, and the rest should (hopefully) be self-explanatory.

Once (if!) granted, the Order will be drawn up, on Form N16, and a blank copy of this is now set out for your delectation. Note that at the end appears the undertaking in damages, which would of course have to be given by Gertrude Housefly when obtaining the injunction. Scant chance of this worrying us in the circumstances.

You may not have forgotten that we are going to have to give various additional undertakings, in view of the fact that we have so far not issued proceedings, or sworn the affidavit in support of the injunction application. These undertakings will be endorsed on Form N117, which form also contains dire warnings of the consequences of breach. As I am by nature a good-hearted chap, I shall now give you another example of how to do this.

Let us say that we have applied without notice, for an injunction against a potential Defendant, restraining him from entering some land until trial or further order. Remember that the undertakings below will be in a different format if the application is for a freezing or search order. I will not bother with the substance of the Order here, but let us assume that such has been the urgency (and it had better have been!), that no formal documentation had been completed prior to the Order being obtained.

IN THE HIGH COURT OF JUSTICE   2006 G No. 0000
QUEEN'S BENCH DIVISION

BETWEEN:

GUNGHO LIMITED

Claimants

— and —

Mr LEON RUMPLESTILTSKIN

Defendant

DRAFT MINUTE OF ORDER

Injunction Order

Between . . . . Claimant

and . . . . Defendant

In the	
	County Court
Claim No.	
Claimant's Ref.	
Defendant Ref.	
For completion by the court **Issued on**	

Seal

If you do not obey this order you will be guilty of contempt of court and you may be sent to prison.

⁽¹⁾The name of the person the order is directed to

On the   of   [20   ] the court considered an application for an injunction

The Court ordered that⁽¹⁾

⁽²⁾The address of the person of the order is directed to

is **forbidden** (whether by himself or by instructing or encouraging any other person)⁽³⁾

⁽³⁾The terms of the injunction order. If the defendant is a limited company, delete the words in brackets and insert "whether by its servants, agents, officers or otherwise"

This order shall remain in force util (the   of   [20   ] at   o' clock

unless before then it is revoked by a) further order of the court

And it is ordered that⁽¹⁾

⁽⁴⁾The terms of any orders requiring acts to be done

Shall⁽⁴⁾

⁽⁵⁾Enter time (and place) as ordered

on or before⁽³⁾

It is further ordered that⁽⁵⁾

⁽⁶⁾The terms of any other orders costs etc.

⁽⁷⁾Use when interim order or order made without notice

Notice of further hearing⁽⁷⁾

The court will re-consider the application and whether the order should continue at a further hearing at

on   the   day of   [20   ] at   o' clock

If you do not attend at the time shown the court may make an injunction order in your absence

⁽⁸⁾Delete if order made on notice

You are entitled to apply to the court to re-consider the order before the day⁽⁸⁾

[The court is satisfied that (the conduct which is prohibited by this injunction, consists of or includes the use or threatened use of violence) (there is a significant risk of harm to a person towards whom the contact prohibited by this injunction is directed).

A power of arrest is attached to terms [   ] of this injunction whereby any constable may under the power given in section 91 of the Anti-social Behaviour Act 2003, arrest without warrant the defendant if the constable has reasonable cause for suspecting the defendant is in breach of any of those terms of this injunction]

If you do not understand anything in this order you should go to a Solicitor, Legal Advice Centre or a Citizens' Advice Bureau

The court office at

is open between 10 am and 4 pm Monday to Friday. When corresponding with the court, please address forms or letters to the Court Manager and quote the claim number.

N16 General form of injuction for interim application or originating application (09.04)

Injunction Order - Record of Hearing   **Claim No.** . . . .

On . . . . the . . . . . . day of . . . . [20   ]

Before (H   Honour)(District) judge . . . .

The court was sitting at . . . .

. . . .

The   ☐   **Claimant**   **(Name)** . . . .

was   ☐   represented by Counsel

☐   represented by a Solicitor

☐   in person

The   ☐   **Defendant**   **(Name)** . . . .

was   ☐   represented by Counsel

☐   represented by a Solicitor

☐   in person

☐   did not appear having been given notice of this hearing

☐   not given notice of this hearing

The court read the written evidence of

☐   the Claimant   (sworn)(signed) on . . . .

☐   the Defendant   (sworn)(signed) on . . . .

And of . . . . (sworn)(signed) on . . . .

. . . .

The court heard spoken evidence on oath from

. . . .

. . . .

The Claimant gave an undertaking (through his counsel or solicitor) promising to pay any damages ordered by the
court if it later decides that the Defendant has suffered loss or damages as a result of this order*
*Delete this paragraph if the court does not require the undertaking

Signed _____ Dated _____

(Judges Clerk)

N16 General form of injunction for interim application or originating application

[We will commence with the usual preliminaries (assuming in this]
[case that Counsel has been briefed):]

Upon hearing Counsel without notice on behalf of the above named Claimant.

And upon reading the draft affidavit of Herb Aceous-Border, and the exhibits thereto, and the draft Claim Form and Particulars of Claim in the Action, and the draft Minute of the Order sought.

Be careful to ensure that the above are properly described. As nothing has been properly sworn or issued, they are no more than proposed documents, or drafts.

Now for all necessary undertakings. Usually they would be as follows:

And upon the Claimant Company by Counsel undertaking:

(1)   To pay any damages ordered by the Court if it later decides that the Defendant has suffered loss or damage as a result of this order;

(2)   To issue a Claim Form and Particulars of Claim forthwith in substantially the same form as the present draft;

(3)   To procure the said Herb Aceous-Border to swear an affidavit [to verify his statement by a statement of truth] in or substantially in the terms of the said draft affidavit [statement], within 24 hours of the making of this Order;

(4)   To inform the Defendant forthwith of the terms of this Order and to serve upon him a copy of the affidavit as sworn together with the exhibits thereto and a copy of the Claim Form and Particulars of Claim in this case, and a copy of this Order;

(5)   To notify the Defendant of his right, if so advised, to apply on notice to discharge or vary this Order.

IT IS ORDERED AND DIRECTED

etc.

Paragraphs (1) and (2) should be self-explanatory. Note that the Claimant Company has given the undertaking through Counsel.

Paragraph (3) contains alternative wording depending on whether or not an affidavit or a statement is to be made. It could simply be worded 'swear an affidavit…' etc. The above example is merely an alternative to take account of the fact that the affidavit itself is not being sworn by the Claimant (which is a company). The above form of wording can also be used when the affidavit is to be sworn by a third party, not presently in Court.

Paragraph (5) is worded so that the Defendant is made aware that he can apply to the Court to set aside or vary the order. Although without notice injunctions are strictly supposed to be indorsed with a return date for a hearing on notice, it is not uncommon for the Order to be 'open-ended' (until trial or further order), save that the Defendant can come back on short notice to apply to discharge or vary the Order. 'If so advised' merely indicates that he does not **have** to make the application — you will, of course, hope that he will not seek to do so!

RECORDING AN AGREEMENT

The recording of an agreement or compromise will obviously vary in format according to the time and circumstances in which it is made.

Where proceedings have not yet been issued, the settlement normally consists of one or both sides agreeing to do (or not to do) certain things in full and final settlement of the dispute between them. As such, this agreement is no more and no less than a contract. Thus, any document recording this agreement will either form the contract itself, or will provide written evidence of its terms. Should someone breach the terms of the settlement, the proper course is not to reopen the original dispute, but to sue on the new agreement.

From a drafting point of view, there are too many imponderables to lay down any general rules. From the enforcement point of view it matters not whether the agreement is recorded in full 'party-dress' form, complete with portentous paragraphs entitled 'WHEREAS…', and the inevitable: 'NOW THIS AGREEMENT WITNESSETH', without which no decent settlement used to be worth its lawyers' fees, or whether the terms are jotted down in note form on the back of an envelope — subject of course to the question of proof. Perhaps the most important thing to remember is that the agreement must be expressed in terms which accurately record the disputes which are being resolved. Just as you would not wish to leave any loopholes open, neither would you want to deny your client the opportunity to deal with other matters of a different nature which may be outstanding with the other side, and which might inadvertently be 'settled' as a result of too enthusiastic a use of the term 'full and final settlement'. Your insurers will be none too pleased either! It goes without saying that the usual principles of clear and concise drafting apply as much here as anywhere else. So avoid overblown phraseology, even if it does sound impressive.

When proceedings have already been started, you are faced with two additional problems. First, how are the proceedings to be resolved? Secondly, who is going to be liable for the costs? This latter question may also, of course, arise even though proceedings have not been commenced, but the costs in such an event will usually (although not invariably) be much less.

If the matter has not advanced very far, a settlement may still be recorded in the same manner as outlined above, with the addition that provision would have to be made for the withdrawal or dismissal of the proceedings, and for costs. Often in such cases, the agreement will merely be recorded in letters between the parties' respective solicitors. If for example, it is agreed that the Defendant will pay the Claimant £7,500 (without prejudice to his contention that the proceedings should never have been commenced in the first place), that this will be in full and final settlement of all disputes, that there will be no order as to costs, and that the Claimant will discontinue his action, this may all have come about in the course of 'without prejudice' correspondence between the solicitors, which, taken altogether amounts to a binding and enforceable agreement, after which the 'without prejudice' is lifted.

Where negotiations take place 'at the door of the Court', or even in the course of the proceedings themselves, the agreement will have to be recorded in a more formal manner, in that the Judge will then be asked to make an Order disposing of the action, and giving effect to the terms agreed by the parties. Technically, such an agreement will have to be subject to the Court's approval, in that the Judge is already seised of the case. However, although this approval should always be sought as a matter of courtesy, it is rare indeed that the Court will not allow the parties to come to terms.

Where an agreement is concluded at the door of the Court, you will have to draw up a draft Order for the approval of the Court. The nature and content of this draft will naturally depend on the nature and content of the agreement that you have reached. Let us take three basic situations:

1. Where there has been an interim agreement — i.e., one which does not mean the conclusion of proceedings.

2. Where there has been a final agreement, which does not require any further execution by either side.

3.   Where there has been a final agreement, which is executory — i.e.,
it requires either or both parties to perform something.

1. The interim agreement
These should not prove difficult to draft. The document should contain:

The title of the action;
Any undertakings given by either party;
The Order by consent.

Occasionally the parties may be agreed on most points, but will leave
outstanding matters to be dealt with by the Court. In such cases,
the order will be drawn up in the above manner, but the Order will
be divided into that made by consent, and that made after hearing
argument.
    As ever, this format is neither exhaustive nor inflexible, and must be
adapted to meet the needs of the instant case. It is, for example, not
uncommon for there to be further 'informal' agreements, which may
either be appended to the draft order, or merely endorsed on Counsels'
briefs (which of course, bind both sides' professional advisers).
    Remember that this is to be a joint document, in that it should reflect
the various concerns of both parties. Unlike other drafting that you may
do, the other side may pick up on matters that you would rather were
omitted, and you will have to argue the toss as you go along. It is of
course for you to ensure that you have not omitted anything of importance to your side. It is at this stage that some tactical advantage may be
gained by showing sufficient understanding of what you are doing for
your opponent to 'leave the draft to you', and simply look over your
shoulder whilst it is being done. Again, a confident display of initiative
and competence may mean that you will be the person proposing
the various terms that should be incorporated into the document, and
essentially you will have conduct of the draft. Whereas you must not of
course take **improper** advantage of this, it will certainly not do your side
any harm!
    You may not, however, be as lucky as I was some time ago, when my
opponent, showing a marked disinclination to get involved with the
minutiae of the agreement, elected to go and get the sandwiches, whilst
I did the draft over lunch. The document (which was approved by him)
was somewhat one-sided whenever it came to anything which could
conceivably have been to the advantage of my client!

EXAMPLE

Stringbag Aviation Ltd, a company registered in Gibraltar, has brought proceedings against Algy Bigglesworth for £92,500, being charges allegedly due in respect of hire of an aircraft. The matter was transferred to the County Court. Due to various reasons (which need not concern us here), the Claimants obtained judgment in default against the Defendant on 23rd May 2005, with damages to be assessed, and a hearing date for such assessment has been set.

The Defendant has made an application for the judgment to be set aside, and has also made an application for the Claimant Company to provide security for costs.

At the door of the Court, the parties reached an agreement on these matters, largely as a result of the Defendant's solicitor stating that he was presently holding £100,000 of the Defendant's money in an account, due to the sale of one of the Defendant's properties. The basic compromise was as follows:

1.   Defendant's solicitors to transfer that sum in a separate account within 7 days, to abide the result of the case.

2.   Judgment in default, and Order of 23rd May 2005 then to be set aside.

3.   Claimant to pay £5,000 into Court by way of security for costs, within 7 days after receiving notification that the sum had been transferred into the separate account.

4.   Interest on both sums to accrue to the party owning the money.

5.   Costs in the case.

Although the above records the basics of the agreement between the parties, it does not take account of the practicalities of the situation. The draft must do so, and, for example, make provision for ensuring that the monies presently held by the Defendant's solicitors are transferred to a separate account in their name, thus preventing the Defendant, should he later change his mind, from requiring repayment from his solicitors, and thus putting them in an embarrassing situation.

We will therefore commence with the title of the action:

<u>IN THE SUNGAR COUNTY COURT</u>   No. GW010000

BETWEEN:

STRINGBAG AVIATION LIMITED
(A Company Registered in Gibraltar)

Claimant

— and —

Mr ALGERNON BIGGLESWORTH

Defendant

(It is not necessary to put any formal title under the heading.)

Now, we must put the various undertakings by the parties which amount to preconditions of the agreed Order. It is essential to differentiate between what should constitute an undertaking, and what should be comprised in the Order. The Order will consist of the various matters which only lie within the authority and jurisdiction of the Court. Thus, for example, the Court will not **order** the Defendant or his solicitors specifically to annex the monies held to a separate account. That is for the parties to decide between them, should they so wish. However, as judgment in default of Defence has already been ordered by the Court, it is not for the parties to set that aside. They may agree that it should be done, but an Order of the Court can only be set aside by the Court.

In the present case, the undertakings will be exclusively from the Defendant, or, to be more accurate, from his solicitors, who will naturally bind him by so doing. In deciding the precise form of these undertakings, we will employ the usual logical analysis of the situation in order to ensure that the interests of all parties are protected.

UPON the Defendant undertaking:

1.   Forthwith to instruct his solicitors to transfer the sum of £100,000 presently held by them, into a separate account

in the name of his solicitors, to abide the outcome of this case, such transfer to be done by [date];

2.   Not to release or otherwise deal with the said sum in any way, save by Order of the Court or the written consent of the Claimant's solicitors;

3.   To notify the Claimant's solicitors immediately upon the said sum being placed in the said account;

I will not analyse the above paragraphs line by line, but they are indicative of the sort of practical considerations which must be given to the agreement, in order to make it workable. Note, however, that the old practice of requiring something to be done 'within 7 days' is no more, due to the difficulty of divining the starting date from which time is to flow. A precise date should be agreed, and, to be extra sure, I would recommend a precise moment on that date, so that there can be no confusion as to when the limit expires — thus 'by 4pm on 3rd December 2005'. Now we must deal with the Orders which we will ask the Court to make.

IT IS ORDERED by consent:

Remember that the consent part of the Order should always be expressed as such. If there is a disagreement at a later stage, it may be relevant to have recorded that part of the Order which was made by consent, and that which was not.

1.   That upon the Defendant's solicitors notifying the Claimant's solicitors in the terms of undertaking 3 above, the Judgment in default herein be set aside, and the Order granted on 23rd May 2005 be discharged.

Undertaking 3 is the notification to the Claimant's solicitors that the monies have been transferred to the separate account in the name of the Defendant's solicitors. This is for the protection of the Claimant, who presently has the benefit not merely of a judgment, but also of a hearing date for the assessment of damages. This date is certainly not going to be vacated until the Defendant's solicitors have confirmed that the monies are now unconditionally appropriated to the agreed purpose.

The word 'herein' is not essential, but ensures that there can be no confusion whatsoever.

Once that has been done, it is the Claimant's turn to perform his bit:

> 2. That upon the setting aside of the said judgment, the
> Claimant pay £5,000 into Court by 4pm on [date] as security
> for the costs of this action;

> 3. That in default of such payment, the Claim be struck out.

The wording of paragraph 3 is to ensure that the Claimant's obligation
to pay money into Court as security for costs arises only in the event of
the judgment being set aside. If it has been set aside, he must then pay
into Court by the due date or have his claim struck out. The sanction is
important as it provides for what is to happen in the event of default by
the Claimant, once the Defendant has effectively given security for the
damages that are being claimed.

> 4. That the costs of today, and of and incidental to
> 23rd May 2005 be costs in the case.

The words 'of and incidental to' are by no means mandatory, as they are,
in any event, subject to assessment if they cannot be agreed. However, it
is a neat phrase which can, in appropriate circumstances, make it clear
that the costs are not just those of the day, but those of other work and
documentation etc. connected with that particular hearing.

I hope you have noticed I have included no provision dealing with the
question of interest, even though that has formed part of our agreement.
That is the sort of administrative consideration that is usually endorsed
on Counsels' briefs, or is the subject of a note exchanged between solicitors. However, you can, should you so wish, include the following words
at the end of the Order, so as to clarify the situation:

> It is further agreed:

> 1. That the interest on the sum of £100,000 be credited to
> the Defendant;

> 2. That the interest on the sum of £5,000 be credited to the
> Claimant.

Again in the interests of clarity, I shall set out the complete order below:

<u>IN THE SUNGAR COUNTY COURT</u>   No. GW010000

BETWEEN:

STRINGBAG AVIATION LIMITED
(A Company Registered in Gibraltar)

<u>Claimant</u>

— and —

ALGERNON BIGGLESWORTH

<u>Defendant</u>

UPON the Defendant through his solicitors undertaking:

1.   Forthwith to instruct his solicitors to transfer the sum of £100,000 presently held by them, into a separate account in the name of his solicitors, to abide the outcome of this case, such transfer to be done by [date];

2.   Not to release or otherwise deal with the said sum in any way, save by Order of the Court or the written consent of the Claimant's solicitors;

3.   To notify the Claimant's solicitors immediately upon the said sum being placed in the said account;

IT IS ORDERED by consent:

1.   That upon the Defendant's solicitors notifying the Claimant's solicitors in the terms of undertaking 3 above, the Judgment in default herein be set aside, and the Order granted on 23rd May 2005 be discharged.

2.   That upon the setting aside of the said judgment, the Claimant pay £5,000 into Court by 4pm on [date] as security for the costs of this action.

3.   That in default of such payment, the Claim be struck out.

4.   That the costs of today, and of and incidental to 23rd May 2005 be costs in the case.

It is further agreed:

1. That the interest on the sum of £100,000 be credited to
the Defendant;

2. That the interest on the sum of £5,000 be credited to the
Claimant.

The agreement will then be signed by Counsel or Solicitors for both
parties and will be formally presented to the Court for approval. Any further
amendments desired by the Court will be inserted, and the document will
then be drawn up as a formal Order.

2. The executed final agreement
This will usually closely follow the format of the above example.
However, as the agreement does not require either party to do anything,
there should be no need for any undertakings. Thus, after the heading,
the draft will merely record the terms of the agreement. How to dispose
of the case in such instances is often a tricky point. Let us take a simple
example:

EXAMPLE

The Claimant claims £7,500, being the balance allegedly due
on goods sold and delivered. The Defendant denies liability
on the grounds that the goods were defective. He has paid
£10,000, but claims to have had to spend £8,000 on repairing
the goods. He thus counterclaims using the Additional
Claim procedure for £8,000, claiming to be able to set that
sum off against the Claimant's claim.
The Claimant thus wants £7,500. The Defendant wants
a further £500, over and above the sum he has kept back.
At the door of the Court, the parties agree that they will
settle on the basis of the status quo, with no order as to costs.
In lawyer's parlance 'everyone goes home'.

One obvious way in which this agreement can be expressed would be for
the Claimant's claim to be dismissed, and for there to be judgment for
the Defendant on the Additional Claim for £8,000, with no order as to
costs in each case.

However appealing that may be to the Defendant, the Claimant may not wish to have a judgment against him, particularly in circumstances in which there have been concessions on both sides. The settlement was almost certainly negotiated on the basis that both parties denied liability, and thus it would be inconsistent with the negotiations to draft the agreed order in the above manner.

Thus, the appropriate way of recording the agreement would require both claim and Additional Claim to be dismissed. This could be done merely by drafting an order to that effect:

(Title of action)
BY CONSENT, IT IS ORDERED THAT:

1. The Claim and Additional Claim herein be dismissed.

2. There be no order for costs on Claim and Additional Claim.

Technically that should take care of the action, in that the Claimant cannot now claim the £7,500 that has been retained by the Defendant, and the Defendant cannot claim the £500 alleged additional expenditure. For the avoidance of any doubt, however, the position could be endorsed on Counsels' briefs, to the effect that:

Defendant is to keep the sum of £7,500 presently retained by him.

As I have said, that is not strictly necessary, but one must always have regard to the feelings of the parties, who may be unhappy unless the position is made absolutely clear, in terms that they can understand.

Should it be desired, however, there is no reason why the agreement could not be drawn up in another manner:

UPON the Claimant and the Defendant agreeing that the Defendant shall keep the sum of £7,500 presently retained by him, and that the same shall be in full and final satisfaction of all disputes between the parties arising out of the sale of the goods the subject of the present action;

IT IS ORDERED BY CONSENT that:

1. The Claim and Additional Claim herein be dismissed. etc.

3. The executory final agreement

In these circumstances, although the matter has supposedly been settled, one or both of the parties still has to perform certain acts. The difficulty remains that should they not, the action would have been dismissed, and the 'innocent' party would thereafter have no alternative but to commence fresh proceedings against the 'guilty' party, with consequent delay and expense. However, if there has been an agreement in settlement of the action, it may not be appropriate to leave things 'hanging in the air', particularly if there is a Judge ready, able and willing to hear the case, once he has finished his cup of coffee.

The standard method of dealing with this situation is by means of a **'Tomlin Order'**. This is essentially an order in standard form, whereby the action is stayed upon certain terms, with liberty to both parties to apply to the Court as to the carrying out of such terms. In other words, the parties are thereafter precluded from re-litigating the action, but can ask the Court to assist in enforcing the terms, without having to commence new proceedings.

The Tomlin Order is very simple to draft, and requires little explanation. It is divided into three parts:

1.   The title of the action.
2.   The Order of the Court in standard form.
3.   The Schedule, detailing the terms of agreement.

The words of the Order are more or less standardised as follows:

> Upon hearing Counsel (or the Solicitor) for the Claimants and for the Defendants;
>
> AND the parties having agreed to the matters set out in the Schedule hereto;
>
> IT IS ORDERED by consent, that the Claim (and Additional Claim) herein be stayed, on the terms set out in the Schedule hereto, and that there be no order as to costs.
>
> Liberty to both parties to apply as to carrying the said terms into effect.

There is then set out a Schedule, containing the terms agreed between the parties. This Schedule need not recite 'upon the Claimant undertaking', etc. as the order has already been made. The Schedule will list the various heads of agreement, such as:

SCHEDULE

1.   Claimants' and Defendant's surveyors will, by 4pm on [date], arrange to meet at the Defendant's premises within a further 7 days of the said arrangement, in order to inspect the double glazing installation therein.

2.   Both surveyors if possible to agree a schedule of defects to be remedied. In the event of entire agreement not being possible, both parties will appoint Mr Slide, of Slide, Slippage and Co., Enfield, as an independent surveyor, to visit the premises as soon as practicable, and report on the said installation. The decision of Mr Slide is to be binding on both parties, and his costs are to be shared equally between them.

3.   Within 14 days of the said schedule of defects being agreed, or imposed by Mr Slide, the Claimants will at their own expense, cause the same to be remedied to the reasonable satisfaction of the Defendant's surveyor.

4.   Upon the said defects being so remedied, the Defendant will pay the Claimants the balance due on the said contract, being £4,250, less a discount of £750, in respect of his costs of this action.

As you can imagine, the Tomlin Order affords considerable flexibility, and yet at the same time allows finality to the action. In the event of there being difficulties in carrying out the terms of the agreement, either party can apply to the Court for directions. Both parties leave the Court in the knowledge that they have settled the proceedings, and can concentrate their efforts on bringing the cause of the dispute between them to an end.

The drafting of agreed orders, or proposed minutes of orders, is often neglected in teaching. Sometimes this is because it is such a large topic — there is very little in the way of standard formats, and the range of material covered by the umbrella title of 'settlements' is obviously vast. Sometimes as well, it may be thought that there is little by way of different or additional techniques, in drafting settlements, from more easily taught areas of drafting. This may to some extent be correct, but the problem with settlements is that you may have very little time indeed to reflect on the format of your draft. It may have to be done at the door of the Court, and in some haste. You may also have been preoccupied with the terms of the settlement, to the exclusion of the format in which it is to be presented. If your mind is alerted to the general principles required when formulating a draft order, this process will become second nature as and when needed.

Chapter Twelve

Bones of Contention
(The Skeleton Argument)

> *'What* IS *the use of repeating all that*
> *stuff,' the Mock Turtle interrupted, 'if you*
> *don't explain it as you go on? It's by far*
> *the most confusing thing I ever heard!'*

In recent years the skeleton argument has progressed from being a useful guide to a difficult argument, to an indispensable part of everyday litigation. This is of course in line with the avowed aims and intentions of the CPR to keep litigation as short and straightforward as possible, but it does mean that we have to master the fine art of the skeleton argument in addition to all the other weapons in our drafting armoury. This, I hope, should not be too difficult!

Now, as usual, I am not going to conduct an analysis of the rules and regulations surrounding the use of skeleton arguments, nor of the manner in which authorities should be cited. You can look all these up in the appropriate tomes. Suffice it to say, for present purposes, that a skeleton argument should provide a concise summary of the party's submissions on the issues raised by the application, and should be as brief as the nature of the case allows. Having regard to the fact that it is unlikely that your meagre fees will be extended to cover the additional work required to draft a skeleton, this latter requirement is probably just as well!

A skeleton argument

It seems to me that there is very little from a tactical point of view that can be achieved during the drafting of a skeleton argument, save that, of course, the clearer and more dazzling your exposition, the greater impact you are likely to make on the persons reading it. Here, you will be endeavouring to impress not so much your opponent (who by this stage of the game should, or ought to, have a pretty fair idea of what your case is all about), but the Judge, who is, as we shall see, a sitting target and fair game for a spot of 'making a good impression'. So I suggest we start by deciding once again, what it is that we are trying to achieve and how best to attain our objectives.

Sitting down to draft our skeleton does actually give us a golden opportunity to take stock of our case and plan how we intend to set it out in Court. After all, the preparation for the skeleton is, or should be, iden-tical to the manner in which we prepare the case for trial. It is not intended to be a substitute for advocacy, but in reality it will take the place of an opening speech, and thus it will be necessary to ensure that we impart to the Judge just those things that he or she needs to know from the outset. So now is the time to sit down, draw a deep breath, and do something completely unusual – have a little tenderness and compas-sion for the poor old Judge!

Now I freely admit that this may not be the most immediate of emotions that go through your mind when thinking of the judiciary. After a hard day in the trenches, having been on the receiving end of everything that His or Her Mightiness can find to throw at you, from sarcasm to volumes of authorities, the thought of making the old gimmer's remaining days anything other than unmitigated hell may require a discipline and maturity that would test the forbearance of a saint. But there are rewards to be won, not just in heaven but even in the County Court! Here's why:

Your average Judge is actually a pretty decent cove. (Yes, I know that there are exceptions, but I wasn't responsible for appointing them, so don't take it out on me!) All he or she wants is a nice quiet life, to be able to go home in the evening in the knowledge that a job has been well done, justice has been served, and that at least some of the manifold wrongs of the world have been put to right through the medium of the due process of law in Her Majesty's Courts. Or whatever! More to the point, there is nothing that worries a Judge more than the thought that he or she has not understood what the case is all about. Workloads are high, time is short. Very often the court file and whatever passes for the 'trial bundle' are put in front of him or her only just before the court day is to start. It is thus essential to be able to get to grips with the basic issues between the parties at the earliest possible opportunity. Your cooperation in enabling this to happen will frequently result in a gratitude which is almost pathetic!

Now of course you will already have got your head around your case when drafting the statements of case etc. in the style so lovingly exemplified in the previous chapters of this work. However, this is the first time that you will really be pulling all the strings together — combining argument and evidence in a manner so irresistible that the Judge will wonder how the other side can possibly have a case at all — until, of course, he or she reads their side of the story! So, a few basic tips at this stage:

Keep it clear.
Keep it short.
Keep it relevant.
Keep it logical.

and above all:

Resist the urge to indulge in flights of rhetoric which will only serve to make your submissions hard to read and difficult to understand, and which ultimately will have the effect of converting your skeleton into an ossuary!

In accordance with previous practice, therefore, let us take a look at an example of a skeleton argument in a case where we are seeking to dispossess a tenant who has been (we say) guilty of anti-social behaviour in breach of the terms of his lease. The tenant will almost certainly not be represented, which will mean that he will not be filing a skeleton argument of his own. It is thus doubly incumbent on us to ensure that the facts and the law are set out in a straightforward and fair manner, making allowances for the fact that the tenant is acting in person.

IN THE ASBO COUNTY COURT   Claim No. 6 AB 4444

BETWEEN:

VERY WONDERFUL HOUSING ASSOCIATION

Claimant

— and —

Mr MICHAEL HARER-STORAR

Defendant

CLAIMANT'S SKELETON ARGUMENT

(Nos. in square brackets refer to page numbers in the
Trial Bundle)

(Note that there is no formal requirement to refer to the pagination in the title as has been done above, but if common sense would dictate it in the circumstances, that is good enough for me!)

Introduction
1.   In this claim the Claimant seeks:—
    (a)   Possession of residential premises at Flat 4, 4 Battle Road, Asbo, Essex ('Flat 4'); see Particulars of Claim [pp. 12–19]; and
    (b)   An injunction pursuant to ss. 153A and 153C of the Housing Act 1996; Application Notice [p. 5].

Here we have commenced, very sensibly you may think, by stating what it is that we are looking for in this action. Some of you, at this advanced stage of this work, may think that it may be more helpful to set out precisely what injunction it is that we are seeking, and if that is what you would like to do, please feel free. We are seeking an anti-social behaviour injunction coupled with an exclusion order and power of arrest, and I suppose it would not hurt to put that in, provided that the terms of the order are not so complex that it would remain more simple just to refer to the relevant page in the bundle.

Now let us move to a little relevant narrative:

2. By a written tenancy agreement dated 29th September 2001 [pp. 24–29], the Defendant became the Claimant's assured tenant of Flat 4 as from 1st October 2001, subject to the provisions of the Housing Act 1988.

3. The Claimant seeks possession under Grounds 12 ('breach of a term of the tenancy other than one relating to rent'), and 14 ('nuisance and annoyance/commission of a criminal offence at the premises'). Both of these grounds are discretionary. The Claimant will be asking the Court to make an outright possession order.

4. On 3rd April 2006 the Claimant obtained a without notice injunction against the Defendant, and the Claimant seeks a continuation of that order for a period of 12 months together with a power of arrest.

Well, that's what the case is all about then. Now it seems logical to turn to the reasons for which we want the order. At this stage it is, you may think, unnecessary to repeat all the evidence — after all, it is there in the witness statements (one hopes), and we will be referring to it in the course of the hearing. What we need here is a **summary** of the allegations, and this is therefore what we shall now provide:

Summary of acts of nuisance and/or breaches relied on [evidence Tab 3 pp. 1–34]

5. In summary, the allegations of breach of tenancy and/or nuisance are as follows:—

(a) Loud noise from Flat 4 late in the evening and in the early hours of the morning, including noise:

(1) of amplified music (witnessed by Environmental Health Officers, and in respect of which abatement notices have been served);

(2) of arguments between the Defendant and his partner/ex partner Thelma Glug;

(b) Threats of violence by the Defendant and his visitors to other residents of, and lawful visitors to Battle Road;

(c)   Other anti-social behaviour, including leaving rubbish
in communal areas etc.

You may have noted that I have been very imprecise in the manner in
which I have dealt with the above. I have not indicated dates, times or
the number of occasions, save in the most general terms. At this stage it
is not necessary — that is all in the evidence and (one hopes!) in the
statements of case. The relevance here is as to the **nature** of the allegations,
so that the argument can be developed.

Having set out what it is we are seeking, and the broad basis why, the
matter that is going to be in the uppermost of the Judge's mind is 'What
are the issues that I am to be asked to decide? Is there a dispute as to the
law? Are the facts agreed, or is there to be a long wrangle over those?'
Let us put the Court out of its misery:

Issues for the Court
6.   Where a claim for possession is brought on discretionary grounds under the Housing Act 1988, the questions
for the Court are as follows:—
(a)   Has the Claimant made out a ground for possession?
(s. 7(1))
(b)   If so, is it reasonable in all the circumstances, including
the effect of nuisance on neighbours (s. 9A), to make a possession
order? (s. 7(4))
(c)   If it is reasonable to make an order, whether the
possession order should be outright or suspended? (s. 9(2))
(d)   If the order is suspended, what terms of such the Court
considers fit. (s. 9(2))

There are some who would say that the above is so basic that you are
being a trifle discourteous to the Court by setting it out. That is of course
a matter for you. Personally, and having spent a lifetime being insulted
by professionals, I don't take offence easily, and would not take it amiss
to be reminded not only of the basic rules, but also of where they are to
be found. Much will of course depend on how much else you have to put
into your skeleton argument, the level and experience of the tribunal in
the field covered by the present case, and the relevance of the principle
to the issues that have to be decided. Anyway, to continue:

7.   There is authority to the effect that:—
(a)   It is not a defence to possession proceedings that the
breach of the tenancy and or the ground for possession is

caused by the behaviour of the tenant's family or visitors; the
tenant is responsible for the behaviour of his visitors and/or
members of his household. The fact that the Defendant himself
is not culpable goes to whether it is reasonable to make an order
and if so any suspension of it (*RLBKC* v *Simmons & Simmons*
(1996) 29 HLR 507, CA; *West Kent Housing Association* v
Davis (1999) 31 HLR 415, CA; and *Portsmouth CC* v *Bryant*
(2000) 32 HLR 906, CA).

(b)   Incidents of repeated swearing/abusive language
should normally result in a possession order being made
(*Woking BC* v *Bistram* (1993) 27 HLR 1, CA).

(c)   The issue in respect of a suspended order is the future
conduct of the tenant, where the inevitable outcome is breach
the order should not be suspended (*Canterbury CC* v *Lowe*
(2001) 33 HLR 53, CA).

The above is almost a 'teaser', in the sense that it is not yet fully
explained in context, but it is clear (one hopes) that the principles set out
are going to be relevant to the argument that follows. We must therefore
now demonstrate this, by dealing with the relevant factual background,
making sure, however, that we do not simply repeat the evidence that
will be given in the course of the case. It never hurts at any stage of our
drafting to pause for a moment and take stock. What we want to do here
is to encapsulate the factual background to show how the above points
are relevant to the issues that the Court has to decide. So:

Factual background

8.   Flat 4 is situated in a building at 4 Battle Road, Asbo,
'the building' containing 4 flats, all of which are let by the
Claimant as residential dwellings; Flat 1 is on the ground
floor, Flats 2 and 3 on the 1st floor, and Flat 4 on the 2nd floor.

9.   The Claimant has received complaints from the neigh-
bours of nuisance and anti-social behaviour caused by the
Defendant. These complaints commenced soon after the
Defendant's tenancy began in October 2001.

10.   At the time of the commencement of the Defendant's
tenancy, the Claimant's tenant of Flat 3 was a Mrs Lottie.

11.   The Claimant wrote to the Defendant in respect of complaints it had received concerning his behaviour on 3.12.01

[p. 263], 14.5.02 (loud music) [p. 264], 31.7.02 (Defendant's children climbing on scaffolding) [p. 265], 27.9.02 (an incident in which it is alleged that the Defendant assaulted Mrs Lottie's husband) [pp. 266–268] and 24.3.05 (in respect of rubbish left by the Defendant in the bin-shed area) [pp. 270–271].

12.   The following incidents are also relied on:—
    (a)   10.7.04, loud amplified music coming from Defendant's premises at about 3.00 am; [diary of Mrs Lottie p. 308]
    (b)   etc.

(I have not set out further incidents, as I hope that by now you have the general idea!)

From a tactical point of view, provided that the matters are set out clearly and succinctly, there is every advantage in setting out each and every allegation on which you are going to rely. After all, you are seeking the exercise of the Court's discretion, and the sheer weight of the behaviour alleged (provided it is admitted or proved) is going to be a powerful influence here in getting what you want. On the other hand, what we don't want to do is to make our skeleton unwieldy, nor to present the Judge with such a basketful of prose as to make it look like our case is a great deal more complex than it is. The answer here I think lies in presentation. If the allegations are, for example, all indented and clearly identifiable as such, they could be typed rather more closely, so that it is their mass rather than the details of their content that become immediately apparent. The fact that you have identified each allegation and cross-referenced it to the bundle means that it is there for ready reference in the event that it is needed. I will show you what I mean in our final draft, when I set it out in a moment.

Let us conclude our narrative background with just a little twist of the Wellington Boot:

13.   As a result of the acts set out above, on 3rd April 2006 the Claimant obtained a 'without notice' injunction against the Defendant.

14.   Since that Order however, the Defendant has made further threats to Mr and Mrs Lottie:—
    (a)   On 9th April 2006 the Defendant threatened to 'kneecap' Mr Lottie [p. 315]
    (b)   etc.

We have now stated what we want, the basis on which our case is founded, the basic law on the subject, and the factual background, together with references to where all the gory details can be found in the trial bundle. All that is really left for us to do now is to encapsulate our argument — not by way of persuasive advocacy, but by a summary of the points that we wish to extrapolate from all the above, which we say should point irresistibly towards giving us what we are after. So:

Submissions

15. The nuisance is persistent and serious.

16. The Defendant has continued to cause nuisance after receipt of letters from the Claimant; after receipt of abatement notices, and after service of an injunction. In the circumstances there is no real prospect of the Defendant complying with such terms of a suspended possession order as would be necessary to ameliorate the nuisance or prevent a recurrence.

17. It would therefore be appropriate for the Court to make an outright possession order.

18. There is a real risk that the Defendant will threaten or assault Mr and Mrs Lottie or any other visitor to the building; in the circumstances it would be appropriate for the injunction to be continued even if the Defendant is evicted from Flat 4.

RAJ ISTAN
Fawlty Chambers, London EC55
Counsel for the Claimants

There is no formal requirement to set out your address, but a little advertising never goes amiss (unless you have made a complete horlicks of the whole thing, in which case you deserve what you get)!

So here, for completeness, is the finished masterpiece:

<u>IN THE ASBO COUNTY COURT</u>   Claim No. 6 AB 4444

BETWEEN:

VERY WONDERFUL HOUSING ASSOCIATION

<u>Claimant</u>

— and —

Mr MICHAEL HARER-STORAR

Defendant

CLAIMANT'S SKELETON ARGUMENT

(Nos. in square brackets refer to page numbers in the Trial Bundle)

Introduction

1. In this claim the Claimant seeks:—

(a) Possession of residential premises at Flat 4, 4 Battle Road, Asbo, Essex ('Flat 4'); see Particulars of Claim [pp. 12–19]; and

(b) An injunction pursuant to ss. 153A and 153C of the Housing Act 1996; Application Notice [p. 5].

2. By a written tenancy agreement dated 29th September 2001 [pp. 24–29], the Defendant became the Claimant's assured tenant of Flat 4 as from 1st October 2001, subject to the provisions of the Housing Act 1988.

3. The Claimant seeks possession under Grounds 12 ('breach of a term of the tenancy other than one relating to rent'), and 14 ('nuisance and annoyance/commission of a criminal offence at the premises'). Both of these grounds are discretionary. The Claimant will be asking the Court to make an outright possession order.

4. On 3rd April 2006 the Claimant obtained a without notice injunction against the Defendant, and the Claimant seeks a continuation of that order for a period of 12 months together with a power of arrest.

Summary of acts of nuisance and/or breaches relied on [evidence Tab 3 pp. 1–34]

5. In summary, the allegations of breach of tenancy and/or nuisance are as follows:—

(a) Loud noise from Flat 4 late in the evening and in the early hours of the morning, including noise:

(1) of amplified music (witnessed by Environmental Health Officers, and in respect of which abatement notices have been served);

(2) of arguments between the Defendant and his partner/ex partner Thelma Glug;

(b)   Threats of violence by the Defendant and his visitors to other residents of, and lawful visitors to Battle Road;

(c)   Other anti-social behaviour, including leaving rubbish in communal areas etc.

Issues for the Court

6.   Where a claim for possession is brought on discretionary grounds under the Housing Act 1988, the questions for the Court are as follows:—

(a)   Has the Claimant made out a ground for possession? (s. 7(1))

(b)   If so, is it reasonable in all the circumstances, including the effect of nuisance on neighbours (s. 9A), to make a possession order? (s. 7(4))

(c)   If it is reasonable to make an order, whether the possession order should be outright or suspended? (s. 9(2))

(d)   If the order is suspended, what terms of such the Court considers fit. (s. 9(2))

7.   There is authority to the effect that:—

(a)   It is not a defence to possession proceedings that the breach of the tenancy and or the ground for possession is caused by the behaviour of the tenant's family or visitors; the tenant is responsible for the behaviour of his visitors and/or members of his household. The fact that the Defendant himself is not culpable goes to whether it is reasonable to make an order and if so any suspension of it (*RLBKC* v *Simmons & Simmons* (1996) 29 HLR 507, CA; *West Kent Housing Association* v *Davis* (1999) 31 HLR 415, CA; and *Portsmouth CC* v *Bryant* (2000) 32 HLR 906, CA).

(b)   Incidents of repeated swearing/abusive language should normally result in a possession order being made (*Woking BC* v *Bistram* (1993) 27 HLR 1, CA).

(c)   The issue in respect of a suspended order is the future conduct of the tenant, where the inevitable outcome is breach the order should not be suspended (*Canterbury CC* v *Lowe* (2001) 33 HLR 53, CA).

Factual background

8.   Flat 4 is situated in a building at 4 Battle Road, Asbo, 'the building' containing 4 flats, all of which are let by the Claimant as residential dwellings; Flat 1 is on the ground floor, Flats 2 and 3 on the 1st floor, and Flat 4 on the 2nd floor.

9.   The Claimant has received complaints from the neighbours of nuisance and anti-social behaviour caused by the Defendant. These complaints commenced soon after the Defendant's tenancy began in October 2001.

10. At the time of the commencement of the Defendant's tenancy, the Claimant's tenant of Flat 3 was a Mrs Lottie.

11. The Claimant wrote to the Defendant in respect of complaints it had received concerning his behaviour on 3.12.01 [p. 263], 14.5.02 (loud music) [p. 264], 31.7.02 (Defendant's children climbing on scaffolding) [p. 265] 27.9.02 (an incident in which it is alleged that the Defendant assaulted Mrs Lottie's husband) [pp. 266–268] and 24.3.05 (in respect of rubbish left by the Defendant in the bin-shed area) [pp. 270–271].

12. The following incidents are also relied on:—

   (a) 10.7.04, loud amplified music coming from Defendant's premises at about 3.00 am; [diary of Mrs Lottie p. 308]

   (b) etc.

13. As a result of the acts set out above, on 3rd April 2006 the Claimant obtained a 'without notice' injunction against the Defendant.

14. Since that Order however, the Defendant has made further threats to Mr and Mrs Lottie:—

   (a) On 9th April 2006 the Defendant threatened to 'kneecap' Mr Lottie [p. 315]

   (b) etc.

Submissions

15. The nuisance is persistent and serious.

16. The Defendant has continued to cause nuisance after receipt of letters from the Claimant; after receipt of abatement notices, and after service of an injunction. In the circumstances there is no real prospect of the Defendant complying with such terms of a suspended possession order as would be necessary to ameliorate the nuisance or prevent a recurrence.

17. It would therefore be appropriate for the Court to make an outright possession order.

18. There is a real risk that the Defendant will threaten or assault Mr and Mrs Lottie or any other visitor to the building; in the circumstances it would be appropriate for the injunction to be continued even if the Defendant is evicted from Flat 4.

RAJ ISTAN
Fawlty Chambers, London EC55
Counsel for the Claimants

The above example is a case which turns on a fairly straightforward point and where it is unlikely that there is going to be any serious legal argument. It may be that the Defendant in person will contend either that he did not commit the acts in question at all, or that he should be given another chance to show that he is capable of abiding by the terms of the tenancy. More realistically, and with the wisdom of bitter experience, it is unlikely that the Defendant will turn up at all, and it will be a matter of formally proving the various acts/breaches alleged and following the argument through to its almost inevitable result. In the next example, however, I will set out respective arguments for an Appellant and a Respondent, where both are represented and where points of law and procedure are in issue. These are adapted from a real case, although I have 'doctored' them so substantially as to make them almost totally unrecognisable.

The case involves an appeal to the County Court against the decision of a local authority holding that the Appellant did not have a priority need for accommodation. Under the Housing Act 1996, such an appeal is heard by way of a form of judicial review, save that the forum is the County Court rather than the Administrative Court. It is worth comparing the format of the following arguments with that of the previous example, remembering the different type of proceedings in which they are being used.

IN THE BOGGLE COUNTY COURT   Case No. BG 123123

BETWEEN:

RAY GINNE-TOOTHAKE

Appellant

— and —

BOGGLE COUNTY COUNCIL

Respondent

APPELLANT'S SKELETON ARGUMENT

Introduction

1.   This is an appeal under s. 204(1)(a) of the Housing Act 1996 against a statutory review decision dated 2nd August 2005 that the Appellant did not have a priority need for accommodation on grounds of vulnerability.

The Jurisdiction

2.   The nature of the Court's task is:

> 'To determine whether any point of law arises on the deci-
> sion which is impugned. Point of law embraces not only
> matters of legal interpretation but also the full range of
> issues which would otherwise be the subject of an appli-
> cation for judicial review, e.g. procedural error, questions
> of *vires*, irrationality and adequacy of reasons.'[1]

3.   If a point of law does arise, the Court's powers are confined to confirming, quashing or varying the decision which
is impugned.[2] The section is permissive and the powers are
discretionary. A decision should be varied only if there is no
realistic prospect of a different decision being reached on a
further review: *Ekwuru* v *Westminster CC* [2003] EWCA
Civ 1293 *per* Schiemann LJ at [30–31]. In the case of procedural irregularity, the decision must be quashed unless the
result would inevitably be the same.[3]

4.   The Court has no fact-finding function and where the
Court is asked to examine factual findings and the exercise of
discretionary powers by a local authority, the Court may intervene only in limited circumstances. The Court's approach has
been explained by Lord Brightman as follows:—

> 'Where the existence or non existence of a fact is left to the
> judgment and discretion of a public body and that fact
> involves a broad spectrum ranging from the obvious to the
> debatable to the just conceivable, it is the duty of the court
> to leave the decision of that fact to the public body to
> whom Parliament has entrusted the decision making power
> save in a case where it is obvious that the public body, con-
> sciously or unconsciously, are acting perversely.'[4]

---

[1] *Nipa Begum* v *LB Tower Hamlets* [2000] 1 WLR 306, 313 *per* Auld LJ.
[2] Section 204(3).
[3] *Ali* v *LB Newham* [2002] HLR 413, para 13 *per* Latham J.
[4] *R* v *LB Hillingdon ex p Puhlhofer* [1986] AC 484, 518 *per* Lord Brightman.

5. The contemporary ambit of a 'judicial review' challenge in the context of a homelessness appeal has more recently been explained by Lord Bingham as follows:—

'... the court may not only quash the authority's decision under s. 204(3) if it is held to be vitiated by legal misdirection or procedural impropriety or unfairness or bias or irrationality or bad faith but also if there was no evidence to support factual findings made or they were plainly untenable or ... if the decision maker is shown to have misunderstood or been ignorant of an established and relevant fact. In the present context I would expect the county court Judge to be alert to any indication that an applicant's case might not have been resolved by the authority in a fair, objective and even-handed way, conscious of the authority's role as decision maker and of the immense importance of its decision to an applicant. But I can see no warrant for applying in this context notions of "anxious scrutiny" ... or more rigorous tha[n] would ordinarily and properly be conducted by a careful and competent Judge determining an application for judicial review.'[5]

6. When a County Court scrutinises a review decision letter, it should bear in mind the following:

'Sections 184(3) and 202(3) of the 1996 Act require an authority when notifying an applicant of its decisions under these and other of its provisions, to give him reasons for any decision adverse to his interests. The reasons should be sufficient to enable him to form a view as to whether to challenge it on a point of law in the sense indicated by Lord Bingham in *Runa Begum* ... However, decision letters under this provision should not be treated as if they were statutes or judgments and subjected to "pedantic exegisis" as Sir Thomas Bingham put it in *R* v *LB Croydon ex p Graham*.[6] It is also important, when looking at the

---

[5] *Runa Begum* v *LB Tower Hamlets* (2003) AC 430 para [7].
[6] 26 HLR 286, 291–2 (1994).

> reasoning in such a letter, to read it as a whole to get its full sense.'[7]

Whew! Now let me say from the beginning, that there's nothing wrong legally with the above exposition. It is a very learned piece of work. However, it has made some very basic points at some considerable length, and in my humble view that is **not** the purposes of a skeleton argument. Indeed, it is hard to see how the argument could actually be **expanded** in any way if and when it was ever presented to the Court! By all means, should you consider it necessary, set out the basic propositions of law on which you submit the Court should act. However, I would resist the temptation in all but the most compelling circumstances to quote from authorities (certainly at length) in the course of a skeleton argument. It defeats the whole object of the exercise, which is to present the bare bones of the argument on which the flesh (ugh) can be put later if required. That is why it is called a skeleton! The above example is more intimidating than helpful and serves little, if any, purpose. Furthermore here, the layout is confusing, with authorities being sometimes quoted within the text and sometimes in the footnotes.

However, note the fact that the example has not set out references to the trial bundle, as was done in the previous one we examined. This particular skeleton was probably drafted well before the bundle came into existence. In any event, where the argument is almost wholly based on law rather than fact, it may only confuse to clutter the skeleton with references which may be unnecessary.

Let's have another go:

Jurisdiction and basic principles
2.   An appeal under s. 204(1)(a) is in the nature of a judicial review on principles similar to that of the Administrative Court. The Court has no fact-finding function, and where the Court is asked to examine factual findings and the exercise of discretionary powers by a local authority, it may intervene only in limited circumstances.[1] Essentially the Court may quash the decision of a local authority under s. 204(3) if it finds the decision to have been vitiated by legal misdirection or procedural impropriety or unfairness, bias, irrationality or

---

[7] *Osmani* v *LB Camden* (2004) EWCA Civ 1706 para [38](9) *per* Auld LJ.
[1] *R* v *LB Hillingdon ex p Puhlhofer* [1986] AC 484.

bad faith; or if there was no evidence to support factual findings made, or such decisions were plainly untenable, or if the decision maker is shown to have misunderstood or been ignorant of an established and relevant fact.[2]

3.   If the Court finds the decision to have been defective for the reasons above or any of them, it may confirm, quash or vary the decision at its discretion.[3] A decision should be varied only if there is no realistic prospect of a different decision being reached on a further review.[4] In the case of procedural irregularity the decision should be quashed unless the result would inevitably be the same.[5]

4.   When a County Court scrutinises a review decision letter it should bear in mind that the applicant is entitled to be notified of the reasons for any decision adverse to his interests, sufficient to enable him to form a view as to whether to challenge it on a point of law. However, such letters should not be treated as if they were statutes or judgments. The letter should be read as a whole to get its full sense when looking at the reasoning.[6]

And that I think is quite enough! The basic points are, I hope, logically set out, and the principles are clear, together with indications as to where the authority for the various statements made can be found.

Let us continue with the original draft:

Priority need for accommodation
7.   When an applicant presents an application under Part 7 of the Housing Act, the housing authority is directed to make such inquiries as are necessary to satisfy itself about a number of issues: s. 184. One such issue is whether the applicant has a priority need for accommodation. Only where the authority is satisfied that the applicant enjoys a priority need will a full housing duty arise: s. 193.

---

[2] *Runa Begum* v *LB Tower Hamlets* [2003] AC 430.

[3] Section 204(3).

[4] *Ekwuru* v *Westminster CC* [2003] EWCA Civ 1293.

[5] *Ali* v *LB Newham* [2002] HLR 413.

[6] *R* v *LB Croydon ex p Graham* (1994) 26 HLR 286 at 291–2; *Osmani* v *LB Camden* [2004] EWCA Civ 1706.

8.   This case concerns vulnerability on medical grounds as defined by s. 189(1)(c) and construed by the Court of Appeal in *R* v *Camden LBC ex p Pereira* (1998) 30 HLR 317, 330 *per* Hobhouse J. That definitive construction has now been further considered by the Court of Appeal in *Osmani* v *Camden LBC* [2004] EWCA Civ 1706 and Auld LJ's judgment at [38] offers a comprehensive explanation.

Frankly, this is not very helpful. Whereas the part about priority need is accurate and informative, it could be put more succinctly, and the second paragraph says nothing about the issues here at all. I suggest thus:

5.   By HA 1996, s. 193, a full housing duty cannot arise unless the authority is satisfied that the applicant enjoys a priority need for accommodation, and fulfils various other criteria. Under s. 184, the housing authority is directed to make such inquiries as are necessary to satisfy itself, amongst other matters, if such a priority need arises. The Appellant in the present case claims that he fulfils the criteria for priority housing on medical grounds as defined by s. 189(1)(c) of the Act as construed in *R* v *Camden LBC ex p Pereira* (1998) 30 HLR 317 and *Osmani* v *Camden LBC* [2004] EWCA Civ 1706, and that the rejection of this contention by the local authority is due to inadequate analysis and consideration such as requires its review decision to be quashed under s. 204.

Now that, it seems to me, is far more helpful. It sets out the basic principles to the extent that they are relevant, and relates them to the subject matter of the appeal, which is not really dealt with in the first draft. In setting this out we are doing no more than exercising the basic principles of drafting that have been discussed in earlier chapters of this work. What we have analysed is:
   (a)   No housing duty arises unless there is a priority need.
   (b)   The authority must see whether there is such a priority need.
   (c)   The Appellant says he has such a need due to medical grounds.
   (d)   The authority rejected this contention.
   (e)   We say that, in rejecting the argument, the authority didn't properly carry out an analysis and consideration of the facts such as the law obliges it to do.
   (f)   Therefore we are entitled to have the decision quashed.

Easy peasy! To continue with the original:

Facts

9.   The Appellant applied for accommodation under Part 7 of the Housing Act and was interviewed on 21st April 2005. Dr Bandage had completed a medical questionnaire dated 18th April. He reported Type 2 diabetes and the absence of any hospital referrals by his practice where the Appellant had been registered since September 2003. A case summary dated 26th April 2005 confirmed Type 2 diabetes but did not report any other significant medical issues. The Respondent's decision under s. 204 was promulgated by a letter dated 22nd April and followed the same pattern as the notes. It concluded 'Your Diabetes Mellitus is tablet controlled and you have not reported any mental health problems and there is no perceived risk of harm to yourself or others. I am of the opinion that the fact that you have been diagnosed with Type 2 Diabetes Mellitus does not render you vulnerable in circumstances where a less vulnerable person would be able to cope without harmful effects.'

10.   By a letter dated 4th May 2005, the Appellant's solicitors requested a review and accommodation pending review. They drew attention to prescriptions for mental health problems. The solicitors sought a further medical opinion and sought extension of time in which to make representations, illustrated by their letter of 3rd June. On 20th June they submitted a report dated 15th June by Dr Nicely, the Appellant's GP.

11.   A case note of 13th July noted the conflicting material from his GP's practice and noted the absence of any 'adequate mental health assessment'.

12.   The review decision was promulgated by a letter dated 2nd August. The letter should be read as a whole.

Now everyone has their own style. After reading the remainder of this chapter you may wish to have a go at setting out the facts here. You might at this stage want to try a few criticisms of the drafting style yourself. (I stress that the whole 'original' draft has been heavily doctored by me to bring out certain points, and bears no relation to the one that was originally used in Court.) However, for those of you who have more pressing things to do, or who find the delights of 'University Challenge' or 'EastEnders' too proximate to attempt a draft at this time, I would venture to suggest that it is not really very clear what the facts are all about, and that it is going to take the reader (the trial Judge) a little time to decipher the matter — and this is not conducive to instilling in him or her the mood of sweetness and light which you would like to have displayed from the bench during the course of the hearing. So:

> 6.   The Appellant applied for accommodation under Part 7 of the Housing Act and was interviewed on 21st April 2005. Before the interview, a member of his GP's practice, Dr Bandage, completed a medical questionnaire which reported that he suffered from Type 2 diabetes, but also stated that he had not been referred to hospital by the practice, at least since September 2003 when the Appellant had first registered. The Respondent's decision was set out in a letter dated 22nd April, and stated that the Appellant's diabetes was tablet controlled, that he had no mental health problems and that there was no perceived risk of harm either to himself or to others. In the circumstances he did not fall within the vulnerability test set out in the Act.

> 7.   On 4th May 2005 the Appellant's solicitors requested a review, and drew attention to prescriptions for mental health problems, which appeared to show that the conclusions drawn by the Respondents as to the Appellant's state of mental health were incorrect. On 20th June 2005 they submitted a report from Dr Nicely, the Appellant's GP, which indicated that the Appellant did have mental health problems. This report was acknowledged by the Respondents, and their case note of 13th July 2005 stated that there was conflicting material from his GP's practice, and also noted the 'absence of any adequate MH assessment'. Notwithstanding this, they upheld the original decision on review in their letter dated 2nd August 2005.

Now the precise facts of the case are not relevant for the purpose of this exercise. However, in accordance with the general principles of clear exposition set out in the earlier part of this book, I would suggest that the

narrative above is far clearer than in the original draft, and that it is therefore more useful and effective.

Continuing with the original:

The argument

13.   Part 7 of the Housing Act 1996 provides a social welfare
scheme for the provision of advice and assistance to homeless persons. The need for accommodation is an important
human need, but in a world of finite resources, Parliament
has not seen fit to provide that local housing authorities should
provide accommodation for all those who are homeless.
Parliament has recognised that some people have a greater
need than others, they have a 'priority need' and, subject to
meeting other qualifications[8] a local housing authority will
have to secure that accommodation is available for them: s. 193.
An applicant will only have a **priority** need for accommodation in circumstances specified in s. 189(1).

14.   Who decides? It is for the local housing authority to
decide: s. 184. It is not for a Judge to decide, nor an applicant, nor his doctors nor the local authority's doctors. When
an authority has reached an adverse decision, an applicant
has an unfettered right to a review: s. 202. When a review is
asked for, all matters of fact and discretion are at large: see
Mohammed v Hammersmith & Fulham LBC [2002] 1 AC
547, 554 at [23] and [26] *per* Lord Slynn.

15.   By what standard does the authority have to decide? The
authority's task is to make such inquiries as are necessary to
satisfy itself whether an applicant is vulnerable. The extent of
any inquiries is a matter for the authority, and, unless an
Appellant can demonstrate that any reasonable authority
would have undertaken further inquiries, the Court will not
intervene. But it follows that an adverse review should be
astute to reason its decision on medical issues with care and
to explain why it has concluded that an applicant will not
suffer the detriment or harm when street homeless rather

---

[8] Eligibility for assistance (s. 185) and not being intentionally homeless (s. 191).

than statutorily homeless but in temporary accommodation. That is the circumstance which the review has to consider.[9] The more open and uncertain the applicant's circumstances, the more important it is that the review should reason its decision with care and explain its reasoning.

16.   In this case, the Appellant had undoubtedly been pre-scribed medication for his diabetes and, although Dr Bandage did not know it, he had also been prescribed medication for depression. The review does not disparage the Appellant's need to maintain a balanced diet in order to avoid complica-tions with his diabetes. While he has been in temporary accommodation, he can be expected to manage. The review supposes without analysis that he would also be able to manage whilst street homeless. It is not just the diabetes though; he would have to manage his diabetes while suffering from depression. Such an applicant might or might not be able to cope; in this case, there is no analysis of why the Appellant would cope when another might not.

17.   Also, when considering his depression, the review sens-ibly recognised that the homeless may well get depressed and that many people lead active lives when prescribed the level of medication taken by the Appellant. That's all very well. But how about the effect of an adverse change of cir-cumstances? The transition from housed to street homeless. Some applicants might be able to cope and others not. There is no analysis of why this applicant can cope beyond a ref-erence to medication and the absence so far of any hospital referral.

18.   Both grounds of appeal challenge the adequacy of rea-soning because the review cannot be shown to have thought through the matters it had to consider. It does not follow that the review would necessarily have been successful if it had, and the Appellant does not suggest that the decision should be varied. But the Appellant does submit that a more careful

---

[9] See *Osmani* at [38](7).

analysis was due to him, and that the Respondent's review should be quashed.

Emma Royd
Farmer Giles Chambers
Old Pile Yard
London EC44

I have set all this out in one piece because I want you to get the flavour of it in its entirety. As an exposition of the duties of a local authority when coming to a decision on homelessness it is textbook. Actually, it could be a textbook! As a piece of advocacy it isn't bad either. Try reading it out loud (make sure nobody is around, or the ladies and gentlemen in white coats will come and take you away!). It declaims pretty well, you may think. The rhetorical questions have a rise and fall about them that would sound pretty good in Court, or in the lecture hall. If you are one of those advocates (and I hope you are not) who has to write everything out in full before opening your mouth in Court, this may be what you would produce. But — a skeleton argument it is not!

Miss Royd has even got a little carried away in the course of her exposition. In paragraph 16, for example, the expression 'It is not just the diabetes though;' is not exactly the phraseology one would (or should) put in an essay or textbook. Also the use of the phrase 'That's all very well' in paragraph 17 evidences, I suggest, that she is in the full flow of her oratory and has forgotten what this particular piece of drafting is all about. Skeleton? This is obesity! Effectively, Miss Royd may as well not turn up to Court and just hand this piece of work in (or at least these few paragraphs). So how do we set about encapsulating all this in skeleton argument form?

I suggest that the first thing we do, is to strip away our argument literally to the bare bones. First, a list of 'don'ts':

(a) No rhetoric or rhetorical questions.

(b) No descriptive preamble, unless it is directly relevant to the argument.

(c) No repetition of points — one good point well made is better than six near misses — likewise (as I am fond of saying), a good point does not need repetition, and a bad one should not be made in the first place.

Now let us consider a structure:

1. Relevant background to such extent as is necessary.
2. What do we say should have been done?

3.   What do we say was in fact done or not done?

4.   What are the consequences that we say flow from the acts or omissions of which we make complaint?

Let us see how these apply here, having regard to the material with which we are faced.

> 8.   Part 7 of HA 1996 provides that a local housing authority will have a duty to secure that accommodation is available for a person who fulfils the criteria for eligibility for assistance, not being intentionally homeless and in priority need, a definition of the last being provided in s. 189(1).

Although the above clearly lacks the comprehensiveness of the original, it is surely sufficient for our purposes.

> 9.   By s. 184 the decision has to be that of the local authority. If it reaches an adverse decision, the applicant has an unfettered right to a review, by s. 202. In such a review, all matters of fact and discretion are at large.

These are pretty basic principles, and so it is not necessary, in my view, to cite chapter and verse for each statement made. If problems arise, this can be done in Court.

> 10.   The housing authority is required to make such inquiries as are necessary to satisfy itself whether an applicant is vulnerable. The extent of any inquiries is a matter for the authority and, unless an Appellant can demonstrate that any reasonable authority would have undertaken further inquiries, the Court will not intervene. However, in the event of an adverse review, the authority should be careful to provide reasoning on medical issues with care, and to explain why it has concluded that an applicant will not suffer detriment or harm when street homeless rather than statutorily homeless but in temporary accommodation. *Osmani* v *LB Camden* [2004] EWCA Civ 1706.

Although there is not a huge difference between this and the original paragraph 15, a close comparison should show the important differences that

I hope make this version clearer and more relevant. In the next passage we should get to grips with our case, which I think can be put quite shortly:

> 11.   In the present case, it is accepted that the Appellant had been prescribed medication for his diabetes. The review does not seek to question the assertion that he requires to maintain a balanced diet in order to avoid complications with this condition. Whilst the Appellant was in temporary accommodation, he can be expected to manage. However, the review also concludes that he would also be able to manage this whilst street homeless. There is no analysis as to why or how this vital decision was reached.

> 12.   Likewise, although the original medical report from Dr Bandage omitted this, the Appellant had been prescribed medication for depression. Although the review sensibly recognised that the homeless may well get depressed and many people lead active lives when prescribed the level of medication taken by the Appellant, there is no analysis in the review of why it is concluded that this Appellant will be able to cope with both depression and diabetes whilst street homeless, nor as to why he would be one of the group who could deal with the depressive effects of street homelessness rather than one of the group who could not.

I hope that this puts our case fairly and squarely. Finally, to round things off:

> 13.   It is not contended that the review would inevitably have been successful had the housing authority demonstrated that it had adequately considered all the necessary matters and given a proper reasoned analysis and explanation of its conclusions. For this reason the Appellant does not contend that the decision should be varied, but that it should be quashed, and the matter remitted for a fresh review to be conducted with the appropriate level of care and analysis that was due to him.

COUNT ERFEET
Laundry Chambers
Washington

Let us see how that all reads when put together:

IN THE BOGGLE COUNTY COURT   Case No. BG 123123

BETWEEN:

RAY GINNE-TOOTHAKE

Appellant

— and —

BOGGLE COUNTY COUNCIL

Respondent

APPELLANT'S SKELETON ARGUMENT

---

1.   This is an appeal under s. 204(1)(a) of the Housing Act 1996 against a statutory review decision dated 2nd August 2005 that the Appellant did not have a priority need for accommodation on grounds of vulnerability.

2.   An appeal under s. 204(1)(a) is in the nature of a judicial review on principles similar to that of the Administrative Court. The Court has no fact-finding function, and where the Court is asked to examine factual findings and the exercise of discretionary powers by a local authority, it may intervene only in limited circumstances.[1] Essentially the Court may quash the decision of a local authority under s. 204(3) if it finds the decision to have been vitiated by legal misdirection or procedural impropriety or unfairness, bias, irrationality or bad faith; or if there was no evidence to support factual findings made, or such decisions were plainly untenable, or if the decision maker is shown to have misunderstood or been ignorant of an established and relevant fact.[2]

3.   If the Court finds the decision to have been defective for the reasons above or any of them, it may confirm, quash or vary the decision at its discretion.[3] A decision should be varied only if there is no realistic

---

[1] *R v LB Hillingdon ex p Puhlhofer* [1986] AC 484.
[2] *Runa Begum* v *LB Tower Hamlets* [2003] AC 430.
[3] Section 204(3).

prospect of a different decision being reached on a further review.[4] In the case of procedural irregularity the decision should be quashed unless the result would inevitably be the same.[5]

4. When a County Court scrutinises a review decision letter it should bear in mind that the applicant is entitled to be notified of the reasons for any decision adverse to his interests, sufficient to enable him to form a view as to whether to challenge it on a point of law. However, such letters should not be treated as if they were statutes or judgments. The letter should be read as a whole to get its full sense when looking at the reasoning.[6]

5. By HA 1996, s. 193, a full housing duty cannot arise unless the authority is satisfied that the applicant enjoys a priority need for accommodation, and fulfils various other criteria. Under s. 184, the housing authority is directed to make such inquiries as are necessary to satisfy itself, amongst other matters, if such a priority need arises. The Appellant in the present case claims that he fulfils the criteria for priority housing on medical grounds as defined by s. 189(1)(c) of the Act as construed in *R v Camden LBC ex p Pereira* (1998) 30 HLR 317 and *Osmani v Camden LBC* [2004] EWCA Civ 1706, and that the rejection of this contention by the local authority is due to inadequate analysis and consideration such as requires its review decision to be quashed under s. 204.

6. The Appellant applied for accommodation under Part 7 of the Housing Act and was interviewed on 21st April 2005. Before the interview, a member of his GP's practice, Dr Bandage, completed a medical questionnaire which reported that he suffered from Type 2 diabetes, but also stated that he had not been referred to hospital by the practice, at least since September 2003 when the Appellant had first registered. The Respondent's decision was set out in a letter dated 22nd April, and stated that the Appellant's diabetes was tablet controlled, that he had no mental health problems and that there was no perceived risk of harm either to himself or to others. In the circumstances he did not fall within the vulnerability test set out in the Act.

---

[4] *Ekwuru v Westminster CC* [2003] EWCA Civ 1293.

[5] *Ali v LB Newham* [2002] HLR 413.

[6] *R v LB Croydon ex p Graham* (1994) 26 HLR 286 at 291–2; *Osmani v LB Camden* [2004] EWCA Civ 1706.

7.   On 4th May 2005 the Appellant's solicitors requested a review, and drew attention to prescriptions for mental health problems, which appeared to show that the conclusions drawn by the Respondents as to the Appellant's state of mental health were incorrect. On 20th June 2005 they submitted a report from Dr Nicely, the Appellant's GP, which indicated that the Appellant did have mental health problems. This report was acknowledged by the Respondents, and their case note of 13th July 2005 stated that there was conflicting material from his GP's practice, and also noted the 'absence of any adequate MH assessment'. Notwithstanding this, they upheld the original decision on review in their letter dated 2nd August 2005.

8.   Part 7 of HA 1996 provides that a local housing authority will have a duty to secure that accommodation is available for a person who fulfils the criteria for eligibility for assistance, not being intentionally homeless and in priority need, a definition of the last being provided in s. 189(1).

9.   By s. 184 the decision has to be that of the local authority. If it reaches an adverse decision, the applicant has an unfettered right to a review, by s. 202. In such a review, all matters of fact and discretion are at large.

10.   The housing authority is required to make such inquiries as are necessary to satisfy itself whether an applicant is vulnerable. The extent of any inquiries is a matter for the authority and, unless an Appellant can demonstrate that any reasonable authority would have undertaken further inquiries, the Court will not intervene. However, in the event of an adverse review, the authority should be careful to provide reasoning on medical issues with care, and to explain why it has concluded that an applicant will not suffer detriment or harm when street homeless rather than statutorily homeless but in temporary accommodation. *Osmani* v *LB Camden* [2004] EWCA Civ 1706.

11.   In the present case, it is accepted that the Appellant had been prescribed medication for his diabetes. The review does not seek to question the assertion that he requires to maintain a balanced diet in order to avoid complications with this condition. Whilst the Appellant was in temporary accommodation, he can be expected to manage. However, the review also concludes that he would also be able to manage this whilst street homeless. There is no analysis as to why or how this vital decision was reached.

12.   Likewise, although the original medical report from Dr Bandage omitted this, the Appellant had been prescribed medication for depression. Although the review sensibly recognised that the homeless may well get

depressed and many people lead active lives when prescribed the level of medication taken by the Appellant, there is no analysis in the review of why it is concluded that this Appellant will be able to cope with both depression and diabetes whilst street homeless, nor as to why he would be one of the group who could deal with the depressive effects of street homelessness rather than one of the group who could not.

13. It is not contended that the review would inevitably have been successful had the housing authority demonstrated that it had adequately considered all the necessary matters and given a proper reasoned analysis and explanation of its conclusions. For this reason the Appellant does not contend that the decision should be varied, but that it should be quashed, and the matter remitted for a fresh review to be conducted with the appropriate level of care and analysis that was due to him.

COUNT ERFEET
Laundry Chambers
Washington

I venture to suggest that this conveys the relevant argument far more succinctly and cogently than the original example — and in a much less space!

Now you may (just) remember that I promised you the other side of the story in this case. This is written in a somewhat different style from either the 'original' or the 'final' example that I have set out above. Let me reproduce it in full so that you can savour its overall effect. I will not seek to redraft it (although you may have a go should you wish), but will just comment on what I consider to be its good and weak points:

IN THE BOGGLE COUNTY COURT   Case No. BG 123123

BETWEEN:

RAY GINNE-TOOTHAK

Appellant

— and —

BOGGLE COUNTY COUNCIL

Respondent

SKELETON ARGUMENT ON BEHALF OF THE
RESPONDENT

Introduction
1.   This is an appeal under s. 204. The Respondent by its s. 184 original decision made on 22nd April 2005 and a s. 202 review decision made on 2nd August 2005 has concluded that the Appellant is not in priority need pursuant to s. 189 HA 1996 and accordingly is owed only limited duties under that Act.

2.   The only decision which can lawfully be challenged is the s. 202 decision of 2nd August 2005.

3.   Applying the established test under s. 189 the Respondent ultimately concluded that the Appellant was not '*vulnerable as a result of mental illness or handicap, physical disability or some other special reason so that <u>when homeless</u> you are less able to fend for yourself than an ordinary homeless person <u>so that</u> injury or detriment <u>will result</u> to you*'.

4.   To succeed the Appellant must demonstrate that the Respondent made an error of law in the review process or decision.

5.   The Appellant contends that the reasoning behind the Respondent's conclusion is inadequate.

Law
6.   The jurisdiction of the County Court under s. 204 Housing Act 1996 is limited to errors of law. The purview of the proceedings is equivalent to judicial review in the High Court: *Nipa Begum* v *LB Tower Hamlets* [2000] WLR 306, CA. For the same reasons the Court has a discretion as to whether to grant relief in any particular case.

7.   Matters of fact, weight and judgment are for the authority: *Puhlhofer* v *Hillingdon London Borough Council* [1986] 1 AC 484 at p. 518 *per* Lord Brightman.

8.   The scope of inquiries is for the authority: *R* v *Royal Borough of Kensington and Chelsea, ex p Bayani* (1990) 22 HLR 406, CA; *R (Cramp)* v *Hastings DC* [2005] EWCA Civ 1005.

9.   The test of vulnerability was authoritatively stated by the Court of Appeal in *R* v *Camden LBC ex p Pereira* (1998) 30 HLR 317 at 330.

10.   The fact that a matter is not mentioned in a decision letter does not mean it was not taken into account. The test is whether the omission was startling. Advisers acting for applicants should take care to ensure all relevant material is before the authority: *R* v *Brent LBC ex p Barisse* (1998) 30 HLR 50 at pp. 57–58.

11.   The correct comparator is the ordinary homeless person who can typically be expected to suffer with a level of depression; and that depression will typically be exacerbated by becoming street homeless: *Yeter* v *LB Enfield* [2001] EWHC Admin 1315.

12.   Authorities are entitled to give their reasons simply. They do not sit in a judicial or quasi-judicial capacity. Those reasons are entitled to a reasonably liberal interpretation: *R* v *Croydon LBC ex p Graham* (1994) 26 HLR 286, CA.

Submissions
13.   There can be no doubt that the reviewer (an experienced review officer of the Respondent) applied the correct *Pereira* test. It is set out in terms in the decision letter. In particular reference is made to conducting the test on the basis of what detriment or injury would result in the situation of homelessness. Nothing in the review decision compels the conclusion that an inappropriate test was being applied. The Appellant explicitly accepts that the conclusion reached in this case would be potentially open to the reviewer. The correct comparator of course is the ordinary homeless person who can typically be expected to suffer with a level of depression: *Yeter* v *LB Enfield* [2001] EWHC Admin 1315.

14.   As the Appellant accepts, the decision letter has to be read as a whole and the guidance in *Graham* applied. The decision letter deals in detail with the Appellant's ability to cope and notes explicitly that the Appellant 'has no major health problems'. There is no appeal against that finding. Further the Appellant remains entitled to all state benefits and that he was able to access services such as health and housing should he need them. There is no appeal against that finding. The same applies to the findings that the Appellant could communicate effectively and was capable of living independently.

15.   Earlier in time, in the s. 184 decision, further reference was made to the ability to secure private accommodation and that was not challenged during the course of the review. The ability to secure accommodation is

recognised as one part of the *Pereira* test (*per* Hobhouse LJ at p. 330). That letter also dealt with the diabetes issue in terms and the Appellant's advisers would have understood the need to persuade the authority to change its mind on this point:— *Barisse/Cramp*.

16.   The review decision letter dealt with each of the items raised by the Appellant. The level of the depression and its management was considered. The reviewer concluded that as a matter of his informed judgment the depression experienced by the Appellant was at a level that could be expected. That was a reasonable conclusion. There was no medical or other suggestion that becoming street homeless would have an impact on the Appellant's depression that was substantially greater than could typically be expected.

17.   The issue of diabetes was identified and dealt with. It was found to be under control by the use of medication. The reasoning on this point has to be read in context and in light of the other factors identified above which indicate that in a number of ways the Appellant was able to access services more readily than others who find themselves street homeless. The reviewer considered in terms whether the nature of the dietary requirements would lead to a detriment and concluded that there was no reason why the Appellant would not be able to eat regularly. That was a reasonable conclusion that an experienced officer was entitled to reach on all the facts of this application.

18.   Looking at the letter as a whole the review decision discloses a careful consideration of the application which is sufficient to comply with *Graham*. For those reasons the appeal should be dismissed.

Ben E. Dictus
Hope and Prayer Chambers
Temple, London EC4

I hope you will agree that this is not a bad piece of work. It is written and structured so that it can be relatively easily absorbed in a short time. Mind you, it is not the most intellectually complex of arguments!

The **Introduction** is concise and logical. Possibly paragraph 5 could be expanded slightly to include the Appellant's principal point that the inadequate reasoning was in respect of the conclusion that his medical condition was not such as to render him vulnerable etc.

However, when it comes to the **Law** section, I think that matters could be improved. The basic principles here are well settled and are not contentious. I would favour a better layout, where the main points were made more punchily, with the authorities relegated to footnotes, in the (unlikely) event that we will need to refer to them in the course of argument. I emphasise that style is very personal; I have said (many times) in the course of this work that I do not want to provide a series of precedents, but to impart the principles and leave you to adapt them to your personal taste. That is why I have included examples which are very different in style and approach. However, my modest effort would read:

Law
6.   The jurisdiction of the County Court under s. 204 is equivalent to judicial review in the High Court.[1] Therefore the Court cannot review matters of fact, weight or judgment,[2] or the scope of the inquiries made by the authority.[3] These are entirely for the authority to decide. The Court is limited to examining errors of law, which includes irrationality and adequacy of reasons given.

7.   The test of vulnerability was authoritatively stated by the Court of Appeal as being [here I would succinctly set out the test — I won't do so now as it is not important for our purposes].[4]

8.   The correct comparator is the ordinary homeless person who can typically be expected to suffer with a level of depression; and that depression will typically be exacerbated by becoming street homeless.[5]

9.   Authorities are entitled to give their reasons simply. They do not sit in a judicial or quasi-judicial capacity. Those

---

[1] *Nipa Begum* v *LB Tower Hamlets* [2000] WLR 306, CA.
[2] *Puhlhofer* v *Hillingdon London Borough Council* [1986] 1 AC 484.
[3] *R* v *Royal Borough of Kensington and Chelsea, ex p Bayani* [1990] 22 HLR 406, CA; *R (Cramp)* v *Hastings DC* [2005] EWCA Civ 1005.
[4] *R* v *Camden LBC, ex p Pereira* (1998) 30 HLR 317.
[5] *Yeter* v *LB Enfield* [2001] EWHC Admin 1315.

reasons are entitled to a reasonably liberal interpretation.[6]
The fact that a matter is not mentioned in a decision letter
does not mean it was not taken into account. The test is
whether the omission was startling.[7]

---

[6] *R* v *Croydon LBC, ex p Graham* (1994) 26 HLR 286.
[7] *R* v *Brent LBC, ex p Barisse* (1998) 30 HLR 50.

Those of you who are still awake will have noticed that not only have
I amalgamated some of the paragraphs in the interests of clarity, but
I have also changed the order in an attempt to make the argument more
logical. You can judge whether or not I have been successful in this.

Turning to the **Submissions** section, ensure that any evidence to
which you refer has actually been given in the course of previous
proceedings. Here, Mr Dictus has stated that the review officer was
experienced. I wouldn't say anything like that if it hasn't been mentioned
before, otherwise you are falling into the old trap of giving evidence for
your own side! Is it necessary to repeat *Yeter* v *LB Enfield*? If possible,
chop down some of the advocacy, avoid any repetition, and ensure that
subjects are dealt with together and in logical order.

I could go on to cite further examples and analyse them, but there
comes a time when the law of diminishing returns applies. (That is the
law that states that if a book becomes too expensive and heavy, it doesn't
sell very well, and my royalties start to dry up!) I hope you have
absorbed the general principles — practice makes perfect and remember,
of course, that the more skeleton arguments you have to draft, the better
your practice is doing — and that can't be bad at all!

Chapter Thirteen

A Matter of Opinions
(Opinion Writing)

> 'Would you tell me, please, which way
> I ought to go from here?'
> 'That depends a good deal on where
> you want to get to', said the Cat.
> 'I don't much care where —' said Alice.
> 'Then it doesn't matter which way you
> go', said the Cat.

I confess to a certain amount of trepidation when approaching this subject. Originally I considered that the format of this work would not allow me to do full justice to this very personal art without a myriad of examples, which would occupy a disproportionate amount of space, and which would raise the cover price of this book to an embarrassing level! However, 'popular demand', as they say, together with the fact that Opinion writing is no longer the exclusive province of the Bar, has prompted me to change my mind, and I hope not too many rain forests will be demolished in the course of the attempt!

At the heart of any good Opinion, of course, is a full understanding of the case, based on careful and thorough preparation, involving the disciplines of legal research and fact management. The former is perhaps obvious, but the latter is equally important, requiring as it does a full comprehension of the factual material at your disposal, its weight and significance, and its particular value in the light of other, possibly undetermined facts. How relevant is a particular fact? May it become relevant? Are there relevant or potentially relevant facts which are presently missing? What are the reasonable and realistic prospects of obtaining such facts? How should they be obtained? What facts do or might the other side have, and how will these affect the material presently or possibly to be in your possession? It is only once all these matters have been considered and you have begun to formulate a clear idea of what it is you wish to say, that the question of the structure and physical expression of the Opinion becomes important.

Most instructions require us to write a general Opinion, although with specific reference to a number of points. Obviously, as you become more senior, the nature of your practice may dictate your ultimate choice of style, and in any event by this time you will have had sufficient experience of writing Opinions such as it would be presumptuous in the extreme for me to offer advice. However, for those setting out on the long hard road through the profession, I would advocate that you start on the basis that you will write an 'entire' Opinion, in which the objectives are recited, the facts of the case are briefly set out, the points of concern are identified, the Opinion is given, together with any necessary analysis of law, and the work is concluded with some good general practical advice.

In contrast to this, however, is the view that Opinions should be short, devoid of narrative, and concerned solely with answering the issue or issues that are causing concern. Such Opinions might commence:

> 1.   I am asked to advise as to the effect of clause 3 of the contract, on the situation prevailing as at 30th August 2005. In *Dogtooth* v *Prime Pet Meats Ltd* (1811) 34 ChD 11998, Woof J stated: …

Now it cannot be said that this type of approach doesn't have its advantages, particularly if you are asked to advise on a fairly short point, concerning a matter of pure law. It is beloved of those of an academic turn of mind, who feel that they are being paid for answers to specific questions, and that it would be a waste of time and money to set out the matter in any great narrative detail. The epitome of this form came several years ago, when an eminent silk was asked to give his learned Opinion as to whether or not the Plaintiff, as he was then called, should commence proceedings against the Defendant. The papers arrived in a pantechnicon, neatly arranged in numbered boxes. Doubts were expressed as to whether the floor of chambers was sufficiently reinforced to stand the weight! The legal world waited on tenterhooks!!

Learned leading Counsel studied the papers at length, and then proffered an Opinion, which when opened, contained the single word: 'Yes.'

Obviously that was considered sufficient by the learned gentleman to comply with his instructions, and such was his pre-eminence in his field that instructing solicitors doubtless swallowed their reservations, swallowed even harder when they received the fee note, and proceeded accordingly!

Very few of us would, I suggest, have the clout (or the sheer audacity) to emulate such a performance, and you may therefore consider that a little more is required of us, even if the net result is the same! So let us take a look at some of the basic considerations.

Even when you have fully understood your case and are ready to give the necessary advice, it is worth pausing for a moment to reflect upon the essential objectives of the task. These are, I suggest, **to give the client advice, together with the basic reasoning behind it**. Such advice should be put forward in a manner which is as straightforward and digestible as possible. I am frequently tempted (and obviously have not resisted it here) to suggest that if you cannot explain something in simple language, the probability is that you do not fully understand it! It may well be that some of the reasoning in a complex issue may be of no interest to the lay client, and might be difficult for a lay person to comprehend even if it was. That does not mean that you have the right to abdicate responsibility for giving the clearest possible explanation. The law is for the benefit of us all, and it will be sad day if it cannot be explained, at least to the greater part, in language which can be understood by those that it exists to serve. I hope that doesn't sound too pompous, but it is so easy to forget in the midst of the pressure and responsibility of attempting to give the right Opinion.

Whilst there is no Rule of Law to the effect, you should always write Opinions in the first person: 'I am asked to advise ...', '... in my opinion', etc. In the bad old days not only was the impersonal form used, but the third person as well: 'Counsel is of the opinion that ...'. Suffice it to say that such a style is wholly unacceptable today. The advantage of using the first person is that it prevents the work from degenerating into an essay with all sorts of discourses on hypothetical and irrelevant matters.

In common with books, letters and my sons' cars, Opinions are notoriously difficult to start. It's best, in my view, to have a formula, as once you have actually got over this hurdle, the rest should (!) start to flow more naturally. My own preference is to begin by outlining the objectives of the Opinion:

> 1.   I am asked to advise Poppop Enterprises Ltd as to the prospects of their being able successfully to appeal a decision

of the Barnes County Court in which they were ordered to
pay damages to the Smoked Salmon Growers Association
under the provisions of section 5 of the Strip Poker and
Underwater Knitting Act 1998.

This having been done, you can then segue into the facts either with
the conventional:

The brief facts are as follows: ...

or more ambitiously (and depending on the circumstances) with the use
of a link phrase such as:

I have had the advantage of seeing Mr Halfwit in conference,
and as a result of this it seems that ...

or

I have read the statements helpfully provided by instructing
solicitors [crawl, crawl] from which it appears that ...

However you choose to do it, you should then be in a position to recite
the relevant facts. Although you should beware of writing an Opinion
which comprises 99% recitation of facts and 1% advice, there are, in my
view, a number of advantages to giving a concise exposition of the basic
problem. In the first place, particularly if you are relatively inexperi-
enced, or not well-known to your instructing solicitors, a résumé of the
facts will assure them not only that you have read the papers fully, but
also that you are fully apprised of the relevant matters. Further, by
basing your Opinion on the facts related, it will immediately become
apparent that it may not apply if the position ultimately proves to be
different, or if (heaven forbid) you have misread the situation.

You will often find that, having rendered your masterpiece, you may
hear no more for a number of months or even longer. During that period
of time, it is to be hoped that you have been rushed off your feet, advising
people left, right and centre, astounding Judges and Masters with the
brilliance both of your oratory and your intellect, and generally Making
a Name for Yourself. Suddenly, out of the blue, the instructions land
back on your desk for some more advice, or with a requirement to draft
a statement of case. The bundle is considerably the more plump, probably

in some disorder, and is wrapped with a short and somewhat disingenuous backsheet commencing:

> You will doubtless recall this matter, having advised (some three hundred years ago) ...

'... astounding Judges and Masters ...'

Of course you have no more recollection of the case than of the scores in the 1599 annual pie-throwing contest at Hampton Court! However, helpfully included with the papers is the earlier Opinion, and by reading that full account of the problem, in your own fair hand, all is suitably brought back to mind!

Opinions are, of course, the product of personal style and taste, and your instructions may perhaps contain matters which you do not consider relevant, or may omit matters which seem very important to you. By setting out a full Advice, complete with basic narrative, you have in effect made a note for yourself of all matters which appear appropriate to you, which should greatly assist you at a later date, either in settling proceedings, or even in providing the foundation of your opening address to the Court.

Unless you are exceptionally brilliant, you will almost certainly find an imbalance between fact and analysis in your first clutch of Opinions, but you will get the hang of it with practice. Remember that there should be proportion in all things — the recipient of your advice will not be desirous of paying to receive a rehashed version of his own instructions.

Try therefore to ensure that your narrative is set out for the purpose of outlining the problems that you are asked to resolve, and in such a form as assists comprehension of your analysis and conclusions.

Just as in drafting a statement of case, your aim should be clarity and simplicity at all times. Never use complicated language or phraseology just for the 'fun of it'. Although good style is very much a matter of personal taste, the basic rules of grammar, structure and, above all, common sense still apply. If at the end of the day you find that you have described something as a wooden handled metal bladed vertically operated manual digging implement, put a line through it and substitute the word 'spade'. Anyone can be complicated — simplicity takes insight and understanding.

At this juncture, I pause to pontificate on the subject of conclusions. There are some who teach that these should be set out in the first or second paragraph of the Opinion, before dealing with your reasoning, in order to concentrate your mind and avoid irrelevance and prolixity. Cynics have also suggested that the reason for adopting this particular style is, not the least, that the recipients of your advice are only interested in the conclusions, and therefore will probably not want to read the rest of the Opinion once they have read the answer! Whatever the rationale, if you are minded to put your conclusions towards the beginning of the work, please ensure that what follows actually does support and lead to such conclusions! Personally, I consider that conclusions should be at the end where they belong. Each paragraph of a well-written Opinion should follow naturally on from the one before, and should lead on naturally to the one following. Even when dealing with a number of separate issues, the Opinion should be a strategic whole and, at the risk of being controversial, I fail to see how this is achieved by putting the natural end at the beginning. Still, I repeat, it is a matter of personal style — just be sure that you get round to putting a conclusion somewhere!!

Never be afraid to ask questions. An Opinion is not an examination essay, in which one assumes that all relevant details have been provided. This is in no way meant to be a criticism of those who have given you your instructions, who may either have taken a different view of the case, or who may simply not have had the time to deal with all matters which seem to you to be relevant.

Ensure that you deal fully with all the matters on which you are asked to advise. Having said that, this should not preclude you from dealing with further points which you may think relevant. You are, after all, being asked to advise, and it would be ludicrous were you not to express your views merely because you may not have been given specific instructions on a point that has occurred to you.

Always be realistic! Do not blindly accept as gospel truth everything that may be said by or on behalf of your client. Without in any way being insulting or implying disbelief, you must deal with questions of credibility, and if you are doubtful that the Court will believe your client's version of events, it is incumbent on you to say so. Again, if you consider your expert evidence to lack the objectivity or even thoroughness which you consider to be essential, do not hesitate to advise, albeit in as constructive a manner as possible, that the report be redrafted.

Never forget that your client is either a human being, or a corporation comprised of human beings. The case may be tedious or trifling in your eyes, and may be so in fact. To the client, however, it is important, and without in any way detracting from the objectivity and relevance of your advice, always express it in an appropriate and, if necessary, diplomatic manner. The fact that you may consider your client to be an unmitigated unpleasant person does not entitle you to express an emotionally clouded view.

Diplomacy is not always easy, particularly as (dare I say it) the law is a profession in which pomposity is not entirely unknown! Often this may be due to an inadvertent or insensitive disregard of the client's own feelings, due to the fact that his or her problem is not our own, and we are advising in the relative comfort, and from the relative distance, of our own offices or chambers. Whereas it is not at all professional to lose objectivity, have regard nevertheless to the fact that, for instance, damages in personal injury cases are often distressingly low in comparison with the pain and inconvenience suffered, and your client may feel very hard done by as a result. It certainly should not hurt you to say '**unfortunate** injuries', or 'I **very much regret to** have to advise Mr Bobsled that his prospects of success are slim in the extreme'. A little tact can go a long way, and may help to soften the blow!

If you find yourself getting bogged down in complexities, consider the intelligent use of sub-headings. These can be useful to direct the mind and the eye to your views on individual matters, e.g., 'The Limitation Acts Point', or 'The Market Garden User Provision'. Remember, however, that sub-headings can also be counter-productive, in that they enable a rapid change of subject, often without any form of explanation, and this can detract from the continuity and flow of the Opinion. Thus, as a tactical device, it is often useful to preface any sub-headings with an introduction, e.g.:

> The present dispute revolves around three separate matters, these being (a) the Limitation Acts, (b) whether or not user was

granted for a market garden, and (c) whether, if such user was not granted, the planning authority should now grant permission for the present user. I will deal with each of these in turn:

(a)   *The Limitation Acts*

When dealing with matters of law, try to do so in a way which will impart practical information to the lay client as well as to the solicitor. However academically fascinating you find the various contrary dicta of the Court of Appeal, try to avoid giving the impression that the law is some mysterious entity only to be understood by the intellectual élite, and to be imparted only condescendingly to those whom it particularly affects. Save detailed legal analysis for the rare occasions which demand it. By all means refer to the relevant authorities. On the other hand, resist the temptation (should you get it!) to cite vast quantities of the judgment and turn your Opinion into an academic treatise. Cite judgments at any length only, for example, if the argument is a difficult one, or where you may be expressing an Opinion contrary to the strongly held views of your professional or lay client.

A common error in Opinion writing is to be too judgmental. After all, remember that an Opinion is just that — it is your professional view as to the likely result of the matter should it come to trial. It is not a judgment. Nothing is certain in life, and (at the risk of sounding jaded) there is even less that is certain in law! Therefore, save in the rarest of circumstances, refrain from stating your views as if they were incontrovertible fact. Rather than:

> The Court will not accede to this application,

try:

> In my opinion it is most unlikely that the Court will accede to this application.

Instead of:

> On the balance of probabilities, the Court will find that Mr Fabric-Stiffener has been negligent,

how about:

> I consider that, if the Court accepts the evidence of Mr Crinkle, there is a high probability that it will then hold that Mr Fabric-Stiffener was in breach of his duty of care to him.

I accept that this can appear somewhat weaselly and wordy, but you must insert the appropriate caveats. All parties in a contested case will often have taken legal advice. That advice may well not agree. Someone will be 'wrong' at the end. Avoid the scenario where the client says 'But you **told** me I would win'. Your advice should therefore contain some qualification in order to take account of the realities and vicissitudes of life.

Never overlook the possibilities of settlement. Even if you are as certain as you can be that your client has a good case, have regard to the hazards and expense of litigation. If it is clear that the case is causing a great deal of worry to the client, see whether you can suggest any form of compromise that may ultimately redound to his or her advantage, if to do so would result in the matter concluding at an early stage. Suggest that it may be worth considering even though it may not be as generous as the award which could be made if it was to go to a full hearing.

Take care to ensure that you actually give advice. Notwithstanding what I have said above about 'hedging your bets', an Opinion which makes a number of tentative conclusions, or which does not really give any direction, is not doing its job. Of course, if you have insufficient instructions on which to come to a view, you must say so, and advise that further information is required.

Your advice should, however, always have regard to the practical elements of the case. Don't get carried away by the exuberance of your own arguments! It is all very well to analyse the law to the 'nth degree' and to craft a carefully argued Opinion as to the probable result should the matter come to trial: always have regard to the common-sense aspects of the case, including costs, the availability of evidence, proportionality, the credibility of witnesses, delays and, above all, the advantages of a compromise settlement should it be possible.

Opinion writing is, when all is said and done, no more than an exercise in analysis and communication. Therefore, ensure that the result is as concise as is compatible with fully carrying out your duties. Make sure that it contains a proper balance between exposition, analysis and conclusion. Ensure that it is well written, and does not contain language which will require two dictionaries and a thesaurus to comprehend! Neither should you use slang or loose language in order to appear 'streetwise'. As ever, the clear use of literate English cannot but assist you in your task.

Using the annotated example set out below, see how I have attempted (and failed dismally) to put these various principles into action. It may well be that you will disagree with the style, or layout, to say nothing of the actual advice given. Never mind — I'm sure that you will learn as much from my errors as from my example!

Re Mr J.E. Sniffy[1]

OPINION

---

1.   I am asked to advise Mr J.E Sniffy in respect of certain difficulties that
have arisen with Wiggley's Bank, over a partnership account in the joint
names of Mr Sniffy, and Mr Pigg. I am greatly obliged to Mr Sniffy for his
clear exposition of events, and for the accompanying documentation.[2]

2.   In June 2002, Mr Sniffy and Mr Pigg commenced trading as
'Sniffypigg', in the retail sale of Nissota car spares. It appears that
Mr Sniffy was very much the sleeping partner, in that he provided the not
inconsiderable finance involved, and Mr Pigg was to run the business.[3]

3.   Once the business was established, Mr Sniffy states that it was not
envisaged that any further purchases of stock would be necessary for
some time, and that special orders were to be purchased out of trading
income. I am not sure how long this state of affairs was proposed to
continue, as it is clear that the stock would have to be replenished at
some time, although Mr Sniffy states that no credit facilities were proposed
to be established with suppliers for at least 2 years.[4]

4.   In June 2002, at the time that trading commenced, a partnership
bank account was opened in the name of 'W. Pigg & J.E. Sniffy t/a
Sniffypigg' with the High Street, Blackstone branch of Wiggley's Bank.
A mandate was signed by both Mr Sniffy and Mr Pigg, and clearly stated
that cheques had to bear the signature of both parties. Indeed, somewhat
unusually, an endorsement to this effect appeared on the face of the
cheques, which made the bank's subsequent conduct particularly strange.

5.   I assume that during the first year of trading, Mr Sniffy was asked
to, and did, sign several cheques. Whether this means that he kept a

---

[1] If proceedings have already commenced I would set out the whole action title.
[2] Basic introduction.
[3] Basic exposition of facts.
[4] Interspersion to raise a query, or to give advice.

'weather eye' on the progress of the business during this time, seems uncertain. However, at the end of the first year of trading, in June 2003, Mr Sniffy apparently requested Mr Pigg to supply the accounts and records of the business for audit, but this was not done for some considerable time. Indeed, 11 months later this had still not been done, and I am presently not instructed as to the degree and extent (if any) to which pressure was exerted by Mr Sniffy to supply the figures.[5]

6.   However, on 3rd May 2004, Mr Sniffy wrote a cheque on the business account, and was surprised (to say the least) when it was returned unpaid, due to lack of funds. At this stage it appears that he had certainly (in his view) sufficient evidence on which safely to assume that the account was well in credit. I am unaware, but assume, that Mr Pigg countersigned the cheque.[6] In any event, Mr Sniffy investigated the situation, and discovered a number of unpalatable facts:

(a)   An overdraft of £7,500 had been obtained by Mr Pigg on 13th October 2003, without Mr Sniffy's knowledge or consent.

(b)   On 26th January 2004, the overdraft limit had been raised to £10,000, again with Mr Sniffy remaining in blissful ignorance.

(c)   The bank was pressing for repayment.

(d)   Mr Pigg was endeavouring to repay the overdraft, by taking out a business development loan, repayable over two years. This required Mr Sniffy's consent.

(e)   The overdraft facility was fully taken up, and the partnership was therefore suffering a liquidity crisis.

(f)   Various suppliers had not been paid, and were threatening proceedings.

(g)   Such purchases as had been made, had not been paid for, and no explanation was forthcoming from Mr Pigg as to why these had not been paid for out of receipts.[7]

7.   At this stage, there was an obvious suspicion that Mr Pigg had not been conducting the affairs of the business with due probity, and Mr Sniffy then dissolved the partnership on 4th May 2004. I am presently

---

[5] This particular case requires a narrative explanation, essential to set out the position clearly. Note that this will assist in opening the case, and/or further research. Advice and queries are inserted at appropriate points.

[6] This makes it clear that the opinion is based on an assumption, which can be corrected if necessary.

[7] Thus, the basic problems leading to the present situation have been summarised.

unaware if the partnership was formally created in writing, or whether it came into existence as a result of an oral agreement between the parties. However, I understand that the agreement to dissolve was minuted and signed by both parties, and I should like, in due course, to see the minutes, and any other pertinent documentation.[8]

8.   At this stage, it may be helpful were I to deal with the question of the overdraft.[9] The only documentation that I have so far seen with regard to the establishment of the account, is the original mandate, and I am not certain whether this comprises the entire document. It makes no mention of any overdraft facility, but does make both partners responsible for all liabilities created.

9.   The purpose of a written mandate should be to avoid arguments as to the extent of the authority given to any person with regard to use of the bank account. Unfortunately, however, it is quite common for very general mandates to be signed nowadays. In *Jacobs* v *Morris* [1902] 1 Ch 816, it was held that, in the absence of express authority to do so, there is no implied authority in an authorised signatory to overdraw the account. Where powers are not spelled out in great detail, the Courts may imply whatever powers are reasonably incidental to the authority given, see *Ashford Shire Council* v *Dependable Motors Pty Ltd* [1961] AC 336.[10] I do not consider that this would give a right to overdraw, but the position here appears to be that the bank was approached by Mr Pigg, and specifically asked to approve an overdraft. The question then arises whether Mr Pigg had any actual or ostensible authority to negotiate the overdraft on behalf of the partnership.[11]

---

[8] It is **always** important to request further information if it is considered necessary. This should not stop you from giving advice, albeit on a presumptive basis.

[9] A different way of introducing a sub-heading. It is a useful device to ensure that the structure of the Opinion does not go by the wayside, in the course of dealing with individual matters.

[10] Note that I have made no attempt to analyse the facts of these cases. They are there to provide authority for the statement made, and of course provide help for you later on, if the case is litigated, and the point has to be argued. Always give full case references.

[11] In drawing a conclusion, e.g., from the authorities, I have then introduced the next topic on which I will give an opinion. This is essential to preserve structure, and keep the aims and objectives in mind.

10.   Under section 5 of the Partnership Act 1890, every general partner
is an agent of the firm for the purpose of the partnership business and,
while acting in the usual business of the partnership, has authority to
bind the firm. Although it has been held that this implied authority does
not extend to borrowing on behalf of the firm, this seems not to be the
case in trading partnerships, see *Higgins* v *Beauchamp* [1914] 3 KB
1192. Thus, in my opinion, Mr Pigg may well be held to have had
prima facie ostensible authority to negotiate an overdraft on behalf of the
partnership.[12]

11.   However, there may, in my opinion, be strong grounds for arguing
that the bank should have appreciated that Mr Pigg did not have authority
to act on his own, such as would rebut what would otherwise have been
his ostensible authority to do so.[13] My present view is provisional only,
as much may depend on the circumstances in which the original mandate was signed.[14] However, it may well be argued that, as the bank was
aware that cheques had to be signed by both partners, it ought to have
appreciated that no individual partner had authority to take financial
decisions that would affect the other. If this construction can be placed
on the relationship between the parties, the bank should not have
allowed overdraft facilities to the partnership (on which Mr Sniffy would
be jointly and severally liable) without his express consent. I should
appreciate a conference with Mr Sniffy, amongst other reasons, to
clarify this point, as it is almost certainly an argument worth running at
the moment.[15]

12.   It does not appear from my instructions, that Mr Sniffy informed the
bank that the partnership had been dissolved. This is perhaps unfortunate,[16]
but in view of the event that then occurred, it may have little or no bearing

---

[12] An illustration of a short point made with the assistance of authority.
[13] Never be blind to the fact that the other side may have an opposing argument.
It is not necessary to anticipate every possible line that they may take, but you
have to use your judgment and deal with the main arguments that may reasonably
be raised against you. If further points come up later on, you can deal with them
in a further Opinion.
[14] An instance of self-preservation!
[15] Never be afraid to ask for further information, particularly if there may be
risks inherent in pursuing a certain line of argument. After all, sometimes it is
easier to discuss matters in a conference rather than in writing.
[16] A little touch of diplomacy.

on the question of liability. What does appear to be strange, however, is the manner in which matters were left between Mr Sniffy and Mr Pigg. It seems that Mr Sniffy allowed Mr Pigg to keep the stock and to dispose of it in order to pay off business debts. Again, the full details of this will presumably be in the minutes. I do not, however, understand why Mr Sniffy allowed himself to continue to be liable on the bank account. At this stage he clearly appreciated that it was considerably overdrawn and that Mr Pigg was not to be trusted. An explanation for this would be helpful, although this may also be appropriate to discuss in conference.

13.   The question may also arise whether Mr Sniffy may have ratified the overdraft as a result of his subsequent actions. Ratification can be implied from the circumstances, and need not be express. The bank would have to show that, within a reasonable time of the overdraft being discovered, Mr Sniffy, in the full knowledge of what had happened, confirmed and adopted it by acting in some way which indicated that he, as a partner, consented to be bound by it. Again, this is a matter which I should wish to investigate further in conference.[17]

14.   As I have said, the bank began to press for payment, and wrote a stiff letter to Mr Sniffy at the beginning of January 2005. Shortly afterwards (and I am somewhat surprised that this was not done some months before),[18] Mr Sniffy investigated the cheques that had been drawn on the account, and discovered that a very large number indeed had apparently been drawn by Mr Pigg on his own, and cleared by the bank, notwithstanding the necessity for these to bear two signatures. Naturally, Mr Sniffy was concerned that some attempt may have been made to forge his signature, but this appears not to have been the case.

15.   The bank has admitted that it erred in allowing the cheques to be cleared. These errors took place over some considerable period — indeed it appears that 112 cheques were written with one signature, compared with only 41 that were properly countersigned. 21 of the cheques were not cleared, but the rest were, in a total sum of £23,161. By this time, the bank appears to have changed its somewhat aggressive attitude towards

---

[17] I didn't consider it necessary to cite any authority for a fairly obvious point.

[18] This is, of course, a criticism of the client, but it is essential to forewarn him of the problems that he may face. Here it gives him an opportunity to consider the matter so that he can give further instructions in due course.

repayment, and seemed to be prevaricating somewhat in its responses to Mr Sniffy's letters. Additionally, although in March 2005 Mr Sniffy requested sight of all cheques drawn on the account, this was not allowed until February 2006, by which time cheques drawn more than 3 years before 18 December 2005 had been destroyed. Thus, the bank has been unable to produce any cheques drawn on the account between the inception of the partnership, in June 2002, and December of that year.

16.   Mr Sniffy considers that he has a claim against the bank in respect of the following items:

(a)   Value of cheques incorrectly paid out: £23,161.

(b)   Cheques paid out before 17th December 2002, which cannot presently be accounted for by the bank: £4,508.

(c)   Interest and service charges on the overdraft and returning the cheque: £5,331.

(d)   Loss of investment, due to the collapse of the business, caused as a result of the bank's activities: £11,550.[19]

I will deal with each of these in turn.[20]

17.   *Cheques incorrectly paid out.*   In my opinion, the partnership has a strong claim against the bank, arising out of the wrongful clearance of the cheques. I emphasise that the action would have to be brought on behalf of the partnership, because the account was in that name. On the other hand, the distribution of any damages between the partners will depend on the legal situation between them, see *Catlin* v *Cyprus Finance Corporation (London) Ltd* [1983] QB 759. In the present case, it seems likely that Mr Pigg[21] would not be able to establish any claim to any sums recovered. The cause of action would be either breach of the contract between the parties, alternatively negligence. However, the degree and extent of loss will depend on the use to which the monies obtained were put. The bank is of the view that the monies benefited the

---

[19] Exposition of the precise matters on which the client wishes an opinion.

[20] A device for introducing sub-headings, which are essential in this case. Of course, many Opinions do not require the facts being set out at such length, but I hope you can see why it is essential here. The Opinion should read as an entire whole, i.e., one should be able to pick it up and understand exactly what the case is all about, what are the main issues and what your view is on them.

[21] An example of giving an **Opinion** rather than being judgmental!

partnership, and that therefore no loss was caused as a result of their error. That is, with respect, an oversimplification of the problem. If there was to be an assumption that the monies went to pay partnership debts etc., there seems little reason why there should have had to have been two signatures on the cheques. Nevertheless, it will be for Mr Sniffy to show that the bank's errors caused damage to the partnership, in that the wrongful clearance of the cheques led to monies being diverted away from partnership business, presumably into the pocket of Mr Pigg.[22] The degree and extent of this should not be too difficult to prove, in that Mr Sniffy has, or should have, copies of the business records, and a full audit should be able to demonstrate the use to which funds obtained from the bank were put. If and to the extent that Mr Pigg drew cheques on his own signature, yet used the monies for partnership business, it cannot be said that the partnership has suffered any loss. On the other hand, if, as seems more likely, some or all of these monies were taken by Mr Pigg, the situation would be very different.[23]

18.   *The destroyed cheques.*   In my opinion, Mr Sniffy cannot claim for all cheques drawn during this period, on the basis that they may have been signed only by one person. It will be for him (or more accurately, the partnership) to establish that the cheques were signed by only one person, and that they were diverted. This is, of course, a matter of evidence, although a strong presumption may be made as to the number of signatories, depending on whether the audit shows that the monies were used for the benefit of the business. It may be that the degree and extent of later unlawful transactions will assist in determining the use of the monies prior to December 2002.

19.   *The interest and service charges.*   I have already dealt with the question of the overdraft. Clearly, if the whole facility was unlawful, the bank will not be entitled to its charges. However, even if the overdraft was lawfully granted, or was subsequently ratified, the fact that a facility has been granted does not mean that it has to be taken up, let alone to the full. Thus, even if the bank can avoid liability on the overdraft itself, it may not be able to avoid liability for the costs etc. if the only reason for the overdraft being taken up was due to its own errors in clearing

---

[22] Analysis of the arguments, from which conclusions will then be drawn.
[23] Always be practical!

unauthorised cheques. As it appears that the total overdraft was in the region of some £11,000, and that the demonstrable value of incorrectly paid-out cheques amounts to nearly twice that sum, there may be a strong case for a refund of service and interest charges that would not have been incurred, but for the bank's breach of contract and/or neglect.[24]

20. *Loss of investment.* I am rather more pessimistic on this ground than I am on the other heads of loss. I fear that the Court will hold that the damage suffered is too remote.[25] For a start, it is based on conjecture however well based. The real reason for the collapse of the business seems to have been the activities of Mr Pigg. It is true that these activities might have been restricted had the bank not cleared the various cheques, but it does not necessarily follow that the business would then have made a profit. It may well have been that Mr Pigg would either have turned to other nefarious activities, or would not have put much effort into the business in any event. There would have been nothing to stop him from failing to meet bills, and from personally pocketing the income from the business in any event. Thus, subject to seeing Mr Sniffy in conference,[26] I am of the view that it is highly unlikely that the bank will be held liable under this head.[27] However, in the event of recovering damages from the bank, the partnership will, of course, be entitled to interest over the period.

21. As I have intimated above, it would be most helpful for me to see Mr Sniffy in conference, once this Opinion has been digested. The matter can then be more fully discussed, and I should also like further information as to the situation *vis-à-vis* the bank between May 2004 and early 2005.[28] In the meantime, I would respectfully advise Instructing Solicitors to write a preliminary letter before action to the bank, advising it of the position, and seeking compensation without recourse to litigation.[29]

---

[24] Note the way in which this has been put. I do not, of course, **know** what the Court will do, but I am expressing an **opinion** as to the likely result.

[25] It's bad news, but again expressed as an opinion, and put in a manner which will, I hope, break the news as gently as is professionally proper.

[26] The appropriate caveat in this case.

[27] Again, note the way in which the advice has been expressed.

[28] Generally drawing the various strings together.

[29] Practical advice.

The claim should, of course, presently include compensation for loss of investment, although this will almost certainly, as I have said, have to be dropped in the course of negotiation.[30] In the meantime, I will be pleased to advise further if required, and hope to see Mr Sniffy and Instructing Solicitors in conference in the near future.[31]

NAME/Address/Date[32]

---

[30] An eye to the practical solution.

[31] General signing off.

[32] It looks more professional if signed with name, professional address, and date for reference purposes.

Epilogue

'But what am I to do?' said Alice.
'Anything you like', said the Footman,
and began whistling.

In the course of the 10 months or so that it originally took to write this book, I was instructed in a civil dispute, in which I drafted what was then called a Statement of Claim. The matter was substantial, and the damages claimed amounted to over £1.5 million.

My opponent was from a very Up Market Set of Civil Chambers, and had a very Fine Mind. He issued an application before the Master, to strike out my pleadings (as they were then known) on the basis that they were frivolous, vexatious, and an abuse of the process of the Court, AND that they disclosed no reasonable cause of action.

I spent several sleepless nights worrying about the matter. It occurred to me that if he was right, I had no business writing a book of this nature. We spent an entertaining (!) four days in Court. For three of them, I listened attentively whilst he went paragraph by paragraph through my Statement of Claim, building up a wonderfully sophisticated argument, using what he frequently described as 'high authority' to support his contentions that, basically, I was totally incompetent.

Fortunately, I escaped both with my life and such reputation as I have, with my pleadings more or less still intact. I was nevertheless severely chastened by my experience, as it made me appreciate that, however much experience I may have under my belt, what I have at most is some gaps in my ignorance, rather than true knowledge.

These gaps, I have tried to share with you. I have no pretensions to being authoritative. Much legal teaching is by way of example, which often conveys its message by evidencing what **not** to do, rather than by encouraging a slavish mimicry of the demonstration.

You will, and indeed must, develop your own style of drafting. The richness and variety of talent within the profession will, I am certain, ensure the integrity of the legal system in an age of rapid and even revolutionary change. The aim of this work has been to provoke thought. In this at least, I hope I have been successful.

William Rose
July 2006